CORONARY-PRONE BEHAVIOR

CORONARY-PRONE BEHAVIOR

Edited by

Theodore M. Dembroski
Stephen M. Weiss
Jim L. Shields
Suzanne G. Haynes
Manning Feinleib

With 6 illustrations

Springer–Verlag   New York   Heidelberg   Berlin

Theodore M. Dembroski, Ph.D.
Associate Professor of Psychology
Behavioral Science Department
Eckerd College
St. Petersburg, Florida 33733

Stephen M. Weiss, Ph.D.
Acting Chief, Behavioral Medicine Branch
National Heart, Lung, and Blood Institute
National Institutes of Health
Bethesda, Maryland 20014

Jim L. Shields, Ph.D.
Deputy Director, Division of Heart and Vascular Diseases
National Heart, Lung, and Blood Institute
National Institutes of Health
Bethesda, Maryland 20014

Suzanne G. Haynes, Ph.D.
Epidemiology Branch
National Heart, Lung, and Blood Institute
National Institutes of Health
Bethesda, Maryland 20014

Manning Feinleib, M.D., Dr. P.H.
Chief, Epidemiology Branch
National Heart, Lung, and Blood Institute
National Institutes of Health
Bethesda, Maryland 20014

Library of Congress Cataloging in Publication Data

Main entry under title:

Coronary-prone behavior.

  Includes bibliographical references and index.
  1. Coronary heart disease—Psychosomatic aspects.
2. Human behavior. I. Dembroski, Theodore M.
RC685.C6C69   616.1'23'0019   78-9947
ISBN 0-387-08876-8

Copyright 1978 by Springer-Verlag New York Inc.

Printed in the United States of America.

9 8 7 6 5 4 3 2 1

ISBN   0-387-**08876**-8 Springer-Verlag New York Heidelberg Berlin
ISBN   3-540-**08876**-8 Springer-Verlag Berlin Heidelberg New York

PREFACE

Almost two decades ago, Drs. Meyer Friedman and Ray Rosenman developed the concept of the Type A coronary-prone behavior pattern and pioneered research in the area. Since then, much effort has been devoted to investigating both medical and psychosocial implications of this phenomenon by an impressive array of biomedical and behavioral scientists.

On the basis of the National Heart, Lung, and Blood Institute's (NHLBI) recent Congressional mandate concerning disease prevention and control, the Division of Heart and Vascular Diseases undertook an intensive review of the existing literature in this area. The review underscored that the very nature of the concept of coronary-prone behavior requires examination by researchers from a variety of disciplines. Publication of findings in both the medical and behavioral literature, however, has created difficulties in gaining a truly comprehensive understanding of the total effort in this area. It became obvious that there was no coherent integration of information regarding the strength of the association between behaviors and disease processes (or outcomes), how behavioral factors associated with coronary heart disease were measured, the possible physiological mechanisms mediating the relationship between behavior and disease, whether intervention could be effective, and what forms of intervention appeared most promising. In short, a clear need existed to organize this information in a more coherent fashion so that it could be subjected to critical review by members of both the medical and behavioral scientific communities.

The first step in accomplishing this goal was to identify major issues and a process by which the issues could be addressed. Five major issues were so identified: (1) What is the specific evidence that suggests a causal link between coronary-prone behavior and coronary heart disease? (2) How is the

coronary-prone behavior pattern assessed? (3) What are the mechanisms that
translate the behavior pattern into coronary heart disease? (4) How does
coronary-prone behavior originate? (5) What can be done to alter coronary-
prone behavior?

Specific questions were derived from each of the major issues listed above
and those scientists clearly equipped to address these issues within the limitations of the "state of the art" were identified. Each of these scientists prepared
a position paper in which the essential theoretical and empirical issues relevant
to the particular question assigned were identified and addressed. In essence,
the contributors to this volume were asked to summarize existing data and
identify areas and issues that needed to be considered to resolve conceptual,
methodological, and controversial problems relevant to their assigned topic.

These papers were then circulated to all contributors for study and com-
ment. The Forum on Coronary-Prone Behavior, sponsored by Eckerd College,
St. Petersburg, Florida with support from the National Heart, Lung, and Blood
Institute and chaired by Dr. Thomas Detre, University of Pittsburg School of
Medicine, brought all of the authors together to collaboratively review and
synthesize the "state of the art" on each of the major issues identified above.
Each of the five "issue" groups, under the direction of the Group Coordinator
and assisted by a Discussant, was requested to prepare a Summary Statement
to capture the essence of each position paper, information from the discussion
during the Forum, and salient elements contained in the Discussant's remarks.
Thus, the Discussants—Drs. Remington, Spielberger, Herd, and Suinn—
played pivotal roles both in facilitating discussion in the Forum and in preparing
summary statements. Each summary statement precedes the chapters for a
particular section. There is some overlap of material among the summary
statements and chapters, but each has its own major focus. Space limitations do
not permit mention and acknowledgment of each participant's contribution to
this field. But, it is obvious that it was their work which provided the *raison
d'être* for this volume.

Theodore M. Dembroski
Stephen M. Weiss
Jim L. Shields
Suzanne G. Haynes
Manning Feinleib

CONTENTS

This volume is dedicated to Bernard Caffrey.

LIST OF CONTRIBUTORS

Richard J. Brand, Ph.D.
Associate Professor of Biostatistics
School of Public Health
University of California
Berkeley, California

Bernard Caffrey, Ph.D.
Professor and Chairman
Dept. of Psychology
Clemson University
Clemson, South Carolina

Joseph H. Chadwick, Ph.D.
Stanford Research Institute
Menlo Park, California

Margaret A. Chesney, Ph.D.
Stanford Research Institute
Menlo Park, California

Judith Blackfield Cohen, Ph.D.
Assistant Professor of Epidemiology
Program in Epidemiology
School of Public Health
University of California
Berkeley, California

Theodore M. Dembroski, Ph.D.
Associate Professor of Psychology
Dept. of Behavioral Science
Eckerd College
St. Petersburg, Florida

Manning Feinleib, M.D., Dr. P.H.
Chief, Epidemiology Branch
National Heart, Lung, and Blood
Institute
National Institutes of Health
Bethesda, Maryland

Meyer Friedman, M.D.
Director, Harold Brunn Institute
Mount Zion Hospital Medical Center
San Francisco, California

W. Doyle Gentry, Ph.D.
Professor of Medical Psychology
Dept. of Psychiatry
Duke University Medical Center
Durham, North Carolina

David C. Glass, Ph.D.
Professor of Psychology
The Graduate Center
City University of New York
New York, New York

J. Alan Herd, M.D.
Associate Professor of Psychobiology
Dept. of Psychiatry
Harvard Medical School
Boston, Massachusetts

C. David Jenkins, Ph.D.
Director, Dept. of Behavioral
Epidemiology and Professor of
Psychiatry
Division of Psychiatry
Boston University School of Medicine
Boston, Massachusetts

Karen A. Matthews, Ph.D.
Assistant Professor of Psychology
Dept. of Psychology
Kansas State University
Manhattan, Kansas

Richard Remington, Ph.D.
Dean, School of Public Health
University of Michigan
Ann Arbor, Michigan

Ray H. Rosenman, M.D.
Associate Director, Harold Brunn
Institute
Mount Zion Hospital Medical Center
San Francisco, California

Neil Schneiderman, Ph.D.
Professor of Psychology
Dept. of Psychology
University of Miami
Coral Gables, Florida

Richard B. Shekelle, Ph.D.
Professor
Dept. of Preventive Medicine
Rush-Presbyterian-St. Luke's
  Medical Center
Chicago, Illinois

Charles D. Spielberger, Ph.D.
Professor of Psychology
Dept. of Psychology
University of South Florida
Tampa, Florida

Richard M. Suinn, Ph.D.
Professor and Head
Dept. of Psychology
Colorado State University
Fort Collins, Colorado

Donald L. Tasto, Ph.D.
Stanford Research Institute
Menlo Park, California

Ingrid Waldron, Ph.D.
Associate Professor of Biology
Dept. of Biology
University of Pennsylvania
Philadelphia, Pennsylvania

Redford B. Williams, Jr., M.D.
Associate Professor of Psychiatry and
Assistant Professor of Medicine
Dept. of Psychiatry,
Duke University Medical Center
Durham, North Carolina

Stephen J. Zyzanski, Ph.D.
Associate Professor of Psychiatry
Dept. of Behavioral Epidemiology
Division of Psychiatry
Boston University School of Medicine
Boston, Massachusetts

INTRODUCTION

Around 1950 there was a widespread albeit simplistic concept that coronary atherosclerosis was caused primarily by intimal deposition of cholesterol from the blood, in turn controlled mainly by the dietary fat intake. This belief appeared to stem from findings such as the arterial damage induced by feeding fat to animals, as well as selected data from population surveys which associated different dietary fat intakes with parallel differences of blood cholesterol levels and prevalence of clinical coronary heart disease (CHD).

Although cholesterol and fat were being generously fed by many investigators to rabbits and other animals to induce a lesion that is very different from human atherosclerosis, little was known about the metabolism of either endogenous or exogenous cholesterol and perhaps even less about triglycerides. In this laboratory we therefore undertook to study the metabolism of cholesterol as well as the mechanisms of its elevation in various hypercholesteremic states. As the result of such studies we found that the level of cholesterol in the serum is not regulated primarily by its rate of input into the circulation from either endogenous sources or the diet, but rather by its rate of egress from the plasma. We also observed that the deposition of lipid on the surface lining of animals fed excess dietary fat was very different from atherosclerosis occurring in humans. Finally, we realized that international population comparisons had many faults of methodology and many exceptions to the almost linear relationship between dietary fat intake, serum cholesterol level, and prevalence of CHD that was claimed by strong proponents of the primary culpability of the diet.

We were aware that the lowest rates of CHD were observed in farming communities in both the United States and the United Kingdom, despite habitual exposure to high saturated fat intakes. It also was clear that patients with CHD had not habitually eaten any differently when compared to individuals with longevity and absence of clinical disease. Finally, our own studies in patients had shown us that there was little relationship in most individuals between dietary fat intake and their blood cholesterol level. Over a period of years, we also found that a significant number of patients exhibited wide fluctuations of serum cholesterol, which clearly could not be ascribed to changes of diet. These and other findings led us to believe that the diet was not the *sine qua non* of the twentieth century "epidemic" of CHD.

I will not attempt to review the early studies relating physical activity to the incidence of CHD. However, whatever its possible role, we again could not find adequate evidence that physical inactivity was the *sine qua non* of the present epidemic. The standard risk factors, such as cigarette smoking, serum cholesterol, and blood pressure were clearly related to the incidence of CHD in all prospective studies, but even taken together, accounted for less than half of the numerical incidence in such studies. Moreover, there did not appear to be valid evidence to show that an increased prevalence of hypercholesteremia or hypertension, or that alterations of either diet or physical activity could explain our high incidence of CHD.

Although coronary atherosclerosis had probably always occurred in man, the clinical incidence of CHD was rather rare until the second or third decades of the twentieth century, as was later pointed out by Dr. Paul White. Moreover, it also became apparent that variables such as diet and physical activity and the standard risk factors were associated with high incidence of CHD only in industrialized societies and in these, the incidence was highest in densely populated urban areas. It was around 1955 that we began to question whether uniquely modern environmental "stress" could be playing a significant causal role in the relatively new "epidemic."

This hypothesis was strengthened when we observed significant and occasionally marked fluctuations of serum cholesterol in patients during certain types of stressful situations. Further support was given by our later finding in a controlled study of tax accountants that many of them exhibited significant increase of serum cholesterol when occupational tax deadlines imposed feelings of urgent time pressure. These fluctuations were clearly not related to dietary alterations. They were widely confirmed by many investigators during the next few years.

In view of these findings we proceeded to observe coronary patients more closely and were impressed by their frequent exhibition of certain personality and behavioral traits. A search of earlier literature revealed that similar characteristics had also been observed by others, including Osler's succinct description at the turn of the century. The Menningers (1936) may have been the first psychiatrists to study patients with CHD, emphasizing their strongly aggressive tendencies. Coronary-prone patients were variously found to be hard-driving, goal-directed individuals who were ambitious and compulsively striving to achieve goals that incorporated power and prestige, according to the observations of Arlow (1945), Dunbar (1948), Gildea (1949), Miles (1954), and Kemple (1975). Gertler and White (1954) found that young patients with CHD were hard-driving and goal-directed, and tended to work excessively, strenuously, and without adequate vacation periods, compared to paired control subjects without CHD. These earlier investigators did not attempt to explain why possibly similar individuals in previous centuries had not often suffered occurrence of clinical CHD. However, these observers did not appear to be cognizant of the possible contributing role of the contemporary environmental milieu in the genesis of the disturbed personalities that they described.

It was in the late 1950s that our thoughts became more crystallized. Influenced by this new reorientation we found that most of our coronary patients under 60 years of age exhibited a particular cluster of behavioral traits that we subsequently called the Type A behavior pattern. From the outset we were rather certain that these traits did not result from clinical disease but definitely preceded it.

We believe that most individuals of both sexes exhibit to a greater or lesser extent either the Type A or the converse Type B behavior pattern, with a relatively small number of persons who exhibit equal characteristics of both patterns. We conceive of Type A behavior pattern as being a particular action–emotion complex which is possessed and exhibited by an individual who is engaged in a relatively chronic and excessive struggle. More often than not this struggle is to obtain a usually unlimited number of things from the environment in the shortest possible period of time and/or against the opposing efforts of other persons or things in the same environment. The chronic struggle might consist of attempts to achieve or to do more and more in less and less time or of other conflicts with one or more persons. Since Type A's rarely despair of losing the chronic struggle, such individuals differ sharply from those with fear, anxiety, or a garden variety of neuroses. Type A's usually exhibit enhanced personality traits of aggressiveness, ambitiousness, and competitiveness, are usually work-oriented, and are often preoccupied with both vocational and avocational deadlines. In this interplay of personality traits and the modern environmental milieu, Type A's lack subtle adaptive response and usually exhibit hostility, chronic impatience, and a strong sense of time urgency. The converse Type B individual is basically free of such enhanced personality traits, generally feels no pressing conflict with either time or other persons, and is therefore without an habitual sense of time urgency.

The contemporary environment that has been associated with the CHD incidence has generally encouraged Type A behavior because it appears to offer special rewards to those who can perform rapidly and aggressively. Moreover, with increasing urbanization and technological progress as well as increasing population density, our modern civilization presents uniquely new challenges never experienced by earlier, less time-conscious generations. Thus, Type A behavior does not stem solely from an individual's personality but emerges when certain challenges or conditions of the milieu arise to elicit this complex of responses in susceptible individuals.

Major facets of Type A behavior are a chronic sense of time urgency and a striving, either by preference or necessity, to accomplish more and to be ever more involved in both vocational and avocational pursuits, despite an ever increasing lack of time. Type A's have an enhanced aggressiveness and drive that are usually associated with or evolve into competitive hostility. Type A behavior occurs when these traits are "activated." Thus, it depends on the nature of environmental stimuli, challenges and demands that confront susceptible individuals, and on both their interpretation and response to these environmental phenomena. When an individual interprets and therefore responds to environmental challenges without feeling impelled to strive against either time or other persons or things, then Type A behavior will not emerge. Conversely, when a subject who initially has only a moderate sense of time urgency and aggressive drive is repetitively confronted with intense environmental demands, which he interprets as necessary to be compiled with, in a minimum of time and with maximum aggressive drive, then Type A behavior usually emerges. Thus, there appears to be a trichotomous origin of Type A behavior. It is not surprising therefore that no particular correlation between job or position, and either type of behavior pattern need exist. Finally, it is important to distinguish Type A behavior from the concept of "stress," which has such different meanings to different people. Type A behavior pattern is neither a stress situation nor a distressed type of response, but is rather a style of overt behavior by which such individuals confront, interpret, and respond to their life situations.

Ray H. Rosenman

SECTION I

ASSOCIATION

Section Summary: Association of the Coronary-Prone Behavior Pattern and Coronary Heart Disease

Manning Feinleib, Richard J. Brand, Richard Remington, and Stephen J. Zyzanski

The emergence of the Type A behavior pattern as a risk factor for coronary heart disease constitutes a fascinating chapter in the history of science. Other risk factors, such as cigarette smoking, serum cholesterol, and high blood pressure, were elucidated in a relatively orderly investigative sequence, involving multiple methodologies. The emergence of Type A behaviors as a risk factor has come about as the result of a series of logical triplets: claim, challenge, and response.

In the 1950s, small-scale investigations of postcoronary patients suggested a behavior pattern characteristic of this group. Criticism and challenge immediately developed: sample sizes were too small; controls were inadequate; the data were retrospective; interviewers were biasing the responses; findings were not consistent with existing behavioral science theory; studies were confined to a single investigative group and not replicated by other scientists. One by one these challenges were addressed: sample sizes were increased; multiple control groups were selected; prospective studies were designed and conducted; a self-administered questionnaire was developed and standardized; behavioral scientists became actively involved; a number of independent investigations were launched in various locations.

Yet, the Type A behavior pattern is still with us. It has survived multiple challenges. The epidemiologic community, often seemingly against its better judgment, has generally admitted that the observed associations of behavior pattern with disease cannot be explained by error or artifact. The questions persist, and as each is answered a new one appears to take its place. While many refinements of inference are still needed, the main conclusion that, in some manner, overt behavior of a particular type is associated with the prevalence, incidence, and recurrence of coronary heart disease seems strongly and consistently supported.

The cornerstone of the evidence regarding the association between the incidence of coronary heart disease (CHD) and A-B behavior assessed by a structured interview is the finding of the Western Collaborative Group Study (WCGS).[1] In this prospective study of 3,154 men aged 39–59 who were followed for 8.5 years, about 50% of the study population comprised men classified Type A. These Type A subjects exhibited 2.37 times the rate of new CHD observed in their Type B counterparts.

Efforts to diagnose the source of this association led to the examination of several possibilities:

Possibility 1:   The association may reflect some systematic difference between Type A and B subjects in their levels of more *traditional* risk factors, such as serum cholesterol, smoking, and systolic blood pressure as assessed in this study.

Possibility 2:   The association may reflect some systematic difference between Type A and B subjects in their levels of nontraditional risk factors or in dynamic aspects of traditional risk factors that are not adequately represented by static assessments that have been employed to obtain available data.

A statistical adjustment procedure provided by the multiple logistic model was used to partition the A-B versus CHD association into two parts corresponding to these two sources. After adjustment for the four traditional factors (age, cholesterol level, systolic blood pressure, and smoking), the approximate relative risk was 1.97.

The reduction from 2.37 to 1.97 may be interpreted as the portion of the association attributable to Possibility 1 and the residual of 1.97 as the portion attributable to Possibility 2. Both of these sources are *consistent with* a causal interpretation in which Type A behavior influences either static or dynamic aspects of traditional risk factors or nontraditional risk factors in an undesirable direction. However, noncausal interpretations are also possible thereby pointing to the serious need for detailed identification and comprehensive examination of new intervening mechanisms and more refined dynamic evaluations of traditional factors as possible intervening variables.

Possibility 3:   The observed association could in principle be the result of a chance fluctuation.

This possibility seems unlikely since both the unadjusted association and the adjusted association between A-B behavior and CHD incidence were highly statistically significant ($p < .0001$).

Possibility 4:   The choice of a statistical model may in some way distort the "true" association.

Statistical goodness-of-fit tests were used to compare two general patterns by which A-B behavior may be operating in the CHD process. In these patterns, Type A behavior is represented either by a constant multiplicative effect or a constant incremental effect applied to the baseline risk level associated with traditional risk factors. The WCGS data are remarkably consistent with the constant multiplicative pattern. Thus, the relative risk measure of association seems to provide an adequate and relatively undistorted model for summarizing the association between A-B behavior treated as a dichotomy and CHD incidence.

Possibility 5: The association may reflect the selection process by which WCGS subjects were initially obtained for study or selective influences affecting the loss to follow-up that occurred at varying times among about 10% of the study population.

Loss to follow-up bias has been examined in detail in the WCGS data by methods of competing risk analysis and has been found to be negligible. Initial selection bias is more troublesome, however, since it cannot be assessed within the context of a single study. Logically, the best insurance against selection bias is the use of study subjects who are randomly chosen from the population to which one would like to generalize results. In the usual absence of this design feature in epidemiological studies, one has only two alternatives. First, the research can be replicated at different times and places. If consistent findings emerge from studies that are not all subject to the same selection bias, then one's confidence is increased that selection bias is not the source for the observed association. In this regard, as discussed below, numerous other studies of varying designs and methods of A-B assessment have shown evidence for an A-B versus CHD association.

Second, the methods of analysis and measures of association used can be examined to see how susceptible they are to selection bias. To the extent that the method of analysis used is invariant under some class of selection bias patterns, then one has at least some insurance against this type of selection bias. In this regard, the multiple logistic model is a particularly favorable form of analysis. Mantel[2] has shown that any selection pattern operating equally among those subjects who go on to develop CHD and those who do not go on to develop CHD will not change the measure of association provided by this form of analysis. The form of selection bias that can be tolerated by this form of analysis is thus consistent with the type that one would expect to occur in a study with prospective assessment of the A-B characteristic and masked assessment of the CHD outcome as was done in the WCGS.

Overall, the thrust of the evidence and methodology speaks against selection and loss to follow-up bias as a major source of the observed association.

Possibility 6: The association may be influenced by some form of misclassification that could either inflate or deflate the "true" association between A-B behavior and CHD incidence.

Since a substantial association exists between A-B behavior and CHD incidence, one would be most concerned with unbalanced misclassification in those destined to become cases compared with noncases that might have inflated the association. There is no direct method for assessing the extent to which unbalanced A-B misclassification in the WCGS incidence study may have inflated the association. There are, however, a number of indirect ways to address this issue. The first source of evidence come from the results obtained prospectively by use of the Jenkins Activity Survey (JAS). The A-B score developed from this instrument was based on interview A-B assessments in the WCGS without regard to CHD case designation. It thereby provides an independent pathway for assessing the relationship between an alternate form of A-B assessment and CHD incidence that is most likely free of differential misclassification among cases and noncases. The JAS A-B assessment was significantly and substantially associated with CHD incidence.[3]

A second line of evidence is provided from analysis of recurrent CHD among survivors of initial heart disease in the WCGS. Type A subjects again show approximately twice the rate of recurrence experienced by Type B subjects. Moreover, one would expect this association to be free from any unbalanced misclassification effects that might be present in the basic incidence results.

Finally, A-B behavior may somehow reflect or forecast soon-to-occur CHD events. This may be examined by using A-B behavior to predict new disease among subjects who have remained free of disease for four and one-half years from the time of A-B assessment. In this form of analysis, despite the time lag involved, the relative risk of new CHD in Type A's is about 1.5 times that of Type B's and is statistically significant at the .01 level.

These considerations provide strong evidence supporting the association between globally assessed A-B behavior and CHD incidence. Further, a large part of this association seems to operate through mechanisms that are not represented by static assessments of traditional risk factors.

Conclusions differ greatly, however, when attention is focused on some of the major attempts that have been made to explore the dimensions of Type A behavior. The initial A-B classification in the WCGS was made at four levels: A_1, A_2, B_3, and B_4. However, no convincing dose-response relationship was observed in the relationship between these four levels and CHD incidence in the WCGS. Subjects classified as A_1 and A_2 had comparable risk. Also, subjects classified B_3 and B_4 had comparable risk at about half the level experienced by the A_1 and A_2 groups. This may be due in part to a reduction of group sizes when one goes beyond a dichotomization into A and B, but further studies in this area are essential.

Further, taken individually, the three factor dimensions (hard-driving, speed and impatience, job involvement) generated from the Jenkins Activity Survey show essentially no prospective predictability for CHD incidence in the WCGS. It appears, then, that much more work is needed to identify predicting traits within the A-B complex, preferably in connection with physiological reactivity, in preparation for future prospective and intervention studies. Nevertheless, the Type A scale of the Jenkins Activity Survey[4] has been related to various cardiovascular endpoints, including myocardial infarction (MI), recurrent MI, and atherosclerosis (as determined by coronary angiography).

The major results concerning the JAS Type A scale are as follows: First, the JAS Type A scale has been found to be consistently related, retrospectively, to coronary heart disease in seven independent studies in this country [5-11] and in one European country as well.[12] However, since response bias and sample selection can, in many ways, influence the results and interpretations in case-control studies, these replications take an added meaning. They assume greater significance in that they speak to the following issues: (1) random phenomena rarely replicate; (2) a variety of population groups were studied, and not simply narrowly defined and selected cases vs. controls; and (3) epidemiological studies have often found that replicated associations based on prevalence data are prospectively related as well.

Second, the JAS Type A scale has been found to have predictive validity for CHD in the WCGS,[13] thereby demonstrating that a self-administered psychological test based on clinical concepts can predict the future emergence of coronary disease. Third, the JAS Type A scale has been shown to be an even stronger predictor of recurrent infarction than initial events in the WCGS.[14,15] Fourth, the JAS Type A scale has been found to be related to the severity of atherosclerosis.[16] Fifth, the JAS Type A scale has been translated with good reliability and shown to relate to coronary heart disease in other cultures.[17] Sixth, most studies have shown the JAS Type A scale to be basically independent of major CHD risk factors for both initial[8] and recurrent CHD events[15].

Limitations on this evidence, however, are suggested by recent data[18] which indicate that the particular set of items used in the 1965, 1966, and 1969 editions of the JAS many not be entirely valid for some groups of subjects, including housewives, students, retired persons, and certain self-employed categories, such as farmers and small business proprietors. Additional validation studies are needed involving both the Structured Interview of Roseman and Friedman and pools of specially-developed questionnaire items so that new scales may be constructed for use with subject groups not adequately measured by the present JAS. The evidence to date suggests the current JAS Type A scale to be most valid for use with employed males between the ages of 25 and 65 who have at least eight years of education. It is thus important to proceed with a new calibration or refinement of the JAS using CHD as the criterion for those groups for whom the current version is not applicable.

Much of the evidence for the consistency of the Type A behavior pattern construct is derived from case-control studies comparing patients who have survived heart attacks with persons who have not experienced such events. Although there are many potential sources of error in such studies, there is little evidence that these have produced spurious results. Thus, case-control studies must deal with surviving patients; fatal events preclude interview. Persons with "silent MI," however, may represent undiscovered CHD events. In fact, Roseman et al.[19] and Jenkins et al.[20] have presented prospective data showing that cases of silent MI do not differ appreciably from cases of symptomatic MI in their frequency of Type A behavior pattern. Additional evidence is needed to substantiate these findings for fatal versus nonfatal coronary events.

Another potential source of bias in case-control studies is nonblind assessment of the behavior pattern. The similarity of results from face-to-face interviews, rating of taped interviews, and use of self-reporting questionnaires such as the JAS mitigate against this being a major problem with the studies cited.

The prospective or cohort study avoids some of these biases but may be subject to others. The major prospective study in this field (WCGS), as noted previously, has tended to avoid most of these other potential problems. When the study was designed in the late 1950s and early 1960s, the investigators already had a clear statement of their hypotheses, a well worked-out operational procedure for classifying Type A behavior at the baseline examination, a fairly large sample free of CHD, and an array of covariates or confounding factors that could be assessed and controlled for. There was a good follow-up over the eight and one-half year period of observation, and objective medical evidence was sought to ascertain end-point events. Thus, the strength and validity of the findings with regard to Type A behavior as a precursor of CHD seems to be as firm as, for example, the evidence regarding blood pressure, cholesterol, and cigarette smoking derived from the early reports of the Framingham Study. However, just as the Framingham findings were confirmed by other population-based studies and by continued surveillance of the Framingham cohort, the WCGS findings would be strengthened by confirmation in other prospective studies. This may be forthcoming from studies currently under way. The Multiple Risk Factor Intervention Trials (MRFIT), for example, will test whether the association of JAS Type A and the incidence of CHD can be replicated. The Aspirin Myocardial Infarction Study (AMIS) will provide an opportunity to cross-validate the relationship of JAS scores to recurrent infarction, and the Coronary Artery Surgery Study (CASS) will examine the replicability of the findings with regard to severity of atherosclerosis.

In developing new approaches to coronary-prone behavior patterns, adequate sample sizes should be used that have sufficient power to differentiate between relevant hypotheses. An effort should also be made to have the samples be representative of relevant general populations. Thus, the use of college students as subjects may be acceptable for initial exploratory studies, but validation should be sought in other more appropriate populations. In addition, new approaches should recognize the importance of identifying as many components of Type A behavior as possible using not only the interview protocol and the JAS but also other indices derived in a heuristic fashion. These components should then be tested against clinical endpoints such as CHD or degree of atherosclerosis in order to identify critical components of the behavior pattern.

Similarly, if there exists a common core of components of Type A behavior which transcends various sociocultural environments, then one way of validating these elements would be to carry out comparative assessments in a variety of cultural settings. In this way a smaller subset more closely associated with elevated CHD risk potentially could be identified. As noted in the development section promising leads already have been uncovered in a study of Japanese-Americans. Factor analyses of JAS responses indicated that these subjects clearly separated questions concerning *hard driving* from those dealing with *hard working*. The latter is consistent with both Type A and Japanese cultural expectations whereas hard-driving is definitely not congruent with these values.

There has been a tendency in most studies of Type A behavior to treat the behavior pattern as a stable characteristic of the individual. Although interview test-retest agreement over a period of one to two years is of the order of magnitude of 80%, it would be of interest to determine how much of this variance is due to unreliability of the assessment procedure versus changeability of the behavior pattern itself. As with smoking or dietary behavior patterns, it is likely that Type A behavior pattern may vary over time. Longitudinal studies are needed to explore the frequency of such changes, their relation to changes in the coronary risk factors, and their relation to the occurrence of coronary heart disease. Such information regarding spontaneous changes should be established before large-scale efforts are launched to intentionally modify behavior patterns.

Good science in this area is only a means to an end. That end is control of the pandemic of coronary heart disease in Western societies. Controlled studies of intervention are needed. Can we modify the Type A behavior pattern in the individual? Is it more important to modify some elements of the pattern than others? Can we reduce the frequency of conversion from Type B to Type A behavior? Can we modify the environment to make it less conducive to the emergence of potentially damaging Type A responses? And if all or any of these alterations in behavioral precursors can be accomplished in a reasonably representative population, will the occurrence of coronary heart disease in that population be reduced?

We can expect over the coming years to see a growing emphasis on the primary prevention of high blood pressure. That is, studies of our ability to prevent the initial conversion of blood pressure from normotensive by hypertensive levels using multiple modes of intervention will increase in number. How about the possibility of primary prevention of Type A behavior pattern? Can this risk factor be controlled at hygienic levels? This is an important possibility which should soon receive major investigative attention.

References

1. Rosenman, R.H., Brand, R.J., Sholtz, R.I., Friedman, M.: Multivariate prediction of coronary heart disease during 8.5 year follow-up in the Western Collaborative Group Study. *Am J Cardiol* **37**:902–910, 1976.
2. Mantel, N.: Synthetic retrospective studies and related topics. *Biometrics* **29**:477–486, 1973.
3. Brand, R.J., Rosenman, R.H., Jenkins, C.D., Sholtz, R.I., Zyzanski, S.J.: Comparison of coronary heart disease prediction in the Western Collaborative Group Study using the structured interview and the Jenkins Activity Survey assessments of the coronary prone Type A behavior pattern. *J Chronic Dis*. (in press).

4. Jenkins, C.D., Friedman, M., Rosenman, R.H.: The Jenkins Activity Survey for Health Prediction. Chapel Hill, N.C.: University of North Carolina, 1965.
5. Jenkins, C.D., Zyzanski, S.J., Rosenman, R.H.: Progress toward validation of a computer-scored test for the Type A coronary-prone behavior pattern. *Psychosom Med* **33**:193–202, 1971.
6. Kenigsberg, D., Zyzanski, S.J., Jenkins, C.D., Wardwell, W.I., et al.: The coronary-prone behavior pattern in hospitalized patients with and without coronary heart disease. *Psychosom Med* **36**:344–351, 1974.
7. Shekelle, R.B., Schoenberger, J.A., Stamler, J.: Correlates of the JAS Type A behavior pattern score. *J Chronic Dis* **29**:381–394, 1976.
8. Hiland, D. Behavioral characteristics of male VA patients with and without coronary disease. Ph.D. Dissertation, University of South Florida, Tampa, 1977.
9. Stokols, J.J.: Life dissatisfaction as a risk factor in coronary heart disease. Ph.D. Dissertation in Psychology, University of North Carolina at Chapel Hill, 1973.
10. Cohen, J.B.: Sociocultural change and behavior patterns in disease etiology: an epidemiologic study of coronary disease among Japanese-Americans. Ph.D. Dissertation in Epidemiology, School of Public Health, University of California at Berkeley, August, 1974.
11. Glass, D.C.: Stress, behavior patterns, and coronary disease. *Am Sci* **65**:177–187, 1977.
12. Zyzanski, S.J., Wazesniewski, K., Jenkins, C.D. Cross-cultural validation of the coronary-prone behavior pattern. Manuscript submitted for publication, 1978.
13. Jenkins, C.D., Rosenman, R.H., Zyzanski, S.J.: Prediction of clinical coronary heart disease by a test for the coronary-prone behavior pattern. *N Engl J Med* **290**:1271–1275, 1974.
14. Jenkins, C.D., Zyzanski, S.J., Rosenman, R.H., Cleveland, G.L.: Association of coronary-prone behavior scores with recurrence of coronary heart disease. *J Chronic Dis* **24**:601–611, 1971.
15. Jenkins, C.D., Zyzanski, S.J., Rosenmen, R.H.: Risk of new myocardial infarction in middle-aged men with manifest coronary heart disease. *Circulation* **53**:342–347, 1976.
16. Zyzanski, S.J., Jenkins, C.D., Ryan, T.J., Flessas, A., et al.: Psychological correlates of coronary angiographic findings. *Arch Intern Med* **136**:1234–1237, 1976.
17. Kittel, F., Kornitzer, M., Zyzanski, S.J., Jenkins, C.D., et al.: Two methods of assessing the Type A coronary-prone behavior pattern in Belgium. *J Chronic Dis* (in press).
18. Blumenthal, J.A., Kong, Y., Rosenman, R.H.: Type A behavior pattern and angiographically documented coronary disease. Presented at the meeting of the American Psychosomatic Society, New Orleans, March 21, 1975.
19. Roseman, R.H., Brand, R.J., Jenkins, C.D., Friedman, M., Straus, R., Wurm, M.: Coronary heart disease in the Western Collaborative Group Study: Final follow-up experience of 8 ½ years. *JAMA* **233**:872–877, 1975.
20. Jenkins, C.D., Rosenman, R.H., Zyzanski, S.J.: Prediction of clinical coronary heart disease by a test for the coronary-prone behavior pattern. *N Engl J Med* **290**:1271–1275, 1974.

Chapter 1

Coronary-Prone Behavior as an Independent Risk Factor for Coronary Heart Disease

Richard J. Brand

To date, there has been little formal research to demonstrate that Type A's can be changed to Type B's. There is even less evidence to show that altering Type A behavior, if it can be effectively accomplished, will in turn reduce the incidence of recurrence of coronary disease. In the absence of these crucial experimental studies, we must be content to attempt causal inferences based on results obtained from a relatively few observational studies. In this, we encounter one of the most challenging phases of epidemiological research. The caveat "association does not imply causation" is familiar to all and serves as a warning to proceed cautiously. Nevertheless, causal interpretation plays an important role in decisions to replicate or refine observational research and in decisions to extend activity to intervention studies or programs. We are, therefore, called upon to exercise our judgment.

It is useful to identify some basic steps involved in making causal inferences. We know that any observed association may derive from various sources. The association may (1) represent a cause and effect relationship, (2) be the result of a chance fluctuation, (3) come from some sort of bias, or (4) derive from some combination of the above. It is therefore sensible to apply a process of elimination to see what noncausal explanations can be reasonably excluded as a basis for an observed association. To the extent that noncausal explanations seem unlikely, our confidence in the causal interpretation is increased.

Methods for assessing chance effects are rather well developed as a result of the extensive statistical theory that is available. However, when an association is inflated by bias, the statistical significance of that association is correspondingly increased. Thus, statistical significance tests can in no way be considered a method for distinguishing between bias and cause and effect. Bias is more difficult to investigate than chance effects since terminology has not yet been standardized. It may, therefore, be helpful to identify the most likely sources of bias.

Bias Due to Selection of Study Subjects

The study subjects may be systematically different in some way from the population to which we would like to generalize results. This may occur through use of the nonrandom convenience samples that are used almost universally in epidemiological research. Selection bias may also result from nonresponse, missing data, and loss to follow-up, which can render nonrepresentative even those samples that were planned to be random samples. In particular, we must be on guard against any process that would tend to overselect Type A cases or underselect Type B noncases. Selection bias can either increase or decrease a true association. One solution to this problem is to choose methods of analysis and accompanying measures of association that are relatively unaffected by likely forms of selection bias.

Bias Due to Measurement Error or Misclassification

Even if we obtain representative study subjects, measurement error and misclassification can influence association. If, for example, net misclassification among cases is toward the Type A category relative to net misclassification among noncases, the behavior pattern–CHD association would be inflated. However, balanced A-B misclassification among both cases and noncases can be shown to dilute association. Bias due to this effect is best controlled by careful masking of the predictor when assessing disease outcome and by masking of the disease outcome when the predictor is assessed.

Bias Due to Covariables

The basic method of epidemiological analysis is statistical comparison of groups such as Type A's versus Type B's to determine differences between CHD rates. To the extent that A's differ from B's according to other covariables (CHD risk factors), we are hard-pressed to isolate the source of differences in CHD rates. If the A's have more CHD than the B's merely because they coincidentally have higher levels of other risk factors, the resulting inflation in the A-B versus CHD association would be called "covariable bias."

It is the method for controlling covariable bias that most clearly distinguishes observational from experimental research. In an experimental study, randomization serves to balance comparison groups for all personal characteristics except the one under study. The effect of chance deviations from exact balance are assessed by a standard test of statistical significance. In observational studies, we can at best adjust for some limited set of covariables that have been measured. This paper emphasizes the use and interpretation of adjustment methods for studying the influence of covariables on the relationship between the behavior pattern and CHD.

Bias Due to Use of an Improper Model

In any data analysis, there are two main sources of information that determine the results. First is the information contained in the data itself, and second is the information implicit in the structural characteristics of the model used to analyze the data. If the "model structure" does not agree with the "reality structure," substantial distortion can occur in the conclusions of the analysis. In CHD risk analysis, the additive multiple logistic model has been widely used. The inherent structure of this model is synergistic in that each risk factor operates by producing a constant multiplicative effect applied to the background risk level corresponding to other factors. This choice of model for assessing the behavior pattern-CHD association will be assessed in some detail.

In the first part of this chapter, I will discuss evidence that suggests a causal link between A-B behavior and coronary heart disease. I have been asked to focus in particular on the following questions:

What is the relationship between A-B behavior and the traditional risk factors in predicting CHD?
Is the behavior pattern an independent risk factor for CHD?

These are, in effect, questions about covariable bias in the observed association between A-B behavior and CHD. Throughout, I am going to focus on behavior pattern data obtained by the Structured Interview conducted at the intake exam of the Western Collaborative Group Study (WCGS). A recent analysis suggests that the interview provides a substantial amount of predictive information that has not been captured by the Jenkins Activity Survey (JAS). Since the WCGS is the only completed large-scale prospective incidence study that has thus far used the Structured Interview the data from this study deserve close scrutiny to see what they can reveal.

Does Behavior Pattern Operate Either Causally or Noncausally Through One of the Traditional Risk Factors?

This issue can be examined by estimating the relationship between behavior pattern and CHD before and after adjustment for the traditional risk factors. Whatever relationship is left after adjustment must operate through some pathway other than the traditional factors. In general, the main purpose of adjustment in observational studies is to partition an observed association to see what part operates through factors for which an adjustment was made versus what part operates through other pathways.

The portion of the behavior pattern-CHD association that operates through the traditional factors may be either causal or noncausal. If any of the traditional factors are causally related to CHD and are in turn causally influenced in an undesirable direction by Type A behavior, then the traditional risk factors are causal intermediaries for the behavior pattern. In this situation, the reduction in behavior pattern-CHD association that results from adjustment can meaningfully be assigned to behavior pattern as the underlying causal factor. If, however, the behavior pattern noncausally covaries with or is causally influenced by traditional risk factors, the adjusted association will also show a reduction that is unfortunately indistinguishable from the previous effect. In this case, no causal contribution accrues to the behavior pattern. One or both of these phenomena may be operating, but with the observational study design we are not able to distinguish between these possibilities. However, supplementary studies of the effects of behavior pattern modification on traditional risk factors could shed some light on this question by demonstrating one link in a causal pathway.

This qualitative discussion can be made more quantitative by an examination of the findings in Table 1.1. These results are based on a multiple logistic analysis of 3, 154 subjects in the WCGS who were free of CHD at intake, 257 of whom experienced CHD events in 8½ years of follow-up. The first line of the table shows the relationship between the behavior pattern and CHD incidence with no adjustment for other factors. Type A subjects have an estimated risk 2.37 times the risk of the Type B subjects. The major traditional risk factors— age, systolic blood pressure, cigarette smoking, and serum cholesterol—are all correlated about .06–.09 with the behavior pattern. Adjustment for any of these factors, one at a time, reduces the relative risk to about 2.25. Adjustment for all of these factors simultaneously reduces the estimated relative risk to 1.97. This reduction from 2.37 to 1.97 represents the portion of the unadjusted behavior pattern association that may be operating through the traditional factors, either causally or noncausally. However, since it seems clear that age cannot be a causal intermediary for behavior pattern, the relative risk of 2.21 after adjustment for age can be viewed as the upper limit of a causal relationship that could conceivably be inferred from WCGS data. It is apparent that a relative risk of about two persists after adjustment that does not seem to operate through those traditional risk factors. To this extent, we can say that the behavior pattern is an independent factor.

Since the major risk factors for CHD were included in this adjustment, it is not surprising that these general conclusions are essentially unchanged by adjustment for a larger list of factors previously studied in WCGS data.[1,2]

The question of causality is, of course, far from settled. The relative risk of 1.97 may be causally based, or it may be the result of some other form of bias such as noncausal covariance with a nontraditional causal factor. This association may, however, represent one or more causal pathways for which intermediary links can be discovered. In any event, the behavior pattern findings represent a new and interesting lead in CHD research. We look to those who will discuss mechanisms for further insight along these lines. It is also impor-

Table 1.1 Relationship between coronary heart disease incidence and behavior pattern assessed by the structured interview, with various adjustments for other major risk factors measured at intake exam.

Age (yrs.)	Systolic Blood Pressure (mm Hg)	Cigarette Smoking (4 level)[a]	Cholesterol (mg/100 ml)	Logistic Coefficient	Significance Probability (P)	Correlation of Factor with Beh. Patt.	Approximate Relative Risk (odds ratio)
yes				.863	<.0001		2.37
	yes			.797	<.0001	.089	2.21
	yes			.805	<.0001	.078	2.23
		yes		.814	<.0001	.078	2.25
			yes	.819	<.0001	.057	2.26
yes	yes			.755	<.0001		2.12
yes		yes		.747	<.0001		2.11
yes			yes	.766	<.0001		2.15
	yes	yes		.749	<.0001		2.11
	yes		yes	.769	<.0001		2.16
		yes	yes	.783	<.0001		2.19
yes	yes	yes		.698	<.0001		2.01
yes	yes		yes	.728	<.0001		2.07
yes		yes	yes	.727	<.0001		2.07
	yes	yes	yes	.727	<.0001		2.07
yes	yes	yes	yes	.682	<.0001		1.97

[a] Smoking status coded: 0 = nonsmoker, 1 = less than a pack per day, 2 = one pack per day, 3 = more than a pack per day.

tant to keep in mind that the portion of the unadjusted relative risk represented by the increment of relative risk from 1.97 to 2.21 may have a causal nature.

Does the Relationship Between A-B Behavior and CHD Incidence Depend on the Level of the Traditional Risk Factors?

There is another aspect of "independence" between risk factors worth considering. The concept to which I am now referring is more often called interaction in biostatistical terminology and synergism or potentiation in the biological sciences. Also, the term "effect-modification" has recently appeared in the epidemiological literature and may be more descriptive. By definition, effect-modification is present if the increment of CHD risk in Type A compared to Type B subjects differs depending on the level of other risk factors. Presence of effect-modification is thereby a form of dependence between risk factors.

Note that the definition of effect-modification depends on the particular choice for the measure of association. In this somewhat arbitrary formulation of the absence of effect-modification, we envision the effect of Type A as a constant increment of risk that adds to whatever background risk level an individual has from levels of traditional risk factors. Alternatively, we may envision the effect of Type A as a constant relative increase that multiples the background risk level of each individual by a constant factor (i.e., by the relative risk). This multiplicative pattern is one form of effect-modification (synergism) since a constant doubling of risk, for example, produces a greater risk increment when applied to a high background level than it does to a low background level.

A number of statistical issues arise when we attempt to see what basic pattern is most consistent with the WCGS data. The nature of statistical tests of goodness-of-fit requires the choice of some pattern as a provisional (null) hypothesis. Then a statistical test can be applied to assess the degree of discrepancy between the hypothesized pattern and the actual data. Furthermore, the only goodness-of-fit test that is well-grounded in statistical theory demands the categorization of the predictors so that a chi-squared method can be used to compare observed and estimated expected CHD rates in the subgroups that result from cross classification of the categorized predictors.

The four major risk factors—age in years (39–49, 50–59); systolic blood pressure in mm Hg (< 126, ≥ 126); cigarette smoking (none, some); and serum cholesterol in mg/100 ml (<233.0, ≥ 223.0)—were dichotomized as indicated to give, along with the dichotomized A-B classification, five two-level risk factors. Cross classification thereby gives $2^5 = 32$ risk subgroups, ranging from one that is low on all five factors to one that is high on all five factors. The numbers of subjects and the CHD events in each of these 32 subgroups are given in Table 1.2.

Table 1.2. Observed and estimated CHD rates in 32 risk subgroups.

Sub-Group	Serum Cholesterol	Behavior Pattern	Systolic B.P.	Cigarette Smoking	Age	Number at Risk	Number of CHD Events	Observed CHD Rate (% in 8.5 yrs.)	Logistic Model	Linear Model
			Dichotomized Risk Factor				Data		Estimated CHD Rate (%) in 8.5 Years	
1						232	1	0.4	1.2	0.1
2					+	45	0	0.0	2.1	0.0
3				+		144	2	1.4	2.1	1.0
4			+			170	7	4.1	2.5	2.6
5		+				147	5	3.4	2.6	2.2
6	+					133	3	2.3	3.1	2.6
7				+	+	31	0	0.0	3.5	3.8
8			+	+	+	47	3	6.4	4.2	5.4
9			+	+		103	4	3.9	4.2	6.3
10		+			+	47	0	0.0	4.3	5.1
11		+		+		118	6	5.1	4.4	6.1
12	+		+			135	7	5.2	5.2	7.7
13	+				+	30	1	3.3	5.2	5.5
14	+			+		126	6	4.8	5.2	6.4
15	+	+	+			122	8	6.6	6.2	8.1
16	+	+				109	6	5.5	6.4	7.7
17		+	+			33	3	9.1	7.1	9.3
18		+		+	+	53	5	9.4	7.3	8.9
19		+	+	+	+	60	7	11.7	8.5	10.5
20		+	+	+		123	8	6.5	8.7	11.5
21	+			+		42	6	14.3	8.7	9.3
22	+		+		+	85	5	5.9	10.1	10.9
23	+		+		+	148	19	12.8	10.3	11.9

continued

Table 1.2. (continued)

	Dichotomized Risk Factor					Data			Estimated CHD Rate (%) in 8.5 Years	
Sub-Group	Serum Cholesterol	Behavior Pattern	Systolic B.P.	Cigarette Smoking	Age	Number at Risk	Number of CHD Events	Observed CHD Rate (% in 8.5 yrs.)	Logistic Model	Linear Model
24	+	+			+	52	7	13.5	10.4	10.6
25	+	+		+		130	18	13.8	10.6	11.5
26	+	+	+			130	15	11.5	12.4	13.2
27		+	+	+	+	63	9	14.3	14.0	14.4
28	+		+	+	+	67	11	16.4	16.4	14.8
29	+	+		+	+	50	7	14.0	16.8	14.4
30	+	+	+		+	103	23	22.3	19.4	16.0
31	+	+	+	+		172	30	17.4	19.7	17.0
32	+	+	+	+	+	92	25	27.2	29.6	19.8
Total						3,142	257	8.2		

+ = high risk level, blank = low risk level

Table 1.3   Coefficients of the linear and logistical models fitted to the WCGS data.

Dichotomous Risk Factor	Prevalence of High-Risk Level (%)	Linear Coefficient[a]	Logistic Coefficient[a]	Approximate Relative Risk
Intercept		−0.0287	−4.402	
Age	28.6	0.0287	.536	1.71
Systolic Blood Pressure	52.6	0.0544	.730	2.08
Cigarette Smoking	47.6	0.0383	.555	1.74
Serum Cholesterol	50.6	0.0548	.952	2.59
Behavior Pattern	50.4	0.0510	.760	2.13

[a] All coefficients are statistically significant at $P < .0001$.

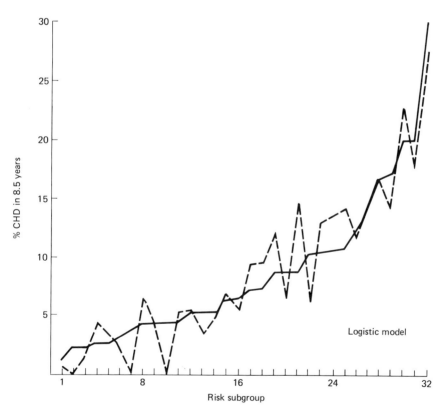

Figure 1.1A: Comparison of CHD rates observed and estimated by the additive logistical risk model. Solid line, estimated rate by logistic model; broken line, observed rate.

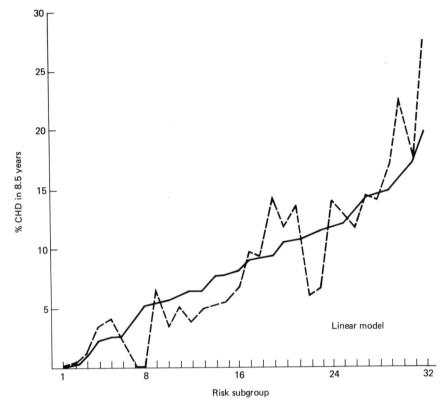

Figure 1.1B: Comparison of CHD rates observed and estimated by the additive linear risk model.
Solid line, estimated rate by linear model; broken line, observed rate.

   The constant risk increment pattern is represented by the additive linear risk
model:

   $R = A_0 + A_1X_1 + \ldots + A_5X_5$

The constant relative risk pattern is well approximated by the additive logistic
risk model:

   $\ln(\dfrac{R}{1 - R}) = B_0 + B_1X_1 + \ldots + B_kX_5$

Here R represents risk, $X_1, \ldots, X_5$ are dummy (0 = low, 1 = high) predictors representing the five dichotomized risk factors, and the $A_0, \ldots, A_5$ and
$B_0, \ldots, B_5$ are the linear and logistic coefficients, respectively, that are the
parameter of the models estimated from CHD status and predictor data. A_j can
be interpreted as the constant risk increment in the high compared to the
low-risk level of factor j, and e^{B_j} can be shown to closely approximate to the
relative risk in high compared to the low risk level for factor j.

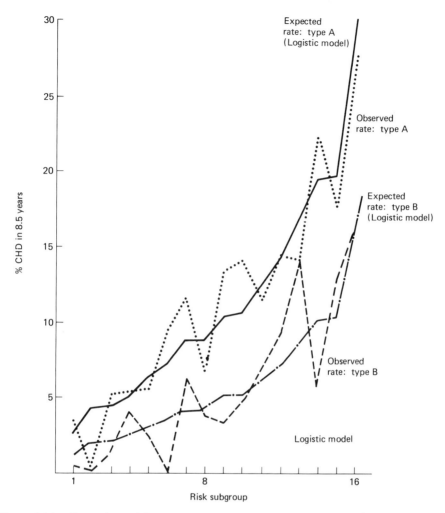

Figure 1.2A: Comparison of CHD rates observed and estimated by the additive logistical risk model, shown separately by behavior pattern classification. Solid line, expected rate; broken line, observed rate.

Each of these models has been applied to the WCGS data to see which fits best. Observed events for the 32 risk subgroups were compared with the expected events estimated from the best fitting versions of these two models. A standard X^2 test of goodness-of-fit with $32 - 6 = 26$ degrees of freedom was used to assess the statistical significance of the discrepancies between observed and expected events.

The linear and logistic coefficients obtained by fitting these two models to the WCGS data are given in Table 1.3. The additive linear model estimates that Type A behavior after adjustment for the other traditional risk factors is associated with an independent CHD rate increment of 5.1% in 8.5 years of

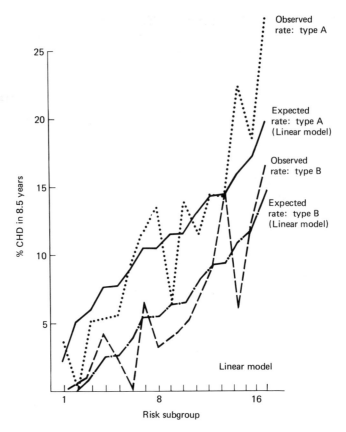

Figure 1.2B: Comparison of CHD rates observed and estimated by the additive linear risk model, shown separately by behavior pattern classification. Solid line, expected rate; broken line, observed rate.

follow-up. For example, the Type A subjects who are low on all factors and who have an estimated CHD risk that is 5.11% in 8.5 years compared to the corresponding Type B subjects who are low on other factors and who have an estimated risk of .1%. Similarly, the Type A subjects who are high on all other factors have an estimated CHD risk of 19.8% in 8.5 years compared to the corresponding Type B subjects who have an estimated risk of 14.7%. By this method, the behavior pattern is very similar in predictive strength to serum cholesterol and systolic blood pressure and somewhat stronger than age and cigarette smoking. (I doubt, however, that any of these differences are very statistically significant, but I have not yet completed the calculations to check this.)

The additive logistic model applied in this way gives the behavior pattern a relative risk of 2.13, which is exceeded only by serum cholesterol with 2.59. For these results, the Type A subjects who are low on all other factors have an estimated CHD risk of 2.5% in 8.5 years, which is 2.13 times the risk of 1.2%

estimated for their Type B counterparts. The estimated risk increment is thus only 1.49%. By comparison, the Type A subjects who are high on all other factors have an estimated risk of 29.6%, which is almost double the estimated risk of 16.4% for their Type B counterparts.* The estimated risk increment is thus quite large at 13.2%.

A comparison of observed and estimated expected CHD rates is shown in Figure 1.1 for each of these models. The 32 subgroups are rank ordered by increasing expected risk estimated by whichever model is under consideration. The logistic model fits the data remarkably well by visual examination and has a goodness-of-fit significance probability of P = .81. The linear model fit is not too bad, however, and it has a significance probability of P = .35. (See the Appendix for a discussion of some more technical points regarding the linear model.)

Further insight into these patterns can be obtained from Figure 1.2, in which the Type A and Type B subgroups are plotted separately for each of these risk models. We see that the linear model tends to underestimate CHD risk for Type A subjects who have a high background risk level from the high levels of traditional risk factors. Corresponding split level representations for the other risk factors give similar results.

Overall, these results leave me with the impression that the data are noticeably more consistent with a synergistic pattern in the heart disease risk, in which not only behavior pattern but also the other risk factors operate with nearly a constant multiplicative effect applied to whatever background level results from other risk factors.

The previous discussion indicates that the dichotomous behavior pattern for the most part does not seem to operate through traditional risk factors. Instead, Type A seems to operate primarily via nontraditional pathways to approximately multiply CHD risk by a factor of 1.97. Furthermore, the 95% confidence interval for this multiplicative factor ranges from 1.49 to 2.62, so this association is not easily explained as a chance fluctuation.

Further examination of possible bias due to selection or misclassification effects is under way.

References

1. Brand, R.J., Rosenman, R.H., Jenkins, C.D., Sholtz, R.I., Zyzanski, S.J.: Comparison of coronary heart disease prediction in the Western Collaborative Group Study using the structured interview and the Jenkins Activity Survey assessments of the coronary prone Type A behavior pattern. *J Chronic Dis,* (in press).

* The shift in the multiplier occurs from the fact that odds ratios derived from the logistic model only approximate relative risk. The ln linear model $\ln(R) = C_0 + C_1 X_1 + . . . + C_5 X_5$ has the pattern in which relative risk given by e^{C_j} for the j-th factor is exactly constant over levels of the remaining factors. For behavior pattern, this relative risk is 1.95 and the goodness-of-fit significance probability for this model is P = .74. The ln linear model and the logistic model are almost indistinguishable since for low risk levels $\ln(R) = \ln(R/(1 - R))$.

2. Rosenman, R.H., Brand, R.J., Sholtz, R.I., Friedman, M.: Multivariate prediction of coronary heart disease during 8.5 year follow-up in the Western Collaborative Group Study. *Am. J. Cardiol.* **37**:902–910, 1976.
3. Walker, S.H., Duncan, D.B.: Estimation of the probability of an event as a function of several independent variables. *Biometrika* **54**:167–179, 1967.

Appendix

Some difficulties occurred in fitting the additive linear model to the WCGS data. The computational algorithm used was a modification of the iterated weighted least squared method described in Section 4 of the paper by Walker and Duncan.[3] The algorithm for the linear model failed because the 232 subjects who were low on all risk factors were estimated to have a CHD rate less than zero. This anomaly in turn produced negative error variances that terminated computation when the program took square roots to get the estimated standard errors of the linear coefficients. Although the calculation of a CHD rate less than zero is mathematically feasible with the linear model, it makes no sense biologically. This result in itself suggests that the linear model does not have the proper structure to represent the multifactor CHD process.

To salvage the linear model, the computational algorithm was then modified to reset rates below zero to the slightly positive value of $R = .001$ (i.e., .1%). Also, the weights on the order of $1/(R(1 - R))$ corresponding to the reset risks were reset to $1/(.5(1 - .5)) = 4$ instead of $1/(.001(1 - .001)) = 1000$ to minimize the impact of the reset risks on the overall estimation.

In this scheme, the linear model assumes a bottom risk threshold at .1% that changes its pattern to be more like a logistic model. Even so, this model does not fit that data as well as the logistic model.

Coronary-Prone Behavior Pattern and Coronary Heart Disease: Epidemiological Evidence

Stephen J. Zyzanski

This chapter addresses the complex issue of whether the observed associations between the coronary-prone behavior pattern (Type A), coronary heart disease (CHD), and traditional CHD risk factors have been consistent across different population groups, sexes, ages, and cultures. In this report, only Type A behavior, as measured by the Type A scale of the Jenkins Activity Survey (JAS), will be considered.[1] Its observed relationships to various cardiovascular endpoints, including myocardial infarction (MI), recurrent infarction, and atherosclerosis (as determined by coronary angiography), will be stressed, as well as its relationships to a variety of demographic indices. The strengths and weaknesses of the Structured Interview, the Bortner scale, and other methods for assessing the behavior pattern will be covered by other sections within this volume. Similarly, the three-factor analytically-derived scales of the JAS, which are related to the coronary-prone behavior pattern but are independent of each other, will also not be considered in this report. The focus, then, will be restricted to an evaluation of the major findings concerning the JAS Type A scale.

Criterion-Based Validity of the JAS Type A Scale

The JAS Type A scale was originally developed for use in the Western Collaborative Group Study (WCGS) to determine whether a precoded self-report instrument could be developed that would measure the Type A coronary-prone behavior pattern. It was derived and cross-validated on independent samples by means of discriminant function analysis. The final 19-item Type A scale of the 1965 JAS represents the subset of items that best discriminated men judged to be Type A from those judged to be Type B by means of the clinical interview administered three and five years earlier in the WCGS.[2] Although the Structured Interview and the JAS do not classify subjects identically (73% agreement was found in the initial calibration), each has been shown in its own right to be a valid predictor of clinical coronary disease. Scoring norms for all JAS scales for all forms of the test were derived from all subjects in the WCGS who completed Activity Surveys in 1965, 1966, and 1969, respectively. Each scale was standardized to have a mean of zero and a standard deviation of 10. Scores in the positive direction indicate Type A predominance and scores in the negative direction indicate Type B tendencies.

In 1975, the very large Belgian Multi-factorial Preventive Project utilized both the Structured Interview and the JAS methods for assessing Type A behavior. This project was a randomized trial involving over 7,000 men who were 40 to 59 years of age at intake. JAS and Structured Interview data were gathered on a subgroup of 726 men. Both procedures were translated into French and Flemish to determine whether the Type A Interview and the self-administered JAS could withstand the effects of translation across languages and nationalities and retain similar distributional properties and relations to one another as in the U.S. population on which they were developed. The project was also carried out to determine whether the Type A concept applies to other populations living in different cultures. Clearly, the validity of assessing Type A behavior in another cultural setting must be established prior to testing whether the behavior pattern's relationship to CHD risk is similar to that found in the United States.

The distribution of interview behavior type ratings, made by trained interviewers in Belgium, was compared with data from North America. They were found to be similarly symmetrical but clustering more towards the central categories (A_2 and B_3) in Belgium. The Activity Survey, when scored by the scoring key developed for the WCGS, yielded averages for this Belgian group that appeared to be more in the Type B direction than the California sample (Table 2.1).[3] JAS Type A scores and the Structured Interview behavior pattern ratings showed a strong correspondence, with 70% agreement observed between the two.

This comparability between findings in Belgium and in the United States suggests that the concept of the Type A behavior pattern has sufficient cross-cultural parallelism to permit the derivation of reliable measurements and to make feasible the determination of whether Type A behavior is a risk factor for coronary disease internationally.

Discrimination of Groups with Coronary
Heart Disease in Prevalence Studies

Since 1970, at least eight studies utilizing the JAS have found evidence supporting the association of Type A behavior with prevalence of coronary disease. In

Table 2.1   Degree of Agreement between Behavior Type Interviews and Activity Survey Scores in Employed Belgian Men.

		BEHAVIOR TYPE by Interview			
		A	B	Total	
JAS type A score divided at Belgian sample mean of −3.05	A	70.1% (195)	30.5% (87)	50.1% (282)	
	B	29.9% (83)	69.5% (198)	49.9% (281)	Overall percentage of agreement: 69.8%
	Total	49.4% (278)	50.6% (285)	100% (563)	

		BEHAVIOR TYPE by Interview			
		A	B	Total	
JAS type A score divided at WCGS sample mean of 0.0	A	60.1% (167)	20.7% (59)	40.1% (226)	
	B	39.9% (111)	79.3% (226)	59.9% (337)	Overall percentage of agreement: 69.8%
	Total	49.4% (278)	50.6% (285)	100% (563)	
Mean JAS type A score		1.5	−7.1	−2.8	
Standard deviation		8.9	7.8	9.4	

a retrospective study in the WCGS, 83 men under the age of 60 who had sustained a first attack of CHD before taking the test were compared with 468 random control subjects.[2] The mean Type A score was significantly higher for the cases than for the controls (P = .01). In a study at Bridgeport Community Hospital in Connecticut, 48 patients with coronary disease (both men and women) scored significantly higher on the Type A scale than 42 patients hospitalized with other diseases.[4] Shekelle et al.[5] studied prevalence of myocardial infarction in 1,209 middle-aged white males entering a screening program of the Chicago Heart Association. They found the Type A score from the Activity Survey significantly related to prevalence of coronary disease after age, cholesterol, diastolic blood pressure, and cigarette smoking were controlled statistically by means of a multiple logistic regression analysis. Glass[5a], in a retrospective study of VA patients, found that the 45 hospitalized coronary patients had significantly higher Type A scores than either the 77 hospitalized or 50 nonhospitalized controls (P < .01). In a 1977 study of 80 VA patients, Hiland[6] found that the 40 CHD cases scored significantly higher on the Type A scale than the 40 matched controls. Wrzesniewski,[7] working in Inowroclaw,

Poland, contrasted 149 MI patients who experienced their first myocardial infarction only 8 to 12 weeks prior to responding to the Activity Survey, with 88 men free of CHD employed in three different companies. The Activity Survey was translated into Polish and back-translated to verify its accuracy in capturing Type A concepts. This is the same procedure that was used with considerable success in the previously cited Belgian study. The Polish MI's scored significantly higher in the Type A direction than the controls (P = .02).

Two unpublished dissertations have reported on patients with coronary disease, one in North Carolina by Jeanne Stokols[8] and the other in Hawaii by Judith B. Cohen.[9] These studies found that men with coronary disease had significantly higher mean scores on the Type A scale than comparison groups without the disease. Dr. Stokols, working with out-patients at the Durham, North Carolina, VA Hospital, found that the 78 patients who experienced a single coronary event scored significantly more often in the Type A direction than the 35 control patients without CHD. Dr. Cohen, working with Americans of Japanese descent who were participating in the Honolulu Heart Program, found in the older (i.e., 56–65 year age group) participants, a CHD rate of 64/1,000 for men rated Type A as compared with a rate of 34/1,000 for men rated Type B.

The consistent cross-validation supplied by these numerous studies lends strong support to the theory underlying the relation of the behavior pattern to CHD, and further documents the validity of the JAS as an objective measure of this life-style. These repeated replications for prevalence data also suggest that the Type A behavior pattern is sufficiently robust to allow for cross-cultural translations, revisions in the item pools, and modifications in the methods of scoring without seriously altering the often-observed relationship between Type A and coronary disease. Whether these associations are greatly influenced by factors known to bias retrospective studies, i.e., selective survival and retrospective bias in answering the questionnaire, can only be established through a prospective study. This would also resolve the issue of whether the behavior preceded the emergence of clinical CHD or whether it followed the illness. This research has also been completed and published.

Prediction of CHD Incidence in the WCGS

Analysis of JAS scores of 120 healthy men from the WCGS who developed CHD after taking the test showed that the Type A scale distinguished cases from healthy controls on a prospective basis.[10] Men scoring in the top third of the Type A distribution incurred nearly twice the incidence of CHD over a four-year period compared with those scoring in the lowest third (the Type B end) of the distribution. The prospective association reported here reinforces earlier retrospective findings that the Type A behavior pattern, both as measured by the Structured Interview and by the JAS, is a genuine precursor of CHD.

The methods of the WCGS were designed to overcome many of the weaknesses found in earlier clinical studies. For example, the study design was prospective, thereby protecting against false inferences caused by selective survival and retrospective biases. It was a double-blind study, protecting against conscious or unconscious biasing of the results for or against the hypothesis being tested. The blinding of subjects further protected against self-fulfilling prophesies and the risk of differential reporting of symptoms by persons who may have believed that they were at high or low risk. Finally, the system for scoring the JAS was derived *a priori* on the basis of the theory of the coronary-prone Type A behavior pattern and clinical judgments of the presence or absence of this pattern, and not after the fact through analyses of items discriminating cases from controls.

Relation to Recurrent Myocardial Infarction and other Causes of Death

The impact of a CHD event on behavior type, particularly on JAS score, has recently been studied. Plausible arguments can be offered that the Type A score might change in either direction after hospitalization for clinical coronary disease. Some CHD cases may consciously attempt to change their life-style toward the Type B direction. The voluntary cessation of cigarette smoking following an MI would be an example of such a therapeutic change. Other persons, however, may feel increased pressure to achieve goals that may now be threatened by a reduced life expectancy. Thus, such individuals may increase rather than decrease their Type A behavior following a return to normal daily activities.

In two overlapping case groups from the WCGS,[11,12] JAS Type A scores were found to be associated with increased risk of reinfarction among persons already having clinical coronary disease. In the latter, more comprehensive group, three risk factors—Type A score, number of cigarettes smoked per day, and serum cholesterol level—significantly discriminated between 220 men surviving a single CHD event and 67 with recurrent events. The Type A score was found to be relatively unaffected by whether the measure was made before or after the initial CHD event. Multiple variable discriminant function equations showed the Type A score to be the single strongest predictor of recurrent CHD among the variables tested. Furthermore, Type A scores significantly discriminated recurrent from single event cases, even after the variables of age, diastolic blood pressure, cholesterol, and number of cigarettes were controlled statistically in a step-wise regression analysis. Finally, a comparison of the magnitude of differences of Type A scores for these clinical groups suggests that scores on the JAS Type A scale distinguish even more effectively between recurrent and single event groups than between the single event and the CHD-free population.

Table 2.2 presents mean Type A scores for various groups of CHD cases and for several different causes of death. The means for initial and recurrent CHD death are of particular interest. The mean Type A score for deaths due to initial

Table 2.2.   Means of JAS Type A Scores for WCGS Population and for Groups of
CHD Prevalence, Incidence and Recurrent Cases and for Causes of Death in the WCGS.

Sample	Sample Size	Mean
WCGS population	2960	0.00
Random sample free of CHD	524	−0.60
CHD survivors for 5+ years	105	0.69
CHD survivors for 1–4 years	98	2.58
CHD incidence for 1–4 years	120	1.70
All recurrent MI before JAS (retrospective)	23	4.77
All recurrent MI after JAS (prospective)	44	4.18
Deaths due to CHD (initial MI)	15	−2.15
Deaths due to CHD (recurrent MI)	26	3.34
Deaths due to violence (accident, suicide, murder)	11	3.44
Deaths due to stroke (CVA)	9	0.78
Deaths due to cancer	35	−0.22
Miscellaneous deaths (liver, renal, pulmonary)	19	0.82

MI is −2.15. This somewhat Type B mean, though, is based only on 15 cases.
However, for deaths due to recurrent MI, the 26 cases have a mean Type A
score of 3.34, suggesting that high intensities of Type A behavior may place
patients at increased risk to a fatal reinfarction. It should be emphasized that
for all causes of death listed in Table 2.2, the number of cases in any one
classification is not large, thereby invoking caution in the interpretation of these
results. Interestingly enough, the Type A scores for the remaining causes of
death, e.g., cancers, are mostly near zero or in the Type B direction. The only
exception to this general pattern is the elevated mean Type A score for deaths
due to accidents and violence. This group has an even higher score on the factor
for speed and impatience. Since the sample has only 11 cases, one cannot say
with any confidence that this trend would continue given a larger sample size,
but it is noted for its interest.

The pattern in the mortality data, however, does suggest that Type A
behavior is indeed quite specific to coronary disease and not associated with
elevated risks of mortality from other common causes.

Relation to Coronary Atherosclerosis

The scientific value of an established association between any risk factor and
the incidence of coronary disease is greatly strengthened when evidence can be
obtained regarding the pathological mechanism linking the associated variables. Evidence along these lines comes from three double-blind studies conducted at about the same time at separate institutions. Ninety-four men with a
variety of cardiological diagnoses who underwent coronary angiography at

Boston University also completed the JAS on admission to the hospital. Fifty-five men with two or more coronary vessels obstructed 50% or more at a point of greatest involvement were found to score significantly higher on all four JAS scales than the remaining 39 men with lesser atherosclerosis.[13] The difference in mean scores observed between men with different degrees of atherosclerosis exceeded in absolute size the difference previously found in JAS studies of incidence and prevalence of coronary disease. Finally, to estimate whether the behavior type preceded or followed overt symptoms or whether these observed relationships might have been mediated by the presence of cardiovascular disability, an analysis of covariance was performed with number of infarctions, age, and angina intensity treated as covariates. The results of this analysis indicate that the initial association between Type A scores and the extent of atherosclerosis cannot be explained in terms of the degree of angina pain reported, age, or prior experience of myocardial infarction.

In the second study, Blumenthal et al.[14] studied 142 men and women of both races who had undergone coronary angiography at Duke University Medical Center. These patients were categorized as manifesting behavior Type A or Type B on the basis of the Structured Interview and also the JAS Type A scale. Patients found to have at least 75% narrowing of one or more coronary arteries had been blindly judged to be Type A in 82% of the cases, whereas only 37% of patients with lesser arterial disease had been judged Type A ($P = .001$). The Type A score did not correlate significantly with angiographic judgments in this group, but unlike most studies using the Activity Survey, the Duke sample included many persons with lower levels of education, persons who were over age 65, and females, all of which differ from the population on which the Activity Survey was standardized.

The findings reported by Zyzanski et al. and Blumenthal et al. have also been replicated by Frank et al. at Columbia University.[15] This research group used only the Structured Interview method in assessing Type A behavior. They reported a similar significant excess of Type A individuals among those men identified as having coronary artery disease. Patients with at least 50% narrowing of one or more coronary arteries were judged to be Type A in 80% of cases, whereas only 47% of patients with lesser disease had been judged Type A. These results are quite similar to those reported by Blumenthal et al., even though 50% rather than 75% narrowing was chosen as the criterion for a diseased vessel.

All three studies, thus, found a strong relation between some measure of Type A and severity of atherosclerosis. This association suggests that one way the Type A behavior raises the risk of coronary disease may be through its association with increased development of atherosclerotic plaques.

Association of JAS Type A Scores with Demographic Characteristics: Sex and Race

Until recently, research studies employing the JAS have almost exclusively focused on white males between the ages of 35 and 64. More specifically, they studied populations that closely resembled the standardizing WCGS population in demographic composition. Perhaps the largest population group to take the JAS, containing substantial numbers of both sexes and blacks as well as whites, was the Chicago Heart Association Detection in Industry Study, which examined over 5,000 persons at intake. Waldron et al.[16] reported sex and race differences in Type A scores for 3,667 white males, 1,149 white females, 265 black males, and 266 black females in the Chicago population. This population had a greater proportion of blue-collar workers than the WCGS population and tended to score a bit more in the Type B direction. White males scored higher than white females ($-.65$ vs. -2.69), and black males scored higher than black females (-3.04 vs. -5.79). Race-specific comparisons for this project showed that blacks scored more Type B than whites for both sexes. It should be emphasized, however, that these mean differences are confounded by disproportionate distributions of age and occupational levels within the four sex-race subgroups. Thus, for example, when Shekelle (in the above study) adjusted these differences for socioeconomic class (measured by occupation and education), men did not differ significantly in Type A score from women. Similarly, black and white males did not differ in mean Type A score once differences in occupational level were taken into account. This underscores the importance of controlling for socioeconomic factors in evaluating the distribution of Type A behavior in demographically-defined subgroups.

In the Bridgeport study, 69 hospitalized males were found to score somewhat higher than 21 hospitalized females, but the differences were not statistically significant. Similarly, a study at Boston City Hospital[17] investigated various treatment modalities for patients with documented myocardial infarction, and found that among the 198 CHD cases screened at intake, 187 were male and 11 female. The mean Type A score was slightly but not significantly higher for females (4.7) than for males (3.1), but again, the number of female cases was too small to draw valid conclusions.

In general, then, males have not been found to score significantly higher than females on the Type A scale in the few studies in which both were tested. In the one study where differences between the two sexes in occupational level and age were controlled statistically, the sex differences were eliminated. However, Waldron in chapter 15 cites additional evidence that the coronary-prone behavior pattern may be less prevalent among women than among men. In addition, it should be noted that the scoring procedures and item response weights were derived from an all-male population, and hence have never been tested against a criterion such as the clinical Structured Interview to see if the item weights and the scoring equation constants need to be recalibrated for working females.

Relation of JAS Type A Scores to Age

Generally, age has not been found to be related to Type A scores in those population groups where the study subjects fall within a restricted but older age range. For example, in the WCGS, for men 39 to 59 years old at intake, no correlation with age was noted for the Type A scale (r = .02). Similar results have been reported for the 442 persons in the 12 Towns Study in England (r = .00) and also for the Polish Prevalence Study (r = .04). However, if the age range is broadened considerably to include much younger persons, then modest to low correlations with age are often observed. Several studies containing subjects within the 20 to 65 years old age range have reported an inverse relationship, with higher Type A scores being observed at younger ages. Shekelle, in the Chicago Detection in Industry Study, found age inversely related to Type A scores for both sexes. Mettlin,[18] in a study of 943 men in five different work organizations, also found an inverse relationship with age (r = −.15). In the Boston study of 390 air traffic controllers[19] between the ages of 30 and 50, the correlation of JAS Type A score and age was (r = −.20). However, in a study of 166 male Georgia food store workers between 20 and 64 years old,[20] no relationship with age was observed (r = −.01). The same lack of association with age was also noted in a group of 64 senior medical students at a southeastern university, all of whom were less than 30 years of age (r = −.10).

Although some statistically significant relationships have been observed, most of these associations are small in magnitude and in the most extreme instances account for less than 4% of the total variance in Type A score (i.e., the air traffic controller study, which found the highest correlation, r = −.20). Age, then, does not seem to be a biasing factor, except for study populations that encompass a wide age range, including young persons.

Relation to Occupation and Education

Most of the studies that have gathered occupational data have found a positive association with Type A scores. For example, in the WCGS, higher occupational levels were associated with higher Type A scores (Table 2.3). This pattern has also been replicated in the study of Georgia food store workers

Table 2.3   Mean JAS Scores in WCGS by Occupational Level in 1965.

Occupational Levels	N	A[a]	S[b]	J[c]	H[d]
Managerial	1405	1.36	0.10	2.58	0.60
Professional/Technical	1050	−0.77	0.28	−0.06	−1.10
Sales	36	2.55	3.64	−1.07	0.47
Clerical	272	−3.23	−1.50	−6.74	−0.06
Foreman	53	−.51	0.47	−7.41	2.25
Skilled, Unskilled Laborers	78	−4.33	−1.74	−13.26	0.75
Totals	2952	0.00	0.01	0.00	−0.01

[a] A: Type A scale
[b] S: Speed and impatience scale
[c] J: Job involvement scale
[d] H: Hard-driving scale

(Table 2.4). In the Buffalo study of five different work organizations, a significant positive correlation was observed between the Type A score and occupational prestige level, with higher Type A scores associated with greater occupational prestige. Shekelle, in the Chicago Detection in Industry Study, also found that Type A scores were positively correlated with socioeconomic status, defined in terms of occupation and education, in each of the four sex and age groups studied.

The relationships observed between Type A score and level of education closely mirror those reported for occupational level. In the WCGS, Type A scores were positively associated with level of education. This positive association was also replicated in the study of the Georgia food store workers. For the food store workers, the highest grade of schooling completed correlated (r = .27) with Type A score. In Mettlin's study of five different Buffalo work organizations, level of education was again positively correlated (r = .16) with the Type A score. Finally, Waldron, in her analysis of data from the Chicago Detection in Industry Study, also observed a highly significant association between educational status and Type A score (P = .001).

The consistency of these findings emphasizes the importance of occupational, educational, or socioeconomic differences in evaluating specific demographic indices. Disproportionate occupational or educational distributions may distort specific zero order correlations due to the confounding effects of these strongly-related socioeconomic factors, and thereby present a biased or spurious picture of the actual relationships.

It is inappropriate, however, in studies of CHD populations to "partial out"

Table 2.4   JAS Means by Occupational Level for 166 Georgia Food Store Workers who completed the 1966 JAS.

Warner's Occupational Levels	N	Means (S.D.'s)			
		A[a]	S[b]	J[c]	H[d]
Administrators (ISC 1,2,3)	39	6.22	−1.09	3.86	6.39
		(9.58)	(11.65)	(5.68)	(12.58)
Managers, Foremen (ISC 4)	57	0.30	−1.42	−1.80	7.96
		(8.96)	(8.40)	(8.16)	(10.79)
Asst. Managers, Clerks (ISC 5)	41	−5.06	−5.27	−5.65	6.28
		(7.25)	(6.79)	(7.88)	(10.66)
Helpers, Truck Drivers, Market Assistants, Laborers (ISC 6,7)	29	−8.47	−5.90	−5.54	2.10
		(6.43)	(7.58)	(6.85)	(9.56)
Analysis of Variance	F	21.21	13.03	13.89	1.83
(df = 3 and 162)	P	.001	.001	.001	N.S.

[a]A: Type A scale
[b]S: Speed and Impatience scale
[c]J: Job-Involvement scale
[d]H: Hard-Driving scale

social status differences and then argue that Type A behavior is not significantly associated with CHD. Reviews of the literature clearly demonstrate that indicators of Type A are often associated with CHD risk but that social status indicators have inconsistent and conflicting associations with CHD. In these instances where social status is positively associated with CHD rates, it may be primarily because the Type A behavior pattern is the mediating mechanism.

Relation to Regions, Cultures, and Special Groups

Table 2.5 provides a listing of both Type A and factor scale scores for a variety of population groups. This listing includes both U.S. and European samples.

For all the European populations studied thus far, the mean Type A score has consistently been negative, for example, Shell Oil employees in the Netherlands (-3.2), postal-telegraph workers in Belgium (-4.5), etc. This implies that, in terms of the U.S. standardizing constants for the JAS, these population groups are more Type B than the WCGS population. The U.S. studies reflect a wide range of mean Type A scores for NASA executives (5.4); for physicians at an AHA postgraduate course (5.3); for senior medical students and for Japanese-Americans in the Honolulu Heart Program (-7.7); for fathers of high school students in Buffalo, New York (-3.7); and for air traffic controllers in the Northeast (-3.1). These varied population groups represent the current range of experience with the JAS. The overall pattern of mean scores is generally consistent with what one would hypothesize from the theory of Type A behavior and from the prior relationships observed between Type A scores and occupation levels, and therefore, contributes to the construct validity of Type A as measured by the JAS.

Relation to Standard CHD Risk Factors

The four basic JAS scales have repeatedly been tested and found to be unrelated to the majority of CHD risk factors. Where correlations have been observed, they have been small. In the WCGS, the Type A score based on 2,952 men correlated only with ponderal index out of the nine risk factors tested, and only at the $r = -.06$ level of magnitude (Table 2.6).

It was similarly unrelated to ratings of physical activity on the job and unrelated to the extent of voluntary exercise in this population. The negative correlation with the ponderal index indicates that shorter, stockier individuals in the WCGS were slightly more likely to score in the Type A direction, but this accounted for less than 1% of the variance in Type A score.

In a sample of 166 male supermarket employees in Georgia, the Type A scale again was uncorrelated with cholesterol ($-.04$), systolic blood pressure (.01), diastolic blood pressure (.08), age ($-.01$), triglycerides (.11), and number of cigarettes smoked (.01). Shekelle et al., in assessing both major CHD risk

Table 2.5   Comparison of Mean Scores on the JAS Observed in Various
Population Groups.

Population	Size	Mean Scores by Scale			
		Type A	Speed-Impatience	Job-Involvement	Hard-Driving
Ten Firms in California	2,952	0.0	0.0	0.0	0.0
Chicago Utility and other Industries (20% sample)	564	−2.6	−3.5	−2.8	1.6
Supermarket Workers in Georgia	178	−1.3	−3.1	−1.8	5.8
Japanese-Americans in Honolulu Heart Program	2,047	−7.7	−5.7	−9.7	4.6
Graduates in Business Administration	113	4.2	0.0	8.7	0.3
North Carolina Senior Medical Students	64	3.6	2.2	8.9	−3.0
Physicians at AHA Postgraduate Course	51	5.4	4.4	4.1	2.0
NASA Executives	84	5.3	4.6	5.7	1.4
Shell Oil Co. in the Netherlands	146	−3.2	−6.0	−6.2	−5.0
Postal-Telegraph Workers in Belgium	318	−4.5	−8.2	−12.4	−3.6
12 Towns Sample in England	442	−1.3	−1.3	−5.2	3.8
British Civil Servants	158	−3.5	−3.4	−3.8	1.3
Pennsylvania State University Exercise Study	539	−1.5	−0.7	−0.5	−1.2
University of Minnesota Exercise Study	225	−2.1	−1.1	−4.1	1.0
University of Wisconsin Exercise Study	86	2.3	0.1	7.3	−2.8
Anti-Coronary Club of New York	1,139	−1.0	1.7	−8.1	4.8
ACC, Oak Ridge National Laboratory	20	−0.1	−2.0	3.9	−3.9
State University of New York at Buffalo, Fathers of High School Students	228	−3.7	−1.8	−5.7	3.3
State University of New York at Buffalo, Five Work Organizations	943	0.6	−0.4	3.1	0.3
Boston Veterans Administration Hospital	106	−1.9	−2.0	−3.7	−1.4
Chicago Heart Association Screening in Industry	5,347	−2.2	−2.9	−3.1	1.5
Rockefeller University Volunteers for Lipid Study	403	−2.3	−2.1	−1.6	0.9
General Motors	201	1.0	−1.7	0.1	3.6
Air Traffic Controllers	392	−3.1	−2.1	−4.8	−0.8
U.S. Air Force Personnel	614	1.1	−2.4	6.6	−0.8
Canadian Industry Study	718	−0.4	1.1	−3.4	0.5
University of Auckland, New Zealand	100	0.5	−1.4	−3.8	7.2
Brussels, Belgium Prevention Project (sample)	726	−3.0	−6.1	−10.4	−0.8
Brussels, Belgium Prevention Project (total)	6,976	−4.7	−7.5	−11.7	−1.1

Table 2.6   Correlations between Traditional CHD Risk Factors and 1965 JAS Scores in the WCGS.

Variables	N	Type A	S	J	H
		Product Moment Correlations			
Age	2,952	.02	$-.07^b$	$-.19^b$	$.06^a$
SBP	2,800	.00	$-.01$	$-.10^b$	.03
DBP	2,800	.02	.01	$-.07^b$	.02
Cholesterol	2,811	.02	.02	$-.03$	.02
Triglycerides	2,796	.02	.02	$-.04$	.03
Cigarettes	2,800	.03	.01	.02	.04
Ponderal Index	2,952	$-.06^a$	$-.08^b$	.03	$-.03$
Lipalbumin	2,941	.00	$-.02$	.03	$-.01$
Beta/Alpha Ratio	2,940	.03	.04	$-.02$	.00

A, Type A Scale; S, Speed-Impatience Scale; J, Job Involvement Scale; H, Hard-driving Scale.
^{a} Correlation $\pm$ .05 are significant at P = .01 (two-tailed)
^{b} Correlations $\pm$ .06 are significant at P = .001 (two-tailed)

factors and JAS Type A, found the Type A score positively though weakly related only to one risk factor—cigarette smoking. Finally, in a sample of 64 senior medical students (Table 2.7), JAS scores were found to correlate with level of achievement (i.e., grade point average and rank in class) and with fasting triglycerides (r = .31), but not with age, cholesterol, or serum uric acid levels.

Thus, in the majority of studies measuring both JAS Type A and standard CHD risk factors, it was found that the Type A score remained consistently uncorrelated with these CHD risk measures. These findings, then, argue that the behavior pattern is an added risk factor, independent of the standard risk factors commonly studied. This issue, plus a comparison of the JAS and Structured Interview methods in predicting future CHD, controlling for the major CHD risk factors, has been presented in more detail by Brand.[21]

Table 2.7   Senior Medical Students at a Southeastern University: 1966 JAS Scores, Risk Factors, and Academic Performance (N = 64).

	Type A^b	S	J	H
	Product Moment Correlations^a			
Age^c	-10	03	-08	-17
Cumulative Grade Average	26^b	21	10	22
Relative Ranking in Class^d	-35^b	-15	-21	-12
Serum Cholesterol	02	06	-09	-15
Fasting Serum Triglycerides	31^b	13	01	14
Serum Uric Acid	-02	-06	-04	09

A, Type A Scale; S, Speed-Impatience Scale; J, Job Involvement Scale; H, Hard-driving Scale.
^{a} Decimals omitted
^{b} Correlations $> \pm$ .25 are significant at P = .05 (two-tailed)
^{c} Very restricted age range in this group
^{d} Lowest numeric ranks indicate best performance

Discussion

To even address the complex question of whether the associations between Type A, CHD, and traditional CHD risk factors have been consistent across different population groups, sexes, ages, and cultures would require the simultaneous collection of data for coronary disease and Type A, in addition to measures of other risk factors from very large and heterogeneous study populations. Unfortunately, this combination of data is currently available for only a few study groups. Nevertheless, one can piece together parts of the picture from those studies that have been completed or are under way.

The evidence is consistent for the prevalence studies, which show a strong association between Type A and CHD. This association has been observed in seven separate studies in this country and in Poland, as well. The only published U.S. studies containing adequate numbers of CHD cases as well as JAS Type A and other CHD risk factors are the WCGS, which found the Type A scale to be an independent risk factor for both the initial and recurrent CHD events, and the Chicago Detection in Industry Study, which also found the Type A scale to be associated with prevalence of CHD once standard CHD risk factors were controlled. The Belgian Multi-factorial Study has also collected risk factor data, but has yet to accumulate CHD endpoints.

Two other groups have compiled both measures of CHD risk factors and the JAS Type A score. The Georgia Food Store Workers Study has shown a lack of correlation between Type A and traditional CHD risk factors, but unfortunately, the cohort was too young and too small to provide significant numbers of CHD cases for statistical analysis. The Polish Prevalence Study gathered selected risk factors, but only for the 149 CHD cases seen at the Center for Cardiac Rehabilitation. These data were then compared with a prevalence sample of cases from the WCGS. It was found that for both samples of cases, Type A was unrelated to age, number of cigarettes smoked, and systolic blood pressure. In the WCGS sample of CHD cases, Type A was correlated with ponderal index ($-.28$), but this was not so for the Polish MI's ($.06$). Shekelle, in the Chicago Detection in Industry Study, also found no relationship between relative body weight and JAS Type A score.

None of the studies thus far reviewed had sufficient numbers of female CHD cases for analysis. The findings for women in the Bridgeport Study, although it was small in size (nine women with CHD and 13 controls), still showed the mean Type A score to be higher for women with CHD than for non-CHD controls. Similarly, preliminary results from the Boston City Hospital Study show the mean Type A score for 11 females with an MI to be as high as the mean for 187 males with an MI. Clearly, these trends need to be replicated on larger samples before any conclusion can be drawn regarding the degree of CHD risk, if any, that Type A confers on women.

In summary, the following major points bear reemphasis. First, the JAS Type A scale has been found to be consistently related, retrospectively, to coronary heart disease in seven independent studies in this country and in one European country. Second, the JAS Type A scale has been found to have predictive validity for CHD in the WCGS, thereby demonstrating that a self-administered psychological test based on a clinical concepts can predict the future emergence of coronary disease. Third, the JAS Type A scale has been shown to be an even stronger predictor of recurrent infarction than it is of the incidence of single events. Fourth, the JAS Type A scale has been found to be related to the severity of atherosclerosis. Fifth, the JAS Type A scale has been translated with good reliability and has been shown to relate to coronary heart disease in other cultures. Sixth, most studies have shown the JAS Type A scale to be basically independent of major CHD risk factors for both initial and recurrent CHD events. Seventh, recent evidence indicates that the particular set of items used in the 1965, 1966, and 1969 editions of the JAS Type A scale may not be entirely valid for some groups of subjects, including housewives, students, retired persons, and certain self-employed categories, such as farmers and small business proprietors. Additional validation studies are needed involving both the Rosenman-Friedman Structured Interview and pools of specially-developed questionnaire items so that a new scale may be constructed for persons not adequately measured by the present JAS. Finally, evidence to date suggests that perhaps the JAS Type A scale currently in use is most valid for those in the population who are employed, male, have at least eight years of education, and are between the ages of 25 and 65.

References

1. Jenkins, C.D., Friedman, M., Rosenman, R.H.: The Jenkins Activity Survey for Health Prediction. Chapel Hill, N.C.: C. David Jenkins (University of North Carolina), 1965.
2. Jenkins, C.D., Zyzanski, S.J., Rosenman, R.H.: Progress toward validation of a computer-scored test for the Type A coronary-prone behavior pattern. *Psychosom Med* **33**:193–202, 1971.
3. Kittel, F., Kornitzer, M., Zyzanski, S.J., Jenkins, C.D., et al.: Two methods of assessing the Type A coronary-prone behavior pattern in Belgium. *J Chronic Dis,* **31**:147–155, 1978.
4. Kenigsberg, D., Zyzanski, S.J., Jenkins, C.D., Wardwell, W.I., et al.: The coronary-prone behavior pattern in hospitalized patients with and without coronary heart disease. *Psychosom Med* **36**:344–351, 1974.
5. Shekelle, R.B., Schoenberger, J.A., Stamler, J.: Correlates of the JAS Type A behavior pattern score. *J Chronic Dis* **29**:381–394, 1976.
5a. Glass, D.C. Stress, behavior patterns, and coronary disease. *Am Sci* **65**:177–184, 1977.
6. Hiland, D.: Behavioral characteristics of male VA patients with and without coronary heart disease. Ph.D. Dissertation, University of South Florida, Tampa, 1977.
7. Zyzanski, S.J., Wrzesniewski, K., Jenkins, C.D.: Cross-validation of the coronary-prone behavior pattern. Manuscript submitted for publication, 1978.
8. Stokols, J.J.: Life dissatisfaction as a risk factor in coronary heart disease. Ph.D. Dissertation in Psychology, University of North Carolina at Chapel Hill, 1973.
9. Cohen, J.B.: Sociocultural change and behavior patterns in disease etiology: an epidemiologic study of coronary disease among Japanese-Americans. Ph.D. Dissertation in Epidemiology, School of Public Health, University of California at Berkeley, August, 1974.
10. Jenkins, C.D., Rosenman, R.H., Zyzanski, S.J.: Prediction of clinical coronary heart disease by a test for the coronary-prone behavior pattern. *N Engl J Med* **290**:1271–1275, 1974.

11. Jenkins, C.D., Zyzanski, S.J., Rosenman, R.H., Cleveland, G.L.: Association of coronary-prone behavior scores with recurrence of coronary heart disease. *J Chronic Dis* **24**:601–611, 1971.

12. Jenkins, C.D., Zyzanski, S.J., Rosenman, R.H.: Risk of new myocardial infarction in middle-aged men with manifest coronary heart disease. *Circulation* **53**:342–347, 1976.

13. Zyzanski, S.J., Jenkins, C.D., Ryan, T.J., Flessas, A., et al.: Psychological correlates of coronary angiographic findings. *Arch Intern Med* **136**:1234–1237, 1976.

14. Blumenthal, J.A., Kong, Y., Rosenman, R.H.: Type A behavior pattern and angiographically documented coronary disease. Presented at the meeting of the American Psychosomatic Society, New Orleans, March 21, 1975.

15. Frank, K.A., Heller, S.S., Kornfeld, D.S., Sporn, A.A., et al.: Type A behavior and coronary artery disease: Angiographic confirmation. *JAMA* (in press).

16. Waldron, I., Zyzanski, S.J., Shekelle, R.B., Jenkins, C.D., et al.: Type A behavior pattern in employed men and women. *J Human Stress* **3**:2–18, 1978.

17. Vokonas, P., Boston City Hospital: Personal communication, 1977.

18. Mettlin, C.: Occupational careers and the prevention of coronary-prone behavior. *Soc Sci Med* **10**:367–372, 1977.

19. Rose, R.M., Boston University School of Medicine: Personal communication, 1977.

20. Hames, C., Evans County Heart Study, Claxton, Georgia: Personal communication, 1977.

21. Brand, R.S., Rosenman, R.H., Jenkins, C.B., et al.: Comparison of coronary heart disease prediction in the Western Collaborative Group Study using the Structured Interview and the Jenkins Activity Survey assessments of the coronary-prone behavior pattern. *J Chronic Dis,* (in press).

Chapter 3

Coronary-Prone Behavior Pattern and Coronary Heart Disease: Methodological Considerations

Richard B. Shekelle

The central logical problem of nonexperimental epidemiological research is to marshal scientifically persuasive arguments showing that a statistically significant association is not an artifact but is due to a causal relationship between the antecedent condition and the disease under investigation. The problem is usually approached by presenting evidence that tends to rule out likely alternate explanations, such as biased sampling procedures, systematic errors in measurement, or the influence of covariates. When a causal mechanism linking the antecedent condition with the disease is not readily apparent or involves many intermediate steps, as is the case with the Type A behavior pattern and coronary heart disease (CHD), the difficulty of persuasively arguing that a causal relationship exists is magnified because the opportunity for error is greater.

Potential sources of error in epidemiological investigations have been described extensively in the literature. For instance, specifying unbiased sampling procedures is one of the most difficult methodological problems to solve with the frequently used case-control method. The goal is to ensure that the sample of cases adequately represents all persons with the disease in a defined population and that the sample of controls represents the remainder. Even if the investigator had a situation in which he could identify all cases of symptomatic CHD in a defined population and if he received full cooperation from all subjects, the sample still would not include cases of silent myocardial infarction (MI) nor cases where death occurred before information about the behavior pattern could be acquired. For at least this reason, it would be useful to know whether cases of silent MI, of suddenly fatal CHD, and of nonfatal symptomatic MI differ in prevalence of the Type A pattern. This could be determined only in a prospective study designed to detect these endpoints, and the number of cases in the several groups would have to be fairly large. For instance, over 130 cases of silent MI and a similar number of nonfatal symptomatic cases would be needed if an investigator wanted to detect a moderately large difference in prevalence of the Type A pattern—say, 50% in one group as compared with 30% or 70% in the other group—at the 0.05 level of significance, and with power of 0.90.

Some data on this point have been presented by Rosenman and colleagues.[1] In the Western Collaborative Group Study (WCGS), the Type A pattern was ascertained at baseline in 68% of 71 men who subsequently had silent MI and in 69% of 135 men who developed symptomatic MI. Jenkins, Rosenman, and Zyzanski[2] have also presented results consistent with the hypothesis that cases of silent MI do not differ appreciably from cases of symptomatic MI in mean JAS Type A score. The question is not entirely answered, however, because in both reports persons who died of the initial CHD event were not reported separately but were included in the group with nonfatal symptomatic MI.

Rarely can the investigator precisely define the population in a case-control study. The only instance I can cite in this area of research is the study by Wardwell and Bahnson.[3] More frequently, a convenience sample is used, such as a series of patients admitted to a hospital. A commonly used procedure for selecting controls, then, is to sample patients admitted to the same hospital during the same period of time for diseases unrelated to the cardiovascular system and, it is hoped, to the antecedent condition under investigation. As Berkson[4] pointed out, however, this sampling procedure can lead to erroneous results. For instance, prevalence of the Type A pattern is correlated with socioeconomic status. If the cardiology section of a hospital drew its patients from a population with a higher socioeconomic status than the population from which the control patients were drawn, a small artificial association between CHD and the Type A pattern could occur.

In addition, results based on differences between convenience samples of hospitalized patients could erroneously indicate no association between CHD and the Type A pattern if both CHD and the diseases included in the control group were truly associated with increased prevalence of the Type A pattern. Conversely, a spurious association could result if the diseases in the control group were truly associated with decreased prevalence of the Type A pattern.

These considerations indicate the desirability of using several control groups, especially when the population from which the cases were selected cannot be defined precisely. Traditionally, these groups would include hospitalized controls, neighborhood controls, and community controls, where the last two groups are probability samples of persons residing in the same neighborhood as the cases and samples of persons residing in the same general community in which the hospital is located. Similar results from comparing the sample of cases with each of these control groups would provide evidence indicating that bias in sampling procedures was not a likely explanation for the results.

Even when it can be shown that the sampling procedure is unbiased, the possibility that the assessments of behavior pattern have been influenced, quite unconsciously, by knowledge of diagnostic category must be ruled out. This is a potential source of error whenever measurement of the antecedent condition is subject to an appreciable amount of unreliability and there is the possibility that the persons making the measurements know, or can guess, the diagnostic categories of cases and controls. Both of these conditions occur when the interview procedure is used to assess behavior pattern in a case-control study of CHD, and this type of error by itself can produce relative risks of a magnitude similar to that found with the Type A pattern, that is, relative risks of about two.

It is extraordinarily difficult to demonstrate that this kind of error has not occurred. For instance, even if the judgments of behavior pattern were made by an auditor who had listened to a recording of the interview, and all possible clues to diagnostic category had been erased from the recording, a critic could still argue that the auditor was listening to material produced by an interviewer whose behavior in eliciting signs of the Type A pattern might have been conditioned by knowledge of diagnostic category.

One way to avoid the possibility of such errors of measurement is to remove the observer entirely and assess the behavior pattern with a self-reporting device such as the JAS. Case-control studies using the JAS have provided valuable supporting evidence that observer bias has not been a significant factor. However, self-reporting procedures could also lead to biased results if the occurrence of CHD systematically altered the tendency of participants to report themselves as possessing Type A characteristics. This possibility has been investigated by Jenkins, Zyzanski, and Rosenman[5]; the results indicated a slight trend among men having only a single CHD event for Type A score to be lowest among cases farthest in the past and highest among men whose first CHD event was to occur in the near future. For men with multiple CHD events, mean Type A scores were similar whether obtained before or after the events.

Prospective epidemiological studies, when correctly designed and conducted, are not subject to these kinds of error because the investigator begins with a defined population, and the measurements of behavior pattern are made when all participants are free of CHD. However, artifical associations between behavior pattern and incidence of CHD could result if the probability of detecting the endpoint was conditioned by the behavior pattern determined at baseline. Differences in probability of ascertainment could occur, for instance, if Type A and Type B participants differed in probability of remaining under observation. However, evidence from the WCGS[1] has indicated that this is an unlikely source of error. About 18% of 1,589 Type A men and 14% of 1,565 Type B men were lost to follow-up during 8½ years.

Another way in which differences in probability of ascertainment could occur is if the follow-up design did not require exactly the same detection and diagnostic procedures for each participant and did not eliminate from every step of the process judgments that could be influenced by knowledge of participants' behavior patterns. Experience in the Pooling Project, for instance, has shown that diagnosis of angina pectoris is subject to an appreciable amount of unreliability, and there seems to be no convincing way by which the persons taking the medical history could be blinded with respect to behavior pattern. For this reason, analyses that include angina pectoris as an endpoint are particularly vulnerable to bias of ascertainment.

At least for analyses aimed at ruling out the possibility of ascertainment bias, the occurrence of nonfatal MI should be based on analysis of ECG's obtained at standard intervals by a standard procedure on all participants. Since the clinical determination of infarct pattern on single ECG tracings also has appreciable unreliability, the procedure for determining whether an infarct pattern has occurred should be an objective one, such as the Minnesota coding method, and should be applied equally to all tracings by persons who have no other knowledge of the participants. The goal in this instance is not to ensure the greatest accuracy in diagnosis of MI, but to ensure that the probability of misclassification cannot have been conditioned by information about behavior pattern.

Some evidence concerning the occurrence of bias in ascertainment can be obtained by using various categories of endpoints in analysis of the data, and the WCGS has provided some data bearing on this question. The Type A pattern in this study was associated with significantly increased risk of symptomatic MI and of silent MI, as well as of angina pectoris.[1] A possible weakness in these results is the reliance on clinical assessment of the ECG. The evidence would be strengthened further if the multivariate analyses were repeated using as the endpoint MI on the interval ECG, as determined by independent coders using the Minnesota criteria.

If these alternate explanations for positive results can be ruled out or shown to be improbable or negligibly small sources of error, the data must be analyzed to show that information about behavior pattern contributes to predicting incidence of CHD over and above information about other factors such as sex, age, plasma lipids, blood pressure, cigarette smoking, and diseases associated with risk of CHD. Fortunately, the technology for accomplishing this has been improved greatly over the past few years by the introduction into epidemiology of multiple logistic regression analysis. This procedure has been employed with skill in the WCGS,[6] and the results have been very helpful in answering this particular question.

Finally, I believe that a more refined definition of the relevant aspects of the Type A pattern and greater objectivity in measuring these aspects are absolutely essential if much progress is to occur in this area of research. The magnitude of this problem can be fully appreciated by trying to describe in writing the interview procedure for assessing behavior pattern in a manner that permits truly independent replication. Further research will need to rely largely on the case-control method, and greater objectivity of measurement would go a long way toward making the results less vulnerable to criticism.

References

1. Rosenman, R.H., Brand, R.J., Jenkins, C.D., Friedman, M., Straus, R., Wurm, M.: Coronary heart disease in the Western Collaborative Group Study: Final follow-up experience of 8 ½ years. *JAMA* **233**:872–877, 1975.

2. Jenkins, C.D., Rosenman, R.H., Zyzanski, S.J.: Prediction of clinical coronary heart disease by a test for the coronary-prone behavior pattern. *N Engl J Med* **290**:1271–1275, 1974.
3. Wardwell, W.I., Bahnson, C.B.: Behavioral variables and myocardial infarction in the Southeastern Connecticut Heart Study. *J Chronic Dis* **26**:447–461, 1973.
4. Berkson, J.: Limitations of the application of four-fold table analysis to hospital data. *Biometrics* **2**:47–53, 1946.
5. Jenkins, C.D., Zyzanski, S.J., Rosenman, R.H.: Risk of new myocardial infarction in middle-aged men with manifest coronary heart disease. *Circulation* **53**:342–247, 1976.
6. Brand, R.J., Rosenman, R.H., Sholtz, R.I., Friedman, M.: Multivariate prediction of coronary heart disease in the Western Collaborative Group Study compared to the findings of the Framingham Study. *Circulation* **53**:348–355, 1976.

SECTION II

ASSESSMENT

Section Summary: Assessment of Coronary-Prone Behavior

Theodore M. Dembroski, Bernard Caffrey, C. David Jenkins, Ray H. Rosenman, Charles D. Spielberger, and Donald L. Tasto

Several methods are available for assessing the coronary-prone behavior pattern designated as Type A. The two most commonly used are the Structured Interview (SI), developed by Rosenman and Friedman,[1] and the Jenkins Activity Survey (JAS),[2] a self-administered computer-scored questionnaire. Several other approaches to assessment have been attempted, such as the Performance Battery and Short Rating Scale developed by Bortner,[3,4] and various assessments of speech stylistics.[5-7] However, since the SI and JAS have been most utilized for research in this field, the comments that follow focus primarily on these two assessment techniques.

There are several criteria by which to evaluate any behavioral measure: (1) utility and cost, (2) objectivity and standardization, (3) reliability, and (4) validity. The chapters by the authors in this section speak in detail to these issues.

Utility and Cost

The behavior pattern is primarily studied as a predictor of coronary heart disease (CHD). Both the SI and the JAS have been replicated as valid discriminators between groups with and without CHD.[8,9] Both measures have also shown a significant ability to predict the future emergence of clinical CHD among healthy men.[10-12] Parenthetically, this may be the first time in the history of medicine that a purely behavioral method, not tapping subclinical signs and symptoms, has successfully and independently predicted future emergence of a somatic disease.

Statistical analysis of data derived from both instruments has shown that the pathogenic contribution of Type A behavior is largely independent of, and in addition to, the risk for CHD associated with other standard risk factors.[10,11] This is the case even though some of these risk factors are more prevalent in Type A persons.[11] In addition, both assessment instruments are predictive of recurrent coronary events in persons who alreeady have CHD.[13,14] Finally, both measures have shown the Type A behavior pattern to be independently associated with severity of atherosclerosis determined angiographically.[15,16]

The SI and the JAS both have their particular strengths and weaknesses. Although the JAS can be used with less cost and more convenience, the SI is the stronger of the two methods in predicting future CHD.[10] In this regard, the JAS seems to obtain most of its predictive strength for CHD from its ability to duplicate the SI. Although the JAS probably does not provide additional predictive power independent of the interview, the combination of both the SI and the JAS provides stronger predictions than those derived from either method alone.[10]

At this juncture, the SI and the JAS are primarily used for research purposes. Until it can be demonstrated that modification of the Type A behavior pattern reduces CHD risk, these measures cannot be recommended for general clinical use.

Objectivity and Standardization

The SI is a highly structured challenge situation in which the assessment is mainly based on the voice stylistics and the psychomotor mannerisms of the respondent, although the actual verbal content is also considered.[1] The JAS is a self-administered questionnaire that yields scores for "Type A," "Hard Driving," "Speed-Impatience," and "Job Involvement" subscales.[17] It depends solely on self ratings for its assessment of Type A or Type B behavior. Thus, a broader spectrum of behavior can be assessed by the SI. The two methods agree in rating persons Type A or B in from 65 to 73% of subjects in a number of studies, with 90% agreement occurring at the more extreme ranges of the Type A versus Type B behavioral continuum.[2,10]

Both methods have adequate agreement between effectively trained raters for the SI and comparability of forms of the JAS.[2,18,19] Both are vulnerable to distortion by subjects who know the pattern and have the desire to deceive. This is probably less true for the SI than for the JAS, because the SI takes into account psychomotor characteristics that are more difficult to disguise than verbal content. However, more research is needed to develop techniques to minimize dissimulation.

Also, further research is necessary to determine how situational testing conditions affect responses to the JAS, how interviewer characterisitcs influence respondent behavior (and vice versa), and how consistently interviewers administer the SI over time. In addition, research on the effectiveness of interviewers trained at the Harold Brunn Institute in teaching others to administer and score the SI would be extremely valuable.[6,7,28]

Although both methods have been used with subjects who differ in sex, age, socioeconomic status, race, etc., most research to date has been conducted with white employed males of middle level socioeconomic status. There is a definite need for more research on the applicability of both methods to different populations of subjects.

Reliability

Reliability of assessment instruments must be established despite the fact that human behavior changes over time. Acceptable test-retest reliabilities over more than a one-year period for both the SI (80% agreement) and the JAS (r = .65–.70) have been reported.[18,19] As different forms of the JAS and new means for scoring the SI and its subcomponents are developed, the reliability of these will need to be determined.[20] As mentioned earlier, good agreement exists between properly trained raters in the SI, but it would be desirable to use more than one rater in efforts designed to further refine scoring procedures for the SI.

Validity

The validity of the SI and the JAS in predicting CHD has received extensive attention in the section on Association. The concurrent and construct validity of these instruments from a psychological standpoint have also been investigated. Both the SI and the JAS appear to measure a unique constellation of attributes, since both measurements generally do not correlate with standard measures of personality.[21,22] The concurrent validity of both methods has received support from significant, albeit modest, correlations between both methods and scales designed to measure such characteristics as activity level, speed, aggression, etc.[21,22] These findings support the concurrent validity of the Type A construct. The construct validity of the Type A pattern has been supported, in the main, by social psychological laboratory research. For example, a unique series of experiments conducted by Glass and associates has demonstrated that Type A subjects are more aggressive, more time urgent, more impatient, and more hard-driving than Type B subjects *when appropriate environmental challenges are made salient.*[21] The latter point underlines the importance of the environmental setting in evoking Type A behavior. Research of this kind has the potential of identifying additional attributes of the Type A pattern. For example, the work of Glass et al. suggests that Type A subjects, compared with Type B subjects, possess a heightened concern with control of their environment, which gives way to helplessness-prone tendencies if prolonged attempts to cope with an aversive noncontrollable situation are unsuccessful.[21] The potentially damaging physiological consequences of these tendencies are discussed in the section on mechanism.

Although the work of Glass et al. has successfully supported the construct validity of the Type A concept, much more research is necessary before a complete understanding of the Type A pattern is established. A priority for future validity research is the inclusion of subjects who differ in age, sex, education, socioeconomic status, etc. Moreover, systematic investigation of behavioral differences between Type A and Type B subjects in natural settings is needed to identify the frequency of Type A behavior and the specific situations or environments that are most likely to evoke it. In addition, no surveys have been conducted on the prevalence of the Type A behavior pattern in the general population. Such research is needed to provide information on the distribution and stability of elements of the Type A pattern in various populations. For example, the Type A behavior pattern has been reported to be as low as 15% in some populations and as high as 70% in others.[23,24] In addition, longitudinal research would be particularly valuable in determining the stability of the pattern and its subcomponents over time.

Social psychological research has demonstrated that Type A subjects respond to certain environmental challenges with greater psychomotor acitvity than Type B subjects. Only a few studies have been conducted on the effect of environmental challenge on *physiological reaction* in Type A and Type B subjects. The results of these studies, however, together with those that have assessed physiologic variables under resting conditions, strongly suggest that Type A subjects, relative to Type B subjects, respond to day-to-day environmental challenges with greater sympathetic arousal.[25-29] Additional research is clearly needed on the range of circumstances that evoke both behavioral *and* physiological arousal in Type A and Type B subjects. Together with more refined analyses of epidemiological data, such research will help clarify those specific components of the coronary-prone behavior pattern most worthy of assessment in future studies.

In this regard, a multidimensional approach to the measurement of coronary-prone behavior can be applied in future research. The following areas may be expanded on in furthering the development of the measurement of coronary-prone behavior: (1) self-report of attitudes and behavior, (2) speech characteristics, (3) motor behavior characteristics, (4) physiological response characteristics, and (5) psychological response characteristics. The purposes of furthering the measurement technology along these lines are primarily to increase the objectivity of the measurement of Type A and Type B behavior, and to explore other potential aspects of the coronary-prone behavior pattern (CPBP) beyond the current definition of Type A and Type B behavior.

With the latter purpose in mind, it is necessary to distinguish between the Type A behavior pattern as a concept and the operational procedures that are used to measure this concept. It is also important to recognize that the Type A concept is not necessarily synonymous with the concept of coronary-prone behavior pattern even though measures of this concept appear to be valid predictors of heart disease. Clarification of these concepts will contribute to the refinement of existing measures and to the construction and validation of new measurement procedures.

A further clarification of the CPBP may be facilitated by content analysis of the SI and item analysis of the JAS using CHD as the clinical endpoint. The data obtained in the WCGS have already proved ideal for this purpose. For example, a recent study found that measures of potential for expressing anger or hostility, competitive drive, and vigorous voice stylistics were more predictive of CHD than other components of the Type A pattern.[20] The interview rated items that significantly discriminated between a group of patients who *prospectively* developed heart disease from those who did not are listed below:

Potential for hostility (p < .003)
Anger directed outward (p < .01)
Competition in games with peers (p < .01)
Gets angry more than once a week (p < .02)
Subject's answers are vigorous (p. < .02)
Irritation at waiting in lines (p < .04)
Explosive voice modulation (p < .05)

It is also of interest to note in this study that reanalyses of data from the WCGS show it is possible to score component resonses in the interview as continuous rather than dichotomous variables, thus increasing the potential for improving the discriminability effectiveness of the SI. Improvement of discriminability will also be important to intervention efforts in order to better determine degrees of change in Type A characteristics.

In summary, although the importance of the Type A pattern in the etiology of CHD appears to be well established, there are many aspects of the behavioral properties of the pattern whose relevance to coronary artery pathology is not yet understood. In addition, probably there are a number of psychosocial contributions to CHD risk that are not included in present measures of Type A behavior. The elucidation and measurement of these will improve prediction of CHD. An important task for future research is to conduct additional component analyses to establish additional attributes that are predictive of CHD and to improve the effective discrimination of assessment instruments. The first steps in assessing the validity of the component measures should involve establishing the concurrent relationship between the component measures and 1) the SI and the JAS, 2) the prevalence of atherosclerosis, 3) the prevalence of clinical CHD, and 4) potentially damaging physiologic states and reactions. In addition, alternate forms for each of the measures should be established. After concurrent validities have been established, prospective epidemiologic *and* intervention studies with CHD as the major endpoint will be necessary to truly assess the predictive validity of any new generation of measures.

References

1. Rosenman, R.H., Friedman, M., Straus, R., et al.: A predictive study of coronary heart disease: The Western Collaborative Group Study. *JAMA* **189**:15–22, 1964.
2. Jenkins, C.D., Rosenman, R.H., Friedman, M.: Development of an objective psychological test for the determination of the coronary-prone behavior pattern in employed men. *J Chronic Dis* **20**:371–379, 1967.

3. Bortner, R.W., Rosenman, R.H.: The measurement of pattern A behavior. *J Chronic Dis* 2:525–533, 1967.
4. Bortner, R.W.: A short rating scale as a potential measure of pattern A behavior. *J Chronic Dis* 22:87–91, 1969.
5. Friedman, M., Brown, A.E., Rosenman, R.H.: Voice analysis test for detection of behavior pattern: responses of normal men and coronary patients. *JAMA* 208:828–836, 1969.
6. Schucker, B., Jacobs, D.R.: Assessment of behavioral risk for coronary disease by voice characteristics. *Psychosom Med* 39:219–228, 1977.
7. Sherwitz, L., Berton, K., Leventhal, H.: Type A assessment in the behavior pattern interview. *Psychosom Med* 39:229–240, 1977.
8. Friedman, M., Rosenman, R.H.: Association of a specific overt behavior pattern with increases in blood cholesterol, blood clotting time, incidence of arcus senilis, and clinical coronary artery disease. *JAMA* 169:1286–1296, 1959.
9. Jenkins, C.D., Zyzanski, S.J., Rosenman, R.H.: Progress toward validation of a computer-scored test for the Type A coronary-prone behavior pattern. *Psychosom Med* 33:193–202, 1971.
10. Brand, R.J., Rosenman, R.H., Jenkins, C.D., Sholtz, R.I., Zyzanski, S.J.: Comparison of coronary heart disease prediction in the Western Collaborative Group Study using the structured interview and the Jenkins Activity Survey assessments of the coronary-prone Type A behavior pattern. *J Chronic Dis* (in press).
11. Brand, R.J., Rosenman, R.H., Sholtz, R.I., Friedman, M.: Multivariate prediction of coronary heart disease in the Western Collaborative Group Study compared to the findings of the Framingham Study. *Circulation* 53:348–355, 1976.
12. Rosenman, R.H., Jenkins, C.D., Brand, R.J., Friedman, M., Straus, R., Wurm, M.: Coronary heart disease in the Western Collaborative Group Study: Final follow-up experience of 8.5 years. *JAMA* 233:872–877, 1975.
13. Jenkins, C.D., Zyzanski, S.J., Rosenman, R.H.: Risk of new myocardial infarction in middle-aged men with manifest coronary heart disease. *Circulation* 53:342–347, 1976.
14. Rosenman, R.H., Friedman, M., Jenkins, C.D., et al.: Recurring and fatal myocardial infarction in the Western Collaborative Group Study. *Am J Cardiol* 19:771–775, 1967.
15. Blumenthal, A., Williams, R.B., Kong, Y., et al.: Coronary-prone behavior and angiographically documented coronary disease. *Circulation* (in press).
16. Zyzanski, S.J., Jenkins, C.D., Ryan, T.J., Flessas, A., Everist, M.: Psychological correlates of coronary angiographic findings. *Arch Intern Med* 136:1234–1237, 1976.
17. Zyzanski, S.J., Jenkins, C.D.: Basic dimensions within the coronary-prone behavior pattern. *J Chronic Dis* 22:781–792, 1970.
18. Jenkins, C.D., Rosenman, R.H., Friedman, M.: Replicability of rating the coronary-prone behavior pattern. *Br J Prev Soc Med* 22:16–22, 1968.
19. Jenkins, C.D., Rosenman, R.H., Zyzanski, S.J.: Prediction of clinical coronary heart disease by a test for the coronary-prone behavior pattern. *N Engl J Med* 290:1271–1275, 1974.
20. Matthews, K.A., Glass, D.C., Rosenman, R.H., Bortner, R.W.: Competitive drive, pattern A, and coronary heart disease: A further analysis of some data from the Western Collaborative Group Study. *J Chronic Dis* 30:489–498, 1977.
21. Glass, D.C.: Behavior Patterns, Stress, and Coronary Disease. Hillsdale, N.J.: Lawrence Erlbaum Associates, 1977.
22. Rosenman, R.H., Rahe, R.H., Borhani, N.O., Feinleib, M.: Heritability of personality and behavior pattern. Paper presented at the meeting of the American Psychosomatic Society, New Orleans, March, 1975.
23. Cohen, J.B.: Sociocultural change and behavior patterns in disease etiology: an epidemiologic study of coronary disease among Japanese Americans. Ph.D. Dissertation in Epidemiology, School of Public Health, University of California at Berkeley, August, 1974.
24. Howard, J.H., Cunningham, D.A., Rechnitzer, P.A.: Health patterns associated with Type A behavior: A managerial population. *J Human Stress* 2:24–32, 1976.
25. Friedman, M., Byers, S., Diamant, J., Rosenman, R.H.: Plasma catecholamine response of coronary-prone subjects (Type A) to a specific challenge. *Metabolism* 24:205–210, 1975.

26. Dembroski, T.M., MacDougall, J.M., Shields, J.L.: Physiologic reactions to social challenge in persons evidencing the Type A coronary-prone behavior pattern. *J Human Stress* **3**:2–10, 1977.

27. Friedman, M.: Type A behavior pattern: Some of its pathophysiological components. *Bull NY Acad Med* **53**:593–604, 1977.

28. Dembroski, T.M., MacDougall, J.M.: Stress effects on affiliation preference among subjects possessing the Type A coronary-prone behavior pattern. *J Pers Soc Psychol* **36**:23–33, 1978.

29. Dembroski, T.M., MacDougall, J.M., Shields, J.L., et al: Components of the type A coronary-prone behavior pattern and cardiovascular responses to psychomotor performance challenge. *J Behav Med* **1**:159–176, 1978.

Chapter 4

The Interview Method of Assessment of the Coronary-Prone Behavior Pattern

Ray H. Rosenman

The structured psychological interview developed at the Harold Brunn Institute[1] for assessment of the Type A behavior pattern evolved over a period of several years and was primarily based on our consistent observations of patients with CHD. We are influenced by earlier descriptions of CHD patients by various psychiatrists who reported remarkably uniform personality traits in their subjects.[2] Our own psychiatric consultants made similar observations.

The coronary-prone Type A behavior pattern appears to be an interplay of certain enhanced personality traits with the environmental milieu that has been increasingly present in 20th century industrialized societies. We speak of it as a behavior pattern because it is an overt syndrome and therefore is best assessed by observing the presence or absence of its characteristics in a given individual. The assessment of the Type A behavior pattern depends upon two factors: (1) the exhibition of this behavior pattern by the subject and, (2) the ability of the interviewer and/or assessor to observe and properly judge the characteristics that comprise this behavioral syndrome. Needless to say, an effective interviewer or assessor must be able to "bring out" the Type A behavior in an individual whose characteristics are less overt. In this regard, the interview is an empirical instrument.

The Structured Interview was conceived and designed to elicit the characteristics of the Type A syndrome. The original interview was structured for the purpose of assessing the behavior pattern of subjects in the Western Collaborative Group Study (WCGS).[1] The Structured Interview and its interpretation are appended. The Structured Interview has been slightly modified since its initial use in 1960, in accordance with subsequent experience by ourselves as well as

These studies were supported by the National Heart and Lung Institute, Research Grant HL-03429 (National Institutes of Health).

other interviewers. It is somewhat shorter, requires about ten minutes to administer, and appears to be more effective than the original interview. The current interview is also appended.

Several of the questions are asked for the specific content of their answers. The content of the answers to the other questions is also useful, but the behavioral assessment is in fact based far more upon the general stylistics and mannerisms of the subject as he answers the questions. Observation is more important in the assessment, i.e., the way something is said, as contrasted with what is said. The assessment also is based upon observation of a number of nonverbal, overt behavior characteristics. The appendix also contains a description of behavior pattern Type A and Type B that has proven useful in teaching prospective interviewers. It describes the various motor and verbal stylistics that characterize the respective behavior patterns.

The interview is used to assess the presence of a behavior pattern that has been found through the use of this methodology to be independently associated with the prevalence and incidence of CHD[3-8] as well as with the severity of underlying coronary atherosclerosis.[9-11] It seems likely that the behavior pattern of most individuals over time is fairly stable. In subjects in the WCGS, 80% showed a similar categorical assessment by the interview method over a period of 12 to 20 months.[12] Keith et al.[13] found replicability of categorical assessment in 74% of 100 subjects who were interviewed from 3 to 18 months after the original interview. Doubtless, Type A individuals might temporarily alter their behavior pattern while on vacation or when hospitalized for acute illness, and more permanently with advancing age or when beset with chronic illness, including the consequences of clinical CHD.

The Structured Interview is not an ideal vehicle since it is an empirical instrument that is not truly objective and does not provide numerical quantification at this juncture. Moreover, it requires a period of training for its effective administration and assessment as well as an observer of adequate intelligence and with certain obvious abilities. Finally, it requires time and expense. In spite of its subjective assessment, it has produced surprisingly high interrater agreement. Thus, categorical agreement of behavior assessment was observed in 84% of a group of WCGS interview assessments between Rosenman and Jenkins[12] and 83.3% between Rosenman and Belmaker in 84 participants in the Type II Intervention Study.[14] The agreement between raters was 79% in the Cleveland Study[15] and 75 to 77% in the studies by Caffrey and associates.[16] The most rigid control was achieved in the Multiple Risk Factor Intervention Trial (MRFIT) study in which two auditors of the Harold Brunn Institute assessed the taped interviews of all participants at five MRFIT centers. In the survey of the first 2,198 subjects, categorical agreement was observed in 83.5% of subjects, with a range of 81 to 85% agreement between the five field interviewers and the two auditors. Rosenman audited a random sample of 285 MRFIT interviews. Categorical agreement with the five field interviewers was found in 86% of their assessments and with the two auditor's assessments in 90% of these subjects.[17]

An important question arises with the consideration that the behavior pattern of the subject might influence the interviewer's technique and more important, that the speech stylistics and mannerisms of the interviewer might significantly influence the subject's responses. Although this has not been adequately investigated, the studies at the University of Wisconsin[18] suggest that little or no bias is introduced in these ways, and particularly, that little effect on the subject's behavioral assessment is engendered by differences in vocal characteristics or in the speed at which the interview is given.

The question is also asked whether an interviewer who was trained at the Harold Brunn Institute but who subsequently worked elsewhere can in turn effectively train others to administer the interview and to assess the behavior pattern. Although this, too, has not been adequately determined, two studies were directed at this question. Scherwitz[18] studied 59 subjects along with several pupils of his own. They independently rated the behavior pattern from content of answers in the interviews as well as from three speech characteristics, reaching categorical agreement of assessment in 91 to 95% of the four characteristics. Schucker,[19] who was the field interviewer for the Minnesota MRFIT group, taught the method of assessment to two naive students. In 100 taped interviews used for validation test purposes in the MRFIT training program, categorical agreement was observed in 87% of instances.

Thus, although the interview developed for the purpose of assessing the behavior pattern[2] suffers from several defects, it appears to be the most suitable vehicle for this purpose at the present time. However, we have attempted over a period of many years to find a questionnaire that would be an adequate substitute for the interview method of assessing the behavior pattern, particularly since this would provide greater objectivity as well as numerical stratification. As a result of our own failures in this regard, we still doubt that a paper and pencil questionnaire can be effective for this purpose.

Assessment of the behavior pattern during the interview is made primarily by observing the subject and the latter's Type A or Type B characteristics. On the other hand, a questionnaire is based upon the content of answers and in this regard it also is *subjective*. In our own extensive experience over two decades, Type A individuals often have little insight into their Pattern A behavior and are often totally inaccurate in their responses to a written questionnaire. Indeed, many Type A's even believe they lack the very qualities from which they already suffer a surfeit. Paradoxically then, the interview method often provides a far more objective method of assessment than can be obtained by the subjective responses to a questionnaire, which negate the value of later objective handling of the written responses. It is thus not surprising that no correlation was found between the content of answers in the interview and vocal stylistics.[18]

The best studied questionnaire is the Jenkins Activity Survey (JAS), which was developed by Jenkins in collaboration with our group.[20] Although many of the questions are similar to those used in the Structured Interview, and were designed to examine personality and behavioral traits assessed in the interview, the JAS is, of course, a paper and pencil questionnaire. Its scoring and quantification depend upon the content of the answers to a series of questions that are asked, and therefore, in the final analysis, depend upon a valid self-appraisal by the subject. As noted above, subjects' responses are often ludicrously inaccurate, particularly those reported by Type A subjects. One of the greater strengths of the JAS as compared to the interview method of assessment is that it can be self-administered and computer-scored and provides a numerical score, for both the global behavioral assessment rating as well as for those components of the behavior pattern that are assessed by various clusters of questions. The problem, of course, is, how accurate is the *subjective* self-appraisal of the subject? As noted above, this type of self-appraisal cannot be said to be an effective observer of the subjects pattern of overt behavior.

The JAS was developed by multivariate statistical methods to provide a computer-scored, continuous scale of Type A-B behavior, based on a weighted combination of the responses to the JAS questions.[20] It was developed using subjects participating in the WCGS.[1] Thus, in both the choice of subjects for constructing JAS scores and in the use of the interview behavior assessment as a criterion, the JAS score was designed to mimic the interview Type A-B assessments as closely as possible. We have used the method of multiple logistical risk analysis[6,7] to make a comparative assessment of CHD predictability in the WCGS[1] by the Structured Interview and the JAS forms of behavior pattern assessment, after adjustment for other risk factors that were found to be significantly associated with the CHD incidence in this population.[5,7] Analyses by Brand et al.[21] showed that the best behavior pattern classification consistency using the different cutpoints for the JAS scores reached 63%, i.e., the JAS misclassified at least one third of the subjects using the interview A-B classification as the criterion. The Type II Intervention Study correctly classified 67% of the subjects, using the same criterion.[14]

Thus, it is clear that the JAS does not completely capture the stylistic mannerism information provided by the interview assessment method. The JAS shows substantial and statisically significant predictive strength for CHD in the WCGS population. However, it is found to capture only a portion of the predictive capability of the interview A-B assessment.[21] In joint analysis of the JAS and interview assessments, the JAS shows a small component of additional predictive information for CHD, but this is not statistically significant. Moreover, the bulk of predictability for CHD by the JAS is found to stem from its ability to mimic the interview A-B assessment. Thus, it was found that the JAS misclassifies a substantial percentage of patients classified as Type A or Type B by the interview method, that its predictive power for CHD largely stems from its ability to mimic the Structured Interview, that its predictive ability is much weaker than that of the interview A-B method, and that it cannot be said to provide additional predictive content that is separate from the interview method. Accordingly, we do not believe that the JAS can replace the interview method for assessment of the A-B behavior pattern.

References

1. Rosenman, R.H., Friedman, M., Straus, R., et al.: A predictive study of coronary heart disease: The Western Collaborative Group Study. *JAMA* **189**:15–22, 1964.

2. Rosenman, R.H., Friedman, M.: Neurogenic factors in pathogenesis of coronary heart disease. *Med Clin North Am* **59**:269–279, 1974.

3. Friedman, M., Rosenman, R.H.: Association of a specific overt behavior pattern with increases in blood cholesterol, blood clotting time, incidence of arcus senilis and clinical coronary artery disease. *JAMA* **169**:1286–1296, 1959.

4. Rosenman, R.H., Friedman, M.: Association of a specific overt behavior pattern in females with blood and cardiovascular findings. *Circulation* **24**:1173–1184, 1961.

5. Rosenman, R.H., Jenkins, C.D., Brand, R.J., Friedman, M., Straus, R., Wurm, M.: Coronary heart disease in the Western Collaborative Group Study: Final follow-up experience of 8-½ years. *JAMA* **233**:872–977, 1975.

6. Brand, R.J., Rosenman, R.H., Sholtz, R.I., Friedman, M.: Multivariate prediction of coronary heart disease in the Western Collaborative Group Study compared to the findings of the Framingham Study. *Circulation* **53**:348–355, 1976.

7. Rosenman, R.H., Brand, R.J., Sholtz, R.I., Friedman, M.: Multivariate prediction of coronary heart disease during 8.5 year follow-up in the Western Collaborative Group Study. *Am J Cardiol* **37**:903–910, 1976.

8a. Jenkins, C.D.: Psychologic and social precursors of coronary disease. *N Engl J Med* **284**:244–255, 307–317, 1971.

8b. Jenkins, C.D.: Recent evidence supporting psychologic and social risk factors for coronary disease. *N Engl J Med* **294**:987–994, 1,033–1,038, 1976.

9. Friedman, M., Rosenman, R.H., Straus, R., Wurm, M., Kositchek, R.: The relationship of behavior pattern A to the state of the coronary vasculature: A study of 51 autopsied subjects. *Am J Med* **44**:525–538, 1968.

10a. Zyzanski, S.J., Jenkins, C.D., Ryan, R.J., Flessas, A., Everist, M.: Psychological correlates of coronary angiographic findings. *Arch Intern Med* **136**:1234–1237, 1976.

10b. Frank, K.A., Heller, S.S., Kornfeld, D.S., Spron, A.A., Weiss, M.B.: Type A behavior and coronary artery disease: Angiographic confirmation. *JAMA*, (in press).

11. Blumenthal, A., Williams, R.B., Kong, Y., et al.: Coronary-prone behavior and angiographically documental coronary disease. *Circulation*, (in press).

12. Jenkins, C.D., Rosenman, R.H., Friedman, M.: Replicability of rating the coronary-prone behavior pattern. *Br J Prev Soc Med* **27**:424–434, 1965.

13. Keith, R.A., Lown, B., Stare, F.J.: Coronary heart disease and behavior patterns: An examination of method. *Psychosom Med* **27**:424–434, 1965.

14. Belmaker, R.H., Pollin, W., Jenkins, C.D., Brensike, J.: Coronary-prone behavior patterns in a sample of Type II hypercholesteremic patients. Submitted for publication, 1977.

15. Friedman, E.H., Hellerstein, H.K., Jones, S.E., et al.: Behavior patterns and serum cholesterol in two groups of normal males. *Circulation* (Supplement II) **32**:89, 1965; *Am J Med Sci* **255**:237–244, 1968.

16. Caffrey, B.: Reliability and validity of personality and behavioral measures in a study of coronary heart disease. *J Chronic Dis* **21**:191–204, 1968.

17. Shekelle, R.: Rush-Presbyterian-St. Luke's Medical Center, Chicago, personal communication.

18. Scherwitz, L., Berton, K., Leventhal, H.: Type A assessment and inter-interaction in the behavior pattern interview. *Psychosom Med* **39**:229–240, 1977.

19. Schucker, R., Jackobs, D.R., Jr.: Assessment of behavioral risk to coronary disease by voice characteristics. *Psychosom Med* **39**:219–228, 1977

20. Jenkins, C.D., Rosenman, R.H., Friedman, M.: Development of an objective psychological test for the determination of the coronary-prone behavior pattern in employed men. *J Chronic Dis* **20**:371–379, 1967.

21. Brand, R.J., Rosenman, R.H., Jenkins, C.D., Sholtz, R.I., Zyzanski, S.J.: Comparison of coronary heart disease prediction in the Western Collaborative Group Study using the structured interview and the Jenkins Activity Survey assessments of the coronary-prone Type A behavior pattern. *J Chronic Dis* (in press).

Appendix 1: Description of Behavior Pattern Types

It is our conviction based upon factual evidence that the presence of a particular behavior pattern accelerates the onset of coronary artery disease. We call this a behavior pattern because it is an overt and observable pattern that reflects an individual's characteristic responses. Moreover, it is determined by the interplay of the individual's own personality facade with the demands, stresses, and distresses of his own environmental milieu, both vocational and avocational. The individual may or may not be aware of his own overt behavior pattern. Therefore, its assessment is far better based on the observations of a trained observer rather than upon the opinion of the subject. In general, individuals exhibit varying degrees of either of two patterns.

The behavior pattern we call Type A is exhibited by persons with impatience and a chronic sense of time urgency, enhanced competitiveness, agressive drive, and often, some hostilities. The behavior pattern we call Type B is characterized by relatively little or nonhabitual sense of time urgency, non-competitiveness, lack of agressive drive, and is exhibited by generally more relaxed, easy-going, and more patient individuals. There is an intermediate behavior pattern, Type X, that is found in persons who exhibit some of the characteristics of both the incompletely developed A and B types. It is generally possible to classify from 85 to 90% or more of subjects as predominantly Type A or Type B.

The Type A-1

The extreme Type A person (Type A-1) is chronically involved in an almost never ending struggle to achieve poorly defined goals against all odds (aggressive drive). He is overly conscientious and work-oriented and tries to excel at his tasks and avocational activities, sports and hobbies (competitiveness). He tries to utilize almost every minute of the day in purposeful, goal-oriented activity since he regards most other things as "a waste of time." While often frustrated by circumstances of time, people, and things that impede his progress, the Type A person continues to strive with the belief that he will overcome his difficulties and opposing forces and often develops impatience and a chronic sense of time urgency that makes him accelerate the rate of all activities, whether eating, talking, walking, and makes him excessively punctual and time-oriented.

What are some of the frustrations a Type A-1 person experiences? Sometimes it is a person such as a fellow employee or boss who obstructs or competes with him, and very often it is a lack of *time* to do everything each day that *he* thinks should get done. Why is the offender so often time conscious? Because Type A-1 persons are either born with, learn early, or are parent-trained and instilled with the desire to achieve. We can often detect this excessive desire to achieve from the patient's recall of his high school or earlier days, e.g., in athletic *competitive* drive (competition being nothing more than a wish to achieve at the expense of someone else). An A-1 individual often will be found to have played on a high school or college team and what is more, to have been the captain or manager of some type.

Our example goes into a business, and here again, he tries to excel, to achieve beyond all others, and he feels that he has the ability to do too many things and do them well, except he is obstructed too often by a *dearth of time*. And so, he begins his never-ending struggle with time. Rarely does he attempt to defeat his adversary by lightening his load. No, he tries to *accelerate* the usual rate of doing things and thus believes he can accomplish more in a given frame of time. Besides this acceleration effort, he attempts to make every minute count. He is apt to dissociate himself from all trivia and irrelevancies as he surges to his goals. Think of a finely poised arrow, always going faster, except the target likewise is always receding too, (the Sisyphus complex). Moreover, he believes he can succeed and rarely seeks help or counsel from physicians, priests, psychiatrists, etc.

Profile

The Type A-1 individual walks briskly. His face looks extraordinarily alert; that is, his eyes are very much alive, more quickly seeking to take in the situation at a glance. He may employ a tense, teeth-clenching, and jaw-grinding posture. His smile has a lateral extension rather than an oval, and his laughter is rarely a "belly-laugh." He tends to look you straight and quite unflinchingly in the eye. He frequently sits poised on the edge of a chair. He may stretch out his feet, cross them, or just keep them bent under this chair.

Rarely do his hands hang limply, with fingers widely spaced. He is apt, whenever he is *enthused* about a subject, to gesture, and particularly, to clench his fist. He will rarely clench his fist as you talk, only when he talks, and then particularly when enthused and excited or when angry and upset. He is apt to give you the impression that he is impatient, and even more, he may make you feel slightly uneasy in your own slowness when you are near him. This is a subtle point but it is very important. Whenever you feel that you are with a person who is harboring a fast "revolving series of motors" and he produces a sensation in you that you must hurry the interview or process you are engaged in, you probably are dealing with an "A" person. One of the ways he gives the interviewer this impression is his frequent habit to trying to hurry your questions, explanations, etc., by saying, "Yes, yes" almost before you finish your sentences or other expressions such as "I see, I see," "Mmm," "Right, right." He may squirm or move about if you talk too slowly for him or tap fingers on legs or desk with impatience.

His speech is not necessarily fast, but often may carry explosive intonations and it accelerates in longer sentences. He tends to put punch in key words of a sentence. He never whines, rarely talks in a whisper and rarely pauses in the middle of sentences. If he begins to talk about a subject that interests him, and if he is interrupted, usually he will bring the conversation back to the subject that interested him or where he was talking when he was interrupted.

To return to his face, very often (particularly in laborers, truck drivers, plumbers, etc.) one senses that there is a set type of hostility in the face, mostly evidenced by the eyes. However, one never feels that one is looking at a "wistful" face.

Rarely will he dally about after an interview. He may ask several pointed questions, and sometimes leave before you have answered him. He really does not often hear you if you speak of subjects that have no bearing on his way of life or of interest to him.

If adroitly questioned, he will admit that he is possessed by a chronic sense of time urgency and he will express it perhaps like this: "Yes, I wish there were more time for me to do things, I always feel that there is not enough time." "I like to be in there pitching." "I like to get things done; no sense dilly-dallying around." "There is not enough time in the day." He will admit that he hates to wait in a line. In fact, he will avoid banks, restaurants, and supermarkets or other places where he knows he will have to wait in line. The Type A-1 will often reveal his competitive attitude in remarks about his work: "If you are not moving up in the business world, you are moving down," is the way one Type A-1 expressed it.

He hates to lose any sort of contest, even with his own children. "When I play a game, I play to win," and then he might add, "Isn't that what a game is for?" He does not like to do routine things around the house, like cleaning dishes, mopping floors, cleaning, etc. He usually does not like to garden. In short, anything that does not appear to be a worthwhile achievement leaves him cold.

He frequently will attempt to indulge in "polyhedral, multiphasic thinking." That is, he may be forced to talk to someone about a subject that he thinks is trivial or irrelevant, and then he will pay lip service to this conversation, whereas he is still attempting to carry on his own thinking about another subject. He certainly likes people to come to the point quickly and he may encourage others, especially family members, to do so.

Summary of Characteristics
After many years of a competitive, driving, unending quest for constantly receding goals, the Type A-1 subject exhibits mannerisms and various motor actions that very often allow him to be identified.

Outstanding motor and behavioral characteristics of the Type A-1 include:

1. A general expression of vigor and energy, alertness, and confidence.
2. A firm handshake and brisk walking pace.
3. Loud and/or vigorous voice.
4. Terse speech, abbreviated responses.
5. Clipped speech (a failure to pronounce the ending sounds of words).
6. Rapid speech and acceleration of speech at the end of a longer sentence.
7. Explosive speech (speech punctuated with certain words spoken emphatically and this is established as the speaker's general pattern) that may contain swear words.
8. Interrupting by frequent rapid responses given before another speaker has completed his question or statement.

9. Speech hurrying in the form of saying "yes, yes," or "mm, mm," or "right, right" or by nodding his head in assent while another person speaks.
10. Vehement reactions to questions relating to impedance of time-progress (i.e., driving slowly, waiting in lines).
11. Use of clenched fist or pointing his finger at you to emphasize his verbalizations.
12. Frequent sighing especially related to questions about his work. It is important to differentiate this from the sighs of a depressed person.
13. Hostility directed at the interviewer or at the topics of the interview.
14. Frequent, abrupt and emphatic one-word responses to your questions. (i.e., Yes! Never! Definitely! Absolutely!).

The Type A-2

All persons with behavior pattern A are not excessively agressive, competitive, achievement-oriented individuals. There must be many persons who happen to be conscientious and presented by an environment that demands incessant haste, hurry, and acceleration. For example, a conscientious telegrapher, television technician, switchboard operator, etc., might not originally have been a Type A person, but the environment, demanding as it is with a constant need of activity under time duress, made him into an A type. It is possible that this is the origin of the less overt, less exaggerated A type behavior pattern designated Type A-2. You can visualize that a relaxed, basically Type B personality becomes Type A if the individual works on an assembly line, is paid on the basis of "piece work," or drives a taxi cab in modern urban environments.

Summary of Characteristics

1. A general impression of some vigor and energy, but not excessive as in an A-1 person.
2. A firm handshake and a fairly brisk walking pace but without severe impatience.
3. Subdued, average, or loud voice quality usually varying from one volume level to another throughout the course of a conversation but not consistently.
4. Usually rather brief responses to questions, but not terse, abrupt, or one-word answers.
5. Clipped speech occasionally in evidence.
6. Rapid speech or accelerating speech sometimes in evidence, especially in longer sentence answers.
7. Explosive speech in some responses.
8. Interrupting in some responses to interviewer's questions.
9. Speech hurrying in the form of "yes, yes," or "m-m-m," or "right, right" or nodding the head in assent usually occurs but not consistently.

10. Occasional vehement reactions to questions relating to impedance of time progress.
11. Rare use of the clenched fist or pointing finger gesture.
12. Occasional sighing.
13. Very infrequently hostility directed at the interviewer or the topics of the questions; however, subject dislikes waiting lines or being held up in traffic.
14. Occasional abrupt and emphatic one-word responses (such as Yes! Definitely! Absolutely!).

The Type B

The Type B person cannot be adequately described as the antithesis of the Type A person because the Type B individual exhibits all or some of the same traits, but not in the exaggerated manner that is so common to the Type A subject. Nor do we find in the Type B person the cluster of these exaggerated characteristics exhibited *simultaneously* as is so often observed in the Type A individual. By way of analogy, if the Type B person were thought of as having a "normal body temperature," then the Type A is the one who has a "a fever." The Type B person is not involved in a *chronic* struggle against time although he may occasionally feel some time pressure. He is not *overly* competitive, and while he may espouse certain ambitions, he pursues his goals in a relatively *nonaggressive* way.

A true "B" is one who from earliest days never cared to compete excessively or to run a race with time. Of course, he might have been a good student and even a superb thinker. He might work long hours and be very conscientious but usually he does not feel the need to compress events in time and get more done "each day." Unlike the "A," the "B" person feels that there is time enough each day to do those things he wishes to do. He cuts a smaller piece of the pie of life. He is not apt to relinquish vacations or take up night school studies for his advancement. He is often very satisfied with his status, both economic and social. He never makes one think of the sharply discharged arrow. He ambles along; he does not run. His whole demeanor suggests relaxation, unhurriedness, and contentment.

Profile
The face of the Type B person is relaxed in expression, lacks muscle rigidity and with relaxed lips. His smile is apt to be broader and his mouth forms roundedness when he laughs. He may have an intelligent face; no hostility is seen.

He usually tends to relax by sitting well back in a chair. You have the idea he is sitting in the chair to remain there and does not seem to regard it as a launching pad or pierced with small nails. His hands usually hang loosely, fingers outstretched; he never clenches his fist. He will shake your hand relatively gently, although in nervousness, he may shake it frequently and rapidly.

He will not give you the idea that he is impatient. You have the impression that you yourself can relax with him. He will rarely attempt to finish your sentences by ad libbing, "yes, yes," or "m-m-m" before you finish your sentences.

His speech is not fast, but not necessarily too slow. But he may hesitate at the start of an answer or in the middle of a sentence to think before he finishes the sentence. One has the impression that he is not indulging in stereotyped, machine-gun-paced responses. He does not punch through various words of a sentence. He may or may not whine; he may speak rather softly or he may not. If he begins to talk about a subject that interests him and you purposely interrupt, he rarely returns to the original subject of his own volition.

He may admit that he occasionally feels a sense of time urgency, but without excessive vehemence or explosive speech. He has no guilt feelings about nonachievement-oriented activities. He does not enjoy working under deadlines or having to accelerate his pace of work. He will laugh and say something like, "After all, it's just a game, I like companionship or the fun of hitting the ball, I don't care about winning or the score." He is apt to do more routine things around the house, apt to garden more, to have hobbies that carry no great goal or purpose. He does not mind if someone takes a long time to come to the point, but sits back and waits it out.

His work record will not be particularly distinguished if he is a laborer, but if he is high echelon, his ability to sit back and think and to delegate may have moved him along very high in corporate status. Many top executives, for example, are Type B.

He tends to linger after the interview is over, and may have to be told "that is all." He may question you about the project, seem to be quite interested in various facets of it, and may even make suggestions. If you speak to him of things that interest you personally, you will usually find him interested, too. He seems to hear and understand you.

Summary of Characteristics

While the Type B occurs in varying degrees, there is no necessity for our purposes to calculate this degree, and thus, a preponderance of Type B characteristics assign a person to the B category. Outstanding motor and behavioral characteristics of the Type B include:

1. A general expression of relaxation, calm and quiet attentiveness.
2. A gentle handshake and a moderate to slow walking pace.
3. A mellow voice usually low in volume.
4. Lengthy, rambling responses.
5. No evidence of clipped speech.
6. Slow to moderate pacing of verbal responses. No acceleration at the end of a sentence.
7. Minimum inflection in general speech, almost a monotone with no explosive quality.
8. Rarely interrupts another speaker.

9. No speech hurrying.
10. No vehement reactions to questions related to impedance of making progress with utilization of time.
11. Never uses the clenched fist or the pointing finger gesture to emphasize his speech.
12. Rarely sighs unless he is "hyperventilating" and showing nervous anxiety.
13. Hostility is rarely, if ever, observed.
14. An absence of emphatic, one-word responses.

The Type X

Occasionally, an individual is observed who exhibits almost equally some of the characteristics that are attributed to both the Type A and Type B patterns. This phenomenon exemplifies the fact that all people are not easily categorized as Type A or Type B. The Type X continues to be an unrelieved compromise in the assessment of the behavior pattern. The important point is that the Type X (whatever may have caused his "blended" response pattern) is not a true or pure Type A or Type B.

The Type X behavior pattern occurs seldom in comparison to the A and B types (about 10% or less of the population). If a preponderance of A pattern characteristics exist, then the subject is rated A; if a preponderance of B characteristics are observed, the subject is rated B. Only when the distribution is so nearly equal that the subject cannot be categorized as really being Type A or Type B should the subject be rated as Type X.

Appendix 2: Interview Directions

1. Try to note posture of individual as he waits for you. (Does he jump up or look up expectantly. Does he read something as he waits?)
2. Watch his stride to your desk? Does he sit on the edge of the chair?
3. Note the handshake. Does he look you squarely in the eye? Is the hand wet or cold?
4. Test microphone placement.
5. Ensure code number is at beginning and end of interview.
6. Insert subject's name several times in questioning.
7. Code stylistics on interview sheet.
8. Ask questions briefly. Do not complicate the questioning.
9. Emphasize technique of emphasis on key words.
10. Watch as well as listen to responses.
    a. Note the speech (explosive-rushes-volume-whining). Close your eyes.
    b. Watch his gestures. (For example, fist clenching when he talks on a particular subject, which you must get him to talk on.)
    c. Watch his face (lips-eyes-jaw muscles-antagonism-alertness-lateral smile).
    d. Does he hurry you along ("Yes, yes. hmmh—I see, I see")?
11. Give one series of questions rapidly.

12. Interrupt and always insert extra meaningless questions. See if subject is annoyed and returns to where left off previous answering. Interrupt on purpose, particularly when subject is excited or in middle of some answers.
13. Do not let subject ramble on and on.
14. Try to audit your own interview by scanning it before assessment is given, particularly if A2 or B3 and if unsure of assessment.

NOTE: One of the secrets of detection of behavior pattern is to find areas of discussion in which the individual can express his inner feelings. This is of particular importance to bring out hand clenching. The latter comes out in a Type A person when he is asked about the irritations of his job with just a bit of challenge as he responds. Remember that a Type A person frequently gives the sort of answers he thinks are standard, rather than how he feels inside. Also remember that many Type A people are not really aware of the fact that they are driving themselves excessively. Do not be afraid of asking leading questions; there is usually a difference in voice response that allows you to discern the true state of affairs. Indeed, sometimes the A person feels a little sheepish about revealing how hard he really does drive.

SCORING

TAPE NO. _____   Participant ID: _____
Tape Counter
Reading _____   Date _____ , 19 _____
Side: IA   2B

BEHAVIOR PATTERN INTERVIEW

HANDSHAKE:	"limp wrist"	weak	average	strong
	moist and cold	average	warm and dry	
ATTITUDE:	friendly	neutral	hostile	
GENERAL APPEARANCE:	calm	nervous	tense	alert
MOTOR PACE:	slow	average	hurried	
SPEECH HURRYING:	none	occasional	frequent	
VOICE QUALITY:	subdued	average	strong	
RHYTHMIC MOVEMENTS HANDS/FEET:	none	occasional	frequent	
FACIAL EXPRESSIONS:	flat	expressive	lateral mouth speech	clenched jaw
LAUGHTER:	none	"round mouth"	lateral smile	
FIST CLENCHING:	none	rare	occasional	frequent
SIGHING:	none	occasional	frequent	

COMMENTS: _____
_____
_____

INTERVIEWER'S ASSESSMENT	FINAL ASSESSMENT
A1 A2 X B	A1 A2 X B
Certain Uncertain	Certain Uncertain
Interviewer's ID/Name _____	Name _____

Appendix 3: Behavior Pattern Interview

Introduction: "I would appreciate it if you would answer the following questions to the best of your ability. Your answers will be kept in the strictest confidence. Most of the questions are concerned with your superficial habits, and none of them will embarrass you." (Begin taping now; emphasize italicized words.)

Your code number is _____ . (Name?)

1. May I ask your age *please?*
2. What is your occupation or job?
   a. How long have you been in this type of work?
3. Are you *satisfied* with your job level? (Why not?)
4. Does your job carry *heavy* responsibility?
   a. Is there any time when you feel particularly *rushed* or under *pressure?*
   b. When you are under *pressure* does it bother you?
5. Would you describe yourself as a *hard-driving, ambitious* type of *man* (*woman*) in accomplishing the things you want, getting things done as *quickly* as possible, *or* would you describe yourself as a relatively *relaxed* and *easy-going* person?
   a. Are you married?
   b. How would your *wife* (*husband*) describe you—as *hard-driving* and *ambitious* or as relaxed and easy-going?
   c. Has she ever asked you to slow down in your work? *never?* How would she put it—in *her*/(*his*) *own* words?
6. When you get *angry* or *upset,* do people around you know about it? How do you show it?
7. Do you think you drive *harder* to *accomplish* things than most of your associates?
8. Do you take work home with you? How often?
9. Do you have any children? When they were around the ages of six and eight, did you *ever* play competitive games with them, like cards, checkers, Monopoly?
   a. Did you *always* allow them to *win* on *purpose?*
   b. *Why* (or *why not*)?
10. When you play games with people your own age, do you play for the fun of it, or are you really in there to *win?*
11. Is there any *competition* in your job? Do you enjoy this?
   a. Are you competitive off the job, sports for example?
12. When you are in your automobile, and there is a car in your lane going *far too slowly* for you, what do you do about it? Would you *mutter* and *complain* to yourself? Would anyone riding with you know that you were *annoyed?*
13. Most people who work have to get up fairly early in the morning—in your particular case, uh-what-time-uh-do-you-uh, ordinarily uh-uh-to-uh-uh-get-up?

14. If you make a *date* with someone for, oh, two o'clock in the afternoon, for example, would you *be there* on *time*?
    a. If you are kept waiting, do you *resent* it?
    b. Would you *say* anything about it?
15. If you see someone doing a job rather *slowly* and you *know* that you could do it faster and better yourself, does it make you *restless* to watch him?
    a. Would you be tempted to *step in and do it* yourself?
16. What *irritates* you most about your work or the people with whom you work?
17. Do you *eat rapidly*? Do you *walk* rapidly? After you've *finished* eating, do you like to sit around the table and chat, or do you like to *get up and get going*?
18. When you go out in the evening to a restaurant and you find eight or ten people *waiting ahead of you* for a table, will you wait? What will you do while you are waiting?
19. How do you feel about waiting in lines: *Bank* lines, or *Supermarket* lines? *Post Office* lines?
20. Do you *always* feel anxious to *get going* and *finish* whatever you have to do?
21. Do you have the feeling that *time* is passing too *rapidly* for you to *accomplish* all the things you'd like to *get done* in one day?
    a. Do you *often* feel a sense of *time urgency*? *Time pressure*?
22. Do you *hurry* in doing most things?
    All right, that completes the interview. Thank you very much.

Interviewers: State: "This completes the interview of Subject (give code numbers)."

Chapter 5

A Comparative Review of the Interview and Questionnaire Methods in the Assessment of the Coronary-Prone Behavior Pattern

C. David Jenkins

Basic Issues in Assessment

What is the coronary-prone behavior pattern *really*? Before we can come to any conclusions regarding the adequacy of methods for assessing a concept, we have to agree on some standard of what that concept really is.

The concepts of the meter and the gram are clearly and completely specified by the golden bar, a meter in length, and the reference gram weight, stored in a vault at the Bureau of Standards. The time concept of a second is more difficult to capture. One must refer to small equal divisions of an astronomically defined period.

What about the coronary-prone behavior pattern (CPBP)? The best calibrated interviewer can hardly be preserved in a bell jar at the Bureau of Standards. The Mount Zion set of 100 tape-recorded interviews sets some sort of unvarying standard, and the printed Activity Survey with its computerized scoring system provides another possible standard—neither of these, however, really define the CPBP in the same sense that the gold bar at the Bureau of Standards defines a meter.

The CPBP is a construct, and hence, criterion validity is helpful but not complete. Coronary-prone behavior is a family of processes existing in nature. It cannot be captured and mounted on a pin under glass like a rare butterfly. The best current measures, including the Structured Interview, are only approximations of clearly real but not totally specified complexes of behavior. We can see most expressions of coronary-prone behavior clearly enough to recognize them, but yet, like late-born colleagues of van Leeuwenhoek, parts of our visual field are blurred, and we are not quite sure about the boundaries of this behavior pattern.

This raises the possibility (really the probability) that the definition of Type A behavior as it now exists is not as complete a definition or as well-refined or as good a predictor of particular pathological processes of the cardiovascular system as will be the definition of coronary-proneness that will have evolved by 1987. The same growth process has been true historically for concepts as varied as "the atom" and "homeostasis."

This call for further research and refinement should not obscure the remarkable utility of the coronary-prone behavior pattern as it is now defined and the surprising strength of several means of assessing it. Never before in the history of medicine has a behavioral rating that is not an expression of subclinical disease ever successfully predicted future emergence of a physical illness, let alone do so repeatedly in such large study populations.

Currently, there are several major independent approaches to assessment of the CPBP: The Structured Interview,[3] the Jenkins Activity Survey,[21,26] the Bortner Performance Battery,[36] the Bortner Rating Scale,[38] and voice analyses.[40-42] Each of these procedures seems to capture some of the general qualities of Type A behavior, and in addition, each seems to assess a unique facet that is truly Type A but not shared by the other assessment techniques. This accounts for the correlations among these approaches that are always positive but usually only moderate in magnitude. Thus, each of these current measures of the CPBP is a potential stepping stone to better conceptualization and better measurement of the general *in vivo* tendency toward coronary-prone behavior.

Characteristics of Good Measure

What are the qualities one looks for in a behavioral measure? How does one judge strengths and weaknesses? We see four sets of criteria as central to evaluating a behavioral measure: First, it should predict something useful; second, it should assist in the explanation of something important; third, the measure it yields should be dependable; and fourth, the measurement process should be convenient and at low cost. Let us consider each of these in more detail.

The Prediction of Something Useful

Some variables are useful predictors in the acturial sense, but give very little in the way of explanation of process. The relation of latitude or gender to coronary heart disease risk are instances of this. Nevertheless, acturial prediction is valuable. The adequacy of such prediction is judged in terms of its sensitivity and specificity. In the first instance, we ask whether the variable in question correctly labels as high risk a high proportion of persons who, in this example, will develop coronary heart disease (CHD) in the near future. The second consideration, specificity, refers to minimization of the rate of designating as high risk those persons who will not develop the disease. A good measure succeeds on both these criteria. It is tempting to call 90% of the population high risk. One maximizes the percentage of future cases properly predicted by this tactic, but one also, at the same time, generates many false positive judgments in that most people thus labeled will remain free of the disease. The goal is, of course, to minimize both false positives and false negatives by setting more balanced thresholds for the designation of high versus low risk.

The Explanation of Something Important

It is possible for the variable to be a good predictor and still give little insight into the processes involved. Yet, it is hardly possible that a variable can really assist in explanation if it is impotent as a predictor. The ability of a variable to be used in explanation is directly associated with the multiplicity of its connections into a nomothetic network of already known relationships. Thus, the greater the number of connections made between the coronary-prone behavior pattern and psychosocial variables on the one hand, and physiological processes on the other, the greater the possibilities for generating a variety of explanations for the role of the CPBP in CHD pathology. Each of these hypothesized processes can then be tested by experimental study.

Associations between a new construct and other bodies of knowledge may also give suggestions for possible forms of intervention. This may be true even if the variable in question does not explain clearly the pathological processes involved. Examples of explanation useful for prediction, although lacking in insight into mechanism, include John Snow's inference about the transmission of cholera, and the miasma theory of malaria. Another quality of a measure related to its potential for explanatory power is the degree to which the ingredients of the variable—or its infrastructure—can be analyzed and related to other variables. Thus, item analysis of the Structural Interview or the Jenkins Activity Survey offers more potential in this respect than the simple one-digit judgment by which the Structural Interview is usually summarized. Perhaps only certain facets of the CPBP are related to CHD, or different facets may associate with different pathological processes. Taking the construct apart into its components can answer these questions.

The Dependability of the Measure

Dependability or reliability refers to the ability of a measure to be unalloyed by the circumstances of measurement, brief passages of time, and irrelevant influences of the external circumstance and the internal set of the respondent. It is desirable to have a high degree of agreement between independent raters or between alternate forms of a test. It is important for measures of enduring characteristics or traits to remain stable over time. It is important that a measure, such as that for the CPBP, assess that construct alone and not get mixed up with such other qualities as social desirability, subcultural values, desire to please an examiner, or other extraneous considerations, such as states of anxiety, "stress," or fatigue.

Convenience and Cost of Making the Measurement

The optimal measure of any characteristic is economical of time and resources. It should be simple, painless, unembarrassing, and not fatiguing to the research subject. It should be convenient, inexpensive, and adaptable to many field conditions for the sake of the project doing the research or clinical work.

Review of Available Measures

Although a number of different procedures have been used at various times and places to assess the Type A coronary-prone behavior pattern, only the Structured Interview of Friedman and Rosenman and the Jenkins Activity Survey have been utilized in a sufficient variety of studies to enable them to be characterized in terms of prediction of CHD endpoints, explanation of process, dependability, convenience, and cost. Table 5.1 summarizes the research based on these two methods and gives subjective ratings by this reviewer to each procedure in terms of the four general areas of criteria described above. The

Table 5.1   Summary of the Performance of the Structured Interview and Activity Survey as Measures of the Coronary-Prone Behavior Pattern

Characteristics of Good Measures	Structured Interview	Jenkins Activity Survey
Prediction of CHD endpoints		
Retrospective	Several studies	7+ studies
Prospective	1	1
Recurrence	1	1
Atherosclerosis	2	1
Sensitivity	+++	++
Specificity	+	++
Explanation of process		
Biological correlates	Many studies	Several studies, few relations
Psychological correlates	Few studies	Many studies
Independence as a CHD risk factor	Yes	Yes
Dependability		
Agreement between raters	+++	"Perfect"
Stability over time	++	++
Resistance to dissimulation	++	+
Freedom from biases and confounding	Largely unknown	Largely unknown
Convenience and low cost		
To research subject	+	++
To research project	+	++

ratings are necessarily impressionistic and open the door to lively debate, but the structure of the table may serve to channel this debate into a short series of justifiable conclusions, and a longer series of needed research studies. At the conclusion of this chapter, available information on other methods of assessing Type A behavior will be briefly summarized.

First, a description of the two primary methods of assessment is in order. The Structured Interview was developed by Friedman and Rosenman on the basis of astute clinical observations and experience in preliminary studies. It was first used on a large scale in the Western Collaborative Group Study (WCGS), which began in 1960. The Structured Interview is less a method for gathering data than it is a challenge situation and a sample of behavior under standard interpersonal circumstances. The content of answers is noted, but even more important to determination of behavior type are the judgments made by the specially trained interviewer regarding the speed and modulation of speech and the impatience and energy revealed by motor mannerisms. The interview method is described in detail in the article by Rosenman and collegues, which introduces the methodology of the Western Collaborative Group Study.[3]

The Jenkins Activity Survey was developed in an effort to duplicate the assessment of behavior Type A by a psychometric method, which was achieved by the Structured Interview. The authors of the Activity Survey worked closely with Drs. Friedman and Rosenman, learning the interview method and becoming sensitized to the many signs and symptoms indicative of Type A and Type B individuals. To maximize convenience and minimize cost of this instrument that was to bring Type A assessment within reach of large-scale industrial and epidemiological studies, the Activity Survey was constructed as a self-administered, precoded, electronically scorable procedure. It achieved "face validity" by including in multiple choice form many of the questions contained in the Structured Interview. It also questioned additional points of behavior and attitude found characteristic of Type A behavior by the clinical work of Friedman and Rosenman. The validity of the Activity Survey does not rest, however, on this duplication of content.

It is known that Type A individuals are particularly lacking in insight regarding their own style of behavior. Similarly, many of them deny possessing Type A traits that embarrass them. On the other hand, Type B persons may feel it socially desirable to portray themselves as hard-driving and achievement oriented. For these reasons, the item pool was not assumed to be a valid measure of Type A behavior once it had been converted into self-report multiple choice questions.

The item pool was first administered in 1964 to 150 men in the WCGS, and each item was analyzed for its empirical ability to discriminate between men previously judged Type A and those judged Type B. Only those items found to be valid discriminators were retained. These formed a 40-item nucleus of the 62-item first edition of the JAS, which appeared in 1965, and was administered to the entire WCGS study population. Better than 92% of the participants completed and returned scorable JAS forms. Again, the empirical approach was used, and each item was tested for its ability to discriminate behavior patterns determined by interview in a sample of 707 WCGS men equally divided between Type A and Type B. These results were then cross-validated in a sample of 984 men and only those items that significantly discriminated Type A's from Type B's in both samples were retained for entry into the discriminant function equation that defined the initial Type A scale of the JAS.

Optimal scaling was performed on the results of the first sample. Discriminant function equations were developed using the second sample, and the product, a discriminant function equation, was applied to a third sample completely independent from the first two; 73% agreement was achieved between the JAS Type A scales thus scored and the interviews conducted in 1960 and in 1962. This is a respectably high degree of agreement considering the change in modality of data gathering and the passage of three years since the most recent interview.

In addition, factor analyses of the JAS items were performed. First, the item pool was limited to those 40 items that significantly discriminated between Type A and Type B men. Then the pool was enlarged to include all 62 items on the 1965 JAS. The two factor analyses were in remarkably close agreement. Then factor analyses were performed separately for Type A and Type B men, and these resulted in the same factor structure for that observed for the entire population. These factor structures in all instances were stable over different numbers of rotations in the varimax solution. Three strong factors were identified and were labelled "speed and impatience," "job involvement," and "hard-driving conscientious." These factors are more fully defined in published reports.[22]

A second edition of the JAS was printed in 1966. This edition included all items that appeared on the Type A discriminant function equation in 1965 and the strong items that helped define the three factors. A number of weak items were dropped and newly written items, based on further clinical experience and psychometric experience with the Type A construct, were added to the pool. Extensive revalidation of the 1966 JAS was undertaken using the same strategies, including multiple replications, as were applied to the 1965 form. A Type A scale was constructed by discriminant function completely based on the 1966 data. This scale contained many of the same items that emerged in 1965, but some differences in the item sequence and in optimal scaling and discriminant function weights occurred. In addition, some new items entered the equation. Despite the somewhat different equations, and the one-year interval between tests, the test-retest correlations across forms was still observed in the range of .60 to .70. This attests to the robustness of the Type A concept, the reliability of the items in the pool, and the statistical soundness of our scale construction procedures. Factor analyses were also performed *de novo* and the same three factors emerged. In fact, it was only after complete replication over two years and two forms of the JAS were completed that we considered the factor scales as psychometrically sound and released them in a publication.[22]

A third edition of the JAS was constructed and administered to the WCGS population in 1969. Because nine years had elapsed since the Structured Interview for Behavior Type conducted at intake into the study, it was deemed inadvisable to attempt to standardize a Type A scale based on a criterion so far distant in time. There was good evidence that the Type A scale from the 1965 and 1966 JAS were reasonably good measures of Type A behavior and for this reason the Type A scale in the 1969 form was derived by discriminant function procedures from items that distinguished those men who scored strong Type A both in 1965 and 1966 on the one hand, from those men who scored strong Type B in these two years on the other hand. This was a similar type of criterion, which based the item selection and their weights upon persons who were stable over time, consistently manifesting Type A or Type B behavior. For the 1965 and 1966 JAS's, the criteria were interviews in 1960 and 1962. For the 1969 JAS, the criteria were the 1965 and 1966 scores. Similarly, in 1969, the factor scores were derived not by repeating the factor analysis, but by using persons who consistently scored high and low on each factor in 1965 and in 1966 as criterion groups for the derivation of discriminant function scales for each of the three factors that compose the Type A behavior pattern. The use of discriminant function scales rather than factor score scales allows for an abbreviation of the scale and its limitation to those items that make strong contributions. The psychometric economies are considerable.

By 1972, it became apparent that a form of the JAS was needed that could be equally applicable to women as well as to men. All items on the 1969 third edition of the JAS that did not appear on the discriminant function scales for Type A or the three factors were eliminated from the item pool. The remaining items that contained gender references (e.g. "your wife") were reworded to be equally appropriate to both sexes (e.g. "your wife" was changed to "your spouse"), and the reference to sports activities in college was broadened to include all extracurricular activities. This became Form B (the B standing for Both sexes), which was printed in 1972 and which has been used in our most recent studies.[20]

Although Form B is equally applicable to both men and women, many of the items are appropriate only to those individuals who are regularly employed in a waged or salaried job. Many items dealing with occupational activities are inappropriate for students, housewives, retired persons, or for certain self-employed persons such as outside salesmen, artists, physicians in private practice, etc. While the JAS in its several forms is not known to be nonvalid for students, housewives, and others, there is, to date, no empirical evidence that all the items mean the same things to these groups as they do to the middle class, employed middle-aged men on whom the test was standardized. Revalidation studies using the standardized interview as a criterion are essential before confidence can be placed in findings generated by groups that are demographically different than the normative study populations.

Despite these elements of uncertainty, new evidence is emerging from several international studies that the Type A concept in general and the JAS in particular are cross-culturally valid when applied to employed men. These data come from recent translation studies involving the JAS and the Structured Interview in Belgium[23] and a prevalence study in Poland[35] that successfully distinguishes coronary cases from healthy controls by use of the Polish version of the JAS scored by US-based equations. These new developments are discussed in Chapter 2.

Evaluation of Available Measures

Let us return now to the earlier discussion of the characteristics of good behavioral measures to see how well the Structured Interview, the Activity Survey, and other behavior-type measures match up to these yard-sticks in terms of prediction of CHD endpoints, explanation of cardiovascular and psychological processes, dependability of measurement, cost, and convenience. (A tabular summary of this section is presented as Table 5.1.)

One aspect of the issue of useful prediction is the question of the degree to which the various measures of the CPBP predict one another. In its final standardization, the 1965 Activity Survey (JAS) Type A scale predicted the Structured Interview judgment 73% of the time for the entire third cross-validation sample.[26] For persons scoring one standard deviation away from the mean on the JAS, there was 90% agreement with the Interview. An earlier published study using a more simple scoring system (the unit scoring system) for the JAS achieved a 72% agreement with the Interview. Subsequent analysis by Brand and others of WCGS data report an association of 63% between the Interview and the JAS. This figure, however, is based on the degree of agreement between the intake interview and the 1965 JAS without consideration of the fact that the degree of agreement between that interview and the same interview as readministered in 1962 was only 80%.[6] Reported degrees of agreement in the articles presenting the JAS standardization are based only on those men who retained the same broad category of Interview rating (either Type A or Type B) for both the 1960 and 1962 Interview judgments. Thus, the 63% agreement reported by Brand et al.[8b] underestimates the true concordance of the two measures when performed concurrently on persons whose behavior type is stable. This conclusion is further supported by recent studies from Belgium that show that despite translation of both the Interview and the JAS into Flemish and French, the degree of agreement remained at 70%.[23] These data for WCGS and Brussels are presented in Table 5.2.

The Belgian study by Rustin, Kornitzer, and colleagues also used R.W. Bortner's Short Rating Scale.[39] It was found that on cross-validation, the Bortner Scale with weighted scores agreed with the Interview 75% of the time. In the same study, the JAS was scored by a locally developed system and agreed with the Standard Interview in 70% of cases on cross-validation. The method of voice analysis developed by Friedman and Brown has been shown to agree with Interview judgment in 84% of cases.[40] Voice analysis by objective rating scales as developed in two different forms by Scherwitz at Wisconsin[42] and by Schucker and Jacobs at Minnesota[41] also show gratifyingly high degrees of agreement with the Interview. The 18-item interview by Wardwell and

Table 5.2   Percentage of Agreement Between JAS and Structured Interview

JAS Type A Score	WCGS[a] Int. A	WCGS[a] Int. B	Percentage Rated in Agreement	Belgium[a] Int. A	Belgium[a] Int. B	Percentage Rated in Agreement
+10.0 and over	75	7	91	56	7	89
+5.0 to +9.9	50	11	82	51	18	74
0.0 to +4.9	31	24	56	60	34	64
−4.9 to −0.1	43	33	43	41	51	55
−5.0 to −9.9	19	41	68	31	48	61
−10 and less	10	75	88	39	127	77
Overall percentage in agreement	68	78	73	60	79	70

[a] Number of individuals

Bahnson[43] has never been validated against the Structured Interview of Friedman and Rosenman. It is also important to note that the very abbreviated set of questions by Caplan and French have never been validated against any of the other more firmly established measures of Type A behavior, and hence, whether they or other similar *ad hoc*, unvalidated procedures really measure Type A remains a matter of conjecture.

The essential quality of measures of the CPBP is their ability to identify retrospectively and predict prospectively individuals who sustain clinical coronary heart disease or other cardiovascular pathologies. The recently developing interest of experimental social psychologists in Type A as a psychological construct has provided an additional area of scientific application for measures of the CPBP.

Most studies associating Type A behavior with CHD prevalence and the only studies associating this behavior type with CHD incidence have been performed using either the Structured Interview or the Activity Survey. The epidemiological and clinical research showing these associations will be reviewed by other participants. But the issue needs mention here because successful prediction is the most important criterion of an assessment procedure.

The Structured Interview has been found associated with prevalence of CHD at intake into the WCGS; in the prevalence study of CHD in 26 North American monasteries by Caffrey,[14] Quinlan,[15] and colleagues; and in a study of women in the San Francisco Bay Area. The JAS has been found associated with CHD prevalence in the WCGS; among inpatients at Bridgeport Hospital, Connecticut[27]; in VA patients in Durham, North Carolina[34]; in VA patients in St. Petersburg, Florida[35b] and when used in combination with measures of social mobility or status incongruity, in Americans of Japanese ancestry in the Honolulu Heart Program.[33] JAS also significantly discriminated CHD cases in the large Chicago Heart Association Screening in Industry project.[32] A Polish translation of the JAS used in Inowroclaw, Poland, by Wrzesniewski also showed significant differences between CHD cases and healthy controls.[35a] Preliminary correspondence from the World Health Organization studies in

Rotterdam, Holland, and Kaunas, Lithuania, reported significantly higher JAS scores in participants with angina pectoris and trends in the correct direction for persons with myocardial infarction.

The only prospective study of the CPBP, to our knowledge, is the WCGS. The behavior type, as determined by the Structured Interview, significantly predicted CHD risk at two and one-half, four and one-half, and the full eight and one-half years of this longitudinal research.[9,10,12] The JAS was available only for the last four years of the project and also proved to be a significant predictor of new cases.[28] The analysis by Brand et al.[8b] showed that in this population, the Structured Interview was a stronger predictor than the JAS and trends in the data suggested that each approach to estimation of Type A may contribute added power to prediction.

Table 5.3 shows that for a given level of JAS score, persons called Type A by interview inevitably had higher CHD incidence than those of the same JAS score level who were interview typed as Type B. In general, within the interview types, those with higher JAS scores incurred more new CHD than those with lower JAS scores. The self-administered multiple choice JAS cannot capture the style of response or the vigor of voice or mannerism, and this may be the missing ingredient that gives the interview its additional predictive power. On the other hand, the JAS may recoup some of its losses by having a more systematized means for making a composite judgment of behavior type based on many pieces of behavior (the items), whereas the many aspects of the interview are weighted and combined solely on the basis of clinical intuition.

In addition to retrospective and prospective studies of CHD, behavior Type A can be an important aspect in research studies of other manifestations of atherosclerosis and myocardial infarction. Both the Structured Interview and the Activity Survey have been shown to be associated with recurrence of

Table 5.3   JAS Type A Scores, The Behavior Type Interview, and CHD Incidence in the Western Collaborative Group Study, 1965–1969

JAS Type A score	Annual CHD Incidence Rate for Employed Men Ages 44–64[a] Interview Type		Total by JAS Score
	A	B	
5.0	15.68 (35/558)	11.78 (13/276)	14.39
5.0 to −4.9	14.79 (30/507)	6.47 (13/502)	10.65
−5.0	8.25 (10/303)	7.86 (19/604)	7.99
Total by interview	13.71	8.14	10.91

[a] This was the age in 1965 of the cohort of men entering WCGS in 1960 at ages 39–59.
Accumulated incidence for the 4-year period has been divided by 4 to give an annual average.

myocardial infarction. This has been shown in the Western Collaborative Group Study both in terms of its early years of experience[16,29] and in terms of the total eight and one-half years of follow-up.[30] That Type A has been associated with underlying disease processes is important corroborative information. The findings indicate an analog to a dose-response relationship in that persons with multiple CHD events are more strongly Type A than those who, over a given period, sustain only one such clinical episode.

At least three studies have now been completed relating Type A to the extent of atherosclerosis in the coronary arteries as determined by angiography. Two of these studies show the Structured Interview assessments of Type A to occur more often among those coronary angiography patients who have a greater number of vessels more seriously obstructed whereas Type B ratings are found in patients with lesser pathology.[18,19] The third study reported a similar finding, but with the JAS as a measure of the CPBP.[31] All four JAS scales were significantly associated with the amount of arterial atherosclerosis. Even after statistical control for amount of anginal pain, age of patient, and history of previous myocardial infarction, the Type A and hard-driving factor scores were still associated with the extent of disease. One of the interview studies also used the JAS and found the interview type but not the JAS score to be associated with the amount of atherosclerosis.[18] The interview obtained much of its predictive strength from the correct identification of women and those men over 60 years of age. Only 53 of the 142 study subjects took the JAS and these were working males in the 30 to 60 age range, the specific group for which this test was developed.

To the best of our knowledge, no other measurement techniques for Type A behavior have been used in studies of recurrent myocardial infarction or atherosclerosis of the coronary arteries. The strength of both the Structured Interview and the Activity Survey in these studies argues first for the basic validity of the Type A concept as a coronary risk factor, and second, for the validity of both these assessment procedures.

A number of other approaches to Type A assessment have been used upon occasion, particularly in retrospective studies of CHD patients and controls. Voice analysis by electronic means developed by Friedman and Brown was found capable of predicting CHD prevalence.[40] The Wardwell-Bahnson Interview found Type A tendencies to be stronger in CHD patients than in either hospitalized or healthy control groups in the Southeast Connecticut Study.[43] An impressive number of other studies using interviews or questionnaires to tap some part of the CPBP have also shown valid associations with the presence of CHD, usually in retrospective studies. These research projects were conducted in several nations and were summarized in 1976 in a review paper in the *New England Journal of Medicine.*[44] These *ad hoc* procedures have not been validated against either the Structured Interview or the JAS, and it is upon their manifest content that we interpret them, in all liklehood, to be measuring selected aspects of the CPBP.

An important characteristic of a behavioral measure is its ability to be used in the studies explaining the pathophysiological processes of cardiac disease or the psychological dynamics of Type A in relation to other psychological characteristics. The Structured Interview has been used in a wide variety of studies and has found Type A behavior to be significantly related to levels of serum cholesterol, to a tendency toward excess cigarette smoking, and to differences in daytime secretion of norepinephrine metabolites. Type A has also been found, in small samples, to be associated with changes in blood clotting and a variety of biological parameters. The JAS has been used in a few studies and has occasionally found Type A behavior to be associated with elevated serum triglycerides. In general, the JAS does not correlate Type A with serum cholesterol. There is little association of JAS scores with cigarette smoking, but weak associations with changes in cigarette habits. In general, the JAS has not been found significantly correlated with most standard CHD risk factors. This lack of correlation together with its significant association with clinical disease supports its position as an independent contributor to the prediction of CHD risk. A series of multiple logistic function studies of the Structured Interview (and also of the JAS) show both these measures of the CPBP to be independent predictors of coronary disease.[8b,13]

Because of its increasing use by psychologists, and also its earlier inclusion in comprehensive studies, the relation of the JAS to a wide variety of psychological and sociological parameters has been examined by a number of research teams. Comprehensive review of this work is beyond the scope of this book, but it is important to note that the JAS does *not* correlate strongly with other measures of standard psychological traits or measures of such states as anxiety, depression, and "stress." There is no way of using standard psychological tests to obtain a good measure of the coronary-prone behavior pattern.

One exception to this general finding is a study by Rosenman and Rahe of a study group of twins in which the Gough Adjective Checklist and certain scales of the Thurstone Temperament Schedule related more strongly than the JAS with interview judgments. This finding has not been replicated, however. The Structured Interview has been incorporated in a number of studies where other psychosocial variables were available. In the Trappist-Benedictine Monastery Study by Caffery et al., the Structured Interview had only modest correlations with scales of Cattell's 16-Personality Factor Inventory.[14] In no instance did these correlations exceed .25 and this is in general agreement that the Type A behavior pattern is a construct quite independent of traditional psychological theorizing and measurement.

Both the Structured Interview and the JAS have a great potential for effective use in studies aimed at explanation of cardiovascular processes or psychological dynamics. The JAS may have a slight edge in this regard inasmuch as it is less expensive to administer and generates separate scores for different aspects of the coronary-prone pattern.

Recent studies of the JAS have shown that different aspects of the general Type A pattern seem to be specifically predictive of acute myocardial infarction, silent myocardial infarction, and angina pectoris without infarction. In fact, on newly derived dimensions, angina and acute infarction patients differ more strongly from each other than either group differs from a control group that remained healthy. This was a prospective study in which all persons completed the JAS before developing CHD and the subsequent development of illness gave rise to the groupings and the extraction of predictive scales. The facility with which item analyses and multidimensional statistical procedures can be applied to the JAS make it a research instrument with great promise.[24]

Recent work by Zyzanski and Jenkins has resulted in the development of three new scales that are distinct from previously published JAS scales, and which, considered simultaneously, define a three-dimensional space that tends to separate persons by the type of clinical CHD they are most likely to develop in the future.[24] This particular work needs replication before further claims may be made. Similarly, a recurrence scale for the JAS is being developed, which should enable clinicians to determine which of their CHD patients has the highest risk of continuing on to a second infarction. The provisional recurrence scale thus far developed has a high correlation with the present Type A scale. Item analyses of the Structured Interview have also been performed, first by Jenkins.[5] Bortner's item-by-item ratings of the interviews of 66 future CHD patients and a control group matched two for one was subjected to detailed analyses by Matthews et al.[7] Both item analyses and factor analyses were performed, and it was found that the two factors, Competitive Drive and Impatience, of the factors extracted, were the only dimensions that correlated either with behavior type interview judgments or with subsequent emergence of coronary disease, and these two factors correlated with both these criteria. This illustrates the value of studies of the infrastructure of the Interview and the JAS and their potential for explanation of important processes.

The next major evaluative characteristic for a behavioral measure is its dependability—referred to by psychologists as reliability. In the present context we consider four issues. These, like the foregoing discussion, are briefly summarized in Table 5.1. Agreement between raters or alternate forms of the test is an important mark of a useful measure. The Structured Interview has been found to evidence a high percentage of interrater agreement on the several occasions it has been studied. The percent of agreement ranges from 76 to 88% in most such studies. Correlations between raters in the Monastery Study were approximately .70. These degrees of agreement placed behavior type as having equal or greater reliability than the reading of chest x-rays by board-certified chest physicians, usual clinical interpretations of ECG tracings, and many other unhesitatingly accepted medical ratings and diagnoses. Quality control is maintained for the JAS through a series of restrictions and requirements made prerequisite to the use of the test. All JAS forms are precoded and punched onto IBM cards, and then verified before further processing. Punching instructions include referral of ambiguous responses to a chief coder and specific conventions for coding missing data or multiple answers to the same item. In addition, raw JAS responses punched onto cards are run through an editing program to catch out-of-range punches before the cards are submitted for computer scoring. An unacceptable percentage of out-of-range punches is considered to be indicative of an unacceptable number of erroneous punches within the ranges provided, and the entire batch of cards is referred for re-punching and reverifying.

Now that several editions of the JAS are being reported in the literature, it is important to determine whether the forms are equivalent. This has been achieved by standardizing all forms currently in use to the WCGS participants as a reference population. It is from this population that the mean and standard deviation of all scales are derived and adjusted to equal 0 and 10, respectively. Thus, even when the JAS is used in a variety of geographic settings and occupational groups, and even in translation, the common scoring algorithm makes comparisons across samples much more reliable than if different inter-viewers were conducting interviews in different settings. The issue of meanings of questions and the meaning of the interview situation, of course, is not resolved in terms of possible cross-cultural differences.

Stability over time is another important consideration in any assessment that purports to measure a stable trait or a characteristic enduring pattern of be-havior. Both the Structured Interview and the JAS have been subjected to test-retest studies and both compare favorably with standard psychological and medical measures. The degree of agreement over a one-year interval is 80% for the Standard Interview. For the continuous scores of the JAS, a correlation coefficient is the most appropriate statistic. Test-retest correlations run gener-ally between .60 and .70. This is about the same range as observed for MMPI scales, scales of the Wechsler-Bellevue test, blood pressure, and serum choles-terol measured at one-year intervals. The JAS shows equal equivalence over long time periods with correlations of the same magnitude being observed for different forms of the test and different scoring equations administered at a four-year interval. Another part of the broader aspect of dependability of measurement is the resistance of a measure to dissimulation. This can be a frank attempt by the subject to misrepresent himself, but it is more often a subtle unconscious desire to place oneself in the best light, depending on the im-mediate circumstances. Although no studies have been done of test-taking bias or dissimulation on measures of the CPBP, it is likely that such an effort would be more likely to be detected and corrected for in the interview situation than would be the case for the JAS. This is an area needing further study, but until it is done, it seems reasonable to consider the Structured Interview as more dependable in this respect.

A good measure of any construct is one that measures that construct alone and remains free of accidental measurement of other variables and free of confounding by other sources of bias. Little study has been done in this regard with respect to the CPBP, but some findings are appropriate to mention. Both the Structured Interview and the JAS are associated with social class. Persons at higher occupational and educational levels are more likely to be assessed as Type A and more likely to be highly involved in their jobs. This seems to be less of an error of measurement or problem of confounding than to reflect validly the tendency for Type A behavior to be more manifest in persons of higher occupational and educational levels. Type A behavior, its achievement orientation, in all likelihood, leads to upward mobility, and similarly, the culture of professions and administration values the same traits that are at the foundation of the Type A value system.

Regional and international comparisons of the JAS suggest considerable variation in mean scores of all the scales, but these differences seem more attributable to socioeconomic and occupational differences among the subgroups under study than to any generalized differences between nations. The most likely instance of a cultural difference on the JAS is the observation of the extreme rarity of Type A behavior among participants of the Honolulu Heart Program. Both the culture and the social setting seem to strongly reinforce the easy-going, polite, cooperative Type B style in the Honolulu participants. In contrast, occupation seems to be a less important determinant of these rather large differences in JAS means.

The developers of the Type A concept have emphasized that the behavior pattern is not a reflection of "stress," anxiety, or psychological disturbance. It is gratifying, therefore, to note that neither the Interview nor the JAS has been found to correlate significantly with a wide variety of measures of emotional distress or psychological dysfunction. The correlations are not all positive, not all negative, but tend to cluster fairly close to 0. Further study is needed to rule out other possible directions of bias or confounding in these measures of the Type A behavior pattern.

A final consideration in the evaluation of an assessment technique is its convenience and cost both to the research subject and to the research project. The Structured Interview requires the services of a specially trained interviewer as well as quality control in the form of periodic monitoring of tape recordings of interviews to prevent tendencies for judgments to drift from fatigue or over the course of a long study. The Interview is interesting and free of embarrassment or stress to the research subject. Originally, the Interview took 20 to 25 minutes, but recent reports indicate that it can be accomplished in as little as 5 to 10 minutes. The effort and costs to the research subjects are relatively small, but the resources and costs to the research project can be considerable, particularly if large populations of persons are to be assessed.

The Activity Survey, on the other hand, is brief, interesting, and non-threatening to the research subject in much the same way as the Interview. Its real economy, however, is in terms of its administration and scoring. Because it is self-administered, there is no need for trained interviewers or calibration nor the quality control that the Structured Interview procedure requires. The expensive developmental work is completed now: printing of forms, keypunching, verifying, computer processing, and printing of scores for each individual are quite inexpensive, with the exact cost depending on the size of the batch processed per computer run. The logistics of administration of the JAS are also quite simple. Study subjects can complete the test in a large room, individually, while waiting for other procedures, or can take the forms home and return them by mail. The latter procedure has been found quite feasible, with a greater than 90% return rate having been achieved. With the self-administered form, thousands can be completed in the same hour, whereas the use of trained interviewers necessarily extends the data collection procedure for many months.

It is impossible to cover, in a brief paper, the scientific yield of nearly two decades of research with the Structured Interview and 13 years of research and development with the JAS. A comprehensive bibliography of the general work with the CPBP can be assembled from other presentations. The appended reference list concentrates primarily on research with the JAS.

References and Selected Bibliography

General References

1. Friedman, M.: Pathogenesis of Coronary Artery Disease. New York: McGraw-Hill, 1969.
2. Jenkins, C.D.: The coronary-prone personality. *In* Psychological Aspects of Myocardial Infarction and Coronary Care. (Gentry, W.D., Williams, R.B., Jr., eds.) St. Louis: C.V. Mosby, 1975, pp. 5–23.

Structured Interview

Methodological:
3. Rosenman, R.H., Friedman, M., Straus, R., et al.: A predictive study of coronary heart disease: the Western Collaborative Group Study. *JAMA* **189**:15–22, 1964.
4. Caffrey, B.: Reliability and validity of personality and behavioral measures in a study of coronary heart disease. *J Chronic Dis* **21**:191–204, 1968.
5. Jenkins, C.D.: Components of the coronary-prone behavior pattern: their relation to silent myocardial infarction and blood lipids. *J Chronic Dis* **19**:599–609, 1966.
6. Jenkins, C.D., Rosenman, R.H., Friedman, M.: Replicability of rating the coronary-prone behaviour pattern. *Br J Prev Soc Med* **22**:16–22, 1968.
7. Matthews, K., Glass, D.C., Rosenman, R.H., et al.: Competitive drive, pattern A and coronary heart disease: a further analysis of some data from the Western Collaborative Group Study. *J Chronic Dis* **30**:489–498, 1977.
8a. Howard, J.H., Cunningham, D.A., Rechnitzer, P.A.: Health patterns associated with Type A behavior: a managerial population. *J Human Stress* **2**:24–32, 1976.
8b. Brand, R., Rosenman, R.H., Jenkins, C.D., et al.: Comparison of coronary heart disease prediction in the Western Collaborative Group Study using the Standard Interview and the Jenkins Activity Survey assessments of the coronary-prone behavior pattern. *J. Chronic Dis* (in press).

Relation to CHD
9. Rosenman, R.H., Friedman, M., Straus, R., et al.: Coronary heart disease in the Western Collaborative Group Study: a follow-up experience of two years. *JAMA* **195**:86–92, 1966.
10. Rosenman, R.H., Friedman, M., Straus, R., et al.: Coronary heart disease in the Western Collaborative Group Study: a follow-up experience of 4½ years. *J Chronic Dis* **23**:173–190, 1970.
11. Jenkins, C.D., Rosenman, R.H., Zyzanski, S.J.: Cigarette smoking: its relationship to coronary heart disease and related risk factors in the Western Collaborative Group Study. *Circulation* **38**:1140–1155, 1968.
12. Rosenman, R.H., Brand, R.J., Jenkins, C.D., et al.: Coronary heart disease in the Western Collaborative Group Study: final follow-up experience of 8½ years. *JAMA* **233**:872–877, 1975.

13. Brand, R.J., Rosenman, R.H., Sholtz, R.I., et al.: Multivariate prediction of coronary heart disease in the Western Collaborative Group Study compared to the findings of the Framingham Study. *Circulation* **53**:348–355, 1976.
14. Caffrey, B.: A multivariate analysis of sociopsychological factors in monks with myocardial infarctions. *Am J Public Health* **60**:452–458, 1970.
15. Quinlan, C.B., Barrow, J.G., Moinuddin, M., et al.: Prevalence of selected coronary heart disease risk factors in Trappist and Benedictine monks. Presented at the Conference on Cardiovascular Epidemiology, American Heart Association, Atlanta, Georgia, February 4, 1968.
16. Rosenman, R.H., Friedman, M., Jenkins, C.D., et al.: Recurring and fatal myocardial infarction in the Western Collaborative Group Study. *Am J Cardiol* **19**:771–775, 1967.
17. Friedman, M., Rosenman, R.H., Straus, R., et al.: The relationship of behavior pattern A to the state of the coronary vasculature: a study of fifty-one autopsy subjects. *Am J Med* **44**:525–537, 1968.
18. Blumenthal, J.A., Kong, Y., Rosenman, R.H., et al.: Type A behavior pattern and angiographically documented coronary disease. Presented at the meeting of the American Psychosomatic Society, New Orleans, March 21, 1975.
19. Frank, K.A., Heller, S.S., Kornfeld, D.S., Sporn, A.A., et al.: Type A behavior and coronary artery disease: angiographic confirmation. Manuscript submitted for publication.

Activity Survey

Methodological
20a. Jenkins, C.D., Zyzanski, S.J., Rosenman, R.H.: The Jenkins Activity Survey for Health Prediction, Chapel Hill, N.C., C.D. Jenkins, 1966, 1969, 1972.
20b. Jenkins, C.D., Zyzanski, S.J., Rosenman, R.H.: *Manual for the Activity Survey.* Psychological Corporation: New York; in press.
21. Jenkins, C.D., Rosenman, R.H., Friedman, M.: Development of an objective psychological test for the determination of the coronary-prone behavior pattern in employed men. *J Chronic Dis* **20**:371–379, 1967.
22. Zyzanski, S.J., Jenkins, C.D.: Basic dimensions within the coronary-prone behavior pattern. *J Chronic Dis* **22**:781–792, 1970.
23. Kittel, F., Kornitzer, M., Zyzanski, S.J., Jenkins, C.D., et al.: Two methods of assessing the Type A coronary-prone behavior pattern in Belgium. *J Chronic Dis* **31**:147–155, 1978.
24. Jenkins, C.D., Zyzanski, S.J., Rosenman, R.H.: Coronary-prone behavior: one pattern or several? *Psychosom Med* **40**:25–43, 1978.
25. Mettlin, C.: Occupational careers and the prevention of coronary-prone behavior. *Soc Sci Med* **10**:367–372, 1976.

Relation to CHD
26. Jenkins, C.D., Zyzanski, S.J., Rosenman, R.H.: Progress toward validation of a computer-scored test for the Type A coronary-prone behavior pattern. *Psychosom Med* **33**:193–202, 1971.
27. Kenigsberg, D., Zyzanski, S.J., Jenkins, C.D., et al.: The coronary-prone behavior pattern in hospitalized patients with and without coronary heart disease. *Psychosom Med* **36**:344–351, 1974.
28. Jenkins, C.D., Rosenman, R.H., Zyzanski, S.J.: Prediction of clinical coronary heart disease by a test for coronary-prone behavior pattern. *N Engl J Med* **290**:1271–1275, 1974.
29. Jenkins, C.D., Zyzanski, S.J., Rosenman, R.H., et al.: Assocation of coronary-prone behavior scores with recurrence of coronary heart disease. *J Chronic Dis* **24**:601–611, 1971.
30. Jenkins, C.D., Zyzanski, S.J., Rosenman, R.H.: Risk of new myocardial infarction in middle-aged men with manifest coronary heart disease. *Circulation* **53**:342–347, 1976.
31. Zyzanski, S.J., Jenkins, C.D., Ryan, T.J., Flessas, A., Everist, M.: Psychological correlates of coronary angiographic findings. *Arch Intern Med* **136**:1234–1237, 1976.

32. Shekelle, R.B., Schoenberger, J.A., Stamler, J.: Correlates of the JAS Type A behavior pattern score. *J Chronic Dis* **29**:381–394, 1976.
33. Cohen, J.B.: Sociocultural change and behavior patterns in disease etiology: an epidemiologic study of coronary disease among Japanese-Americans. Ph.D. Dissertation in Epidemiology, School of Public Health, University of California at Berkeley, August, 1974.
34. Stokols, J.J.: Life dissatisfaction as a risk factor in coronary heart disease. Ph.D. Dissertation in Psychology, University of North Carolina at Chapel Hill, 1973.
35a. Zyzanski, S.J., Wrzesniewski, K., and Jenkins, C.D.: Cross-cultural validation of the coronary-prone behavior pattern in Poland. Submitted for publication, 1978.
35b. Hiland, D. Ph.D. Dissertation. Department of Psychology, University of South Florida, Tampa, Fla., June, 1978.

Bortner Performance Battery

36. Bortner, R.W., Rosenman, R.H.: The measurement of Pattern A behavior. *J Chronic Dis* **20**:525–533, 1967.
37. Bortner, R.W., Rosenman, R.H., Friedman, M.: Familial similarity in pattern A behavior: fathers and sons. *J Chronic Dis* **23**:39–43, 1970.

Bortner Short Rating Scale

38. Bortner, R.W.: A short rating scale as a potential measure of pattern A behavior. *J Chronic Dis* **22**:87–91, 1969.
39. Rustin, R.M., Dramaix, M., Kittel, F., Degre, C., Kornitzer, M., Thilly, C., de Backer, G.: Validation de techniques d'evaluation du profil comportemental "A" utilisees dans de "Projet Belge de Prevention de affections cardiovasculaires," (P.B.S.) *Rev Epidem et Sante Publ* **24**:497–507, 1976.

Voice Analysis

40. Friedman, M., Brown, A.E., Rosenman, R.H.: Voice analysis test for detection of behavior pattern: responses of normal men and coronary patients. *JAMA* **208**:828–836, 1969.
41. Schucker, B., Jacobs, D.R.: Assessment of behavioral risk for coronary disease by voice characteristics. *Psychosom Med* **39**:219–228, 1977.
42. Scherwitz, L., Berton, K., Leventhal, H.: Type A assessment and interaction in the behavior pattern interview. *Psychosom Med* **39**:229–240, 1977.

Other Methods

43. Wardwell, W.I., Bahnson, C.B.: Behavioral variables and myocardial infarction in the South-eastern Connecticut Heart Study. *J Chronic Dis.* **26**:447–461, 1973.
44. Jenkins, C.D.: Recent evidence supporting psychologic and social risk factors for coronary disease. *N Engl J Med* **294**:987–994; 1033–1038, 1976.

Chapter 6

Psychometric Procedures Applied to the Assessment of the Coronary-Prone Behavior Pattern

Bernard Caffrey

Measurement means the assignment of numbers to objects according to some rule. The quantification of some aspects of behavior relevant to human problems has been a difficult task, but behavioral scientists have made notable progress in this area. Application of mathematical principles to problems related to human health have also been difficult, forcing medical scientists to be among the first to use computers for solving the important problems they face. In general, it is possible to identify five characteristics of a good assessment technique: objectivity, standardization, reliability, discriminability, and validity.

Objectivity

The problem of experimental contamination includes all variables that might influence the subject's behavior or the observer's behavior in recording data in a manner that affects the accuracy of the results.[1] For example, the results of a recent study by Scherwitz, Berton, and Leventhal[3] may have been affected by such variables. They interviewed 60 college students selected from the extremes of a distribution of Jenkins Activity Survey scores, who had been involved in a number of laboratory tasks before beginning the interview. This method of selecting study subjects appears to suffer from a combination of interviewer and respondent bias. Although it was not clear what kind of interaction the interviewer had with the respondent prior to the interview, the interviewer must have been aware that 32 of the students had been selected as extreme Type A's and 28 as extreme Type B's on the basis of the JAS scores. The respondents had already completed the JAS scale an indefinite period of time before the interview, and had been subjected to about 30 minutes of psychological measures. Loss of objectivity led to other weaknesses in the study, so it should be no surprise that the study by Schucker and Jacobs[3] which used appropriately objective methods, appeared in some respects to contradict the findings of Scherwitz et al. Unless the criterion of objectivity is met it is impossible to meet the other standards discussed here.

Standardization

Standardization of procedures is especially difficult to achieve in an interview. This is the strength of a paper-and-pencil inventory such as the JAS. In the large study of monks, Caffrey[4] used the assessment technique that he learned from Rosenman and Friedman, interviewing all subjects personally to be certain that procedures were constant. He tape-recorded instructions for the Abbot and a senior monk in each monastery to enable them to rate each monk on a five-point scale of Type A behavior and responsibility level. The interview became a "structured behavioral test" with spoken responses and careful observation of standard behavioral indicators. Although it is difficult to develop standard procedures, developing one's procedures *in detail* will permit greater comparability of studies that use the interview to assess the coronary-prone behavior pattern.

Reliability

Reliability is an extremely important criterion to meet, and most studies have made some effort to do so. Consistency of measurement is vital if the research is to be of any value, but it is not the sole criterion of success. Caffrey[4,5] assessed the reliability of the interview by having the Abbot and another monk make global assessments of the behavior pattern and responsibility levels. This involved a procedural difference, since the interviewer's judgment was based on the interview and they based theirs on their personal experiences with the monks, but the correlation among the three was still 0.75. Many studies use two or more judges, usually listening to taped interviews, whose ratings are then correlated. I am not aware of any studies of the Type A pattern that used multiple judges of the actual interview situation. This should be done, since some stylistics of behavior related to the pattern must be seen while others can be heard. The use of video-taping procedures would seem to be ideal for this purpose.

Discriminability

Discriminability is that quality of a measuring instrument that is related to the magnitude of meaningful differences that the instrument generates. In general, this quality refers to the range of scores that can be obtained by a measuring instrument and the precision required in its application. The case at hand concerns the question of whether subjects should be scored as Type A or Type B (a two-point scale), as A+, A−, A/B, B−, B+ (a five-point scale), on a continuum ranging from −30.0 to +30.0 (as the JAS scale does), or whether some alternate procedure should be used. Although many studies have found the A-B dichotomy adequate for discriminating between those who developed CHD and those who did not, this is not useful for studying other variables that might be related to the behavior pattern and CHD. Perhaps there should be better standardization using a continuous scale, standardized with a mean of 50.0 and a standard deviation of 10.0. This would eliminate the minus sign from the JAS scoring system, for example, which is an easy cause of clerical and coding errors, and would allow the researcher to use standard cut-off points more effectively.

I would like to warn against procedures that are clouded by the "mystery of the missing middle" and risk errors by sampling from a limited range of scores. The excellent work of David Glass[6] is somewhat weakened by his practice of taking extreme groups from a distribution of JAS scores (as did Sherwitz et al.).[2] Future research should use at least three groups, with the optimal size being five groups. Much of the early research on anxiety was weakened by the practice of taking high anxious versus low anxious groups, thus obscuring the curvilinear and interactive effects that are so common in the study of motivation and behavior. A good example of this procedure, but one which used the simple A-B classification, was found in the Jenkins et al.[7] report comparing smoking rates, behavior pattern, and CHD rates. This is shown in Figure 6.1, which clearly illustrates the type of interaction that would have been obscured if the respondents had simply been classed as "smoker versus nonsmoker." Erroneous conclusions could have been drawn from the study, and the interaction effect gave the authors a lot to write about, especially when it was absent in the 50 to 59 year age-group. Interactions are sometimes not pleasant to find, but if they exist, instruments should have the discriminating power to determine the effect.

Validity

The most important criterion for any measuring instrument is that it be valid. All of the other standards aim at this as their ultimate goal. It is possible to discuss three types of validity: predictive, content, and construct. Predictive validity refers to the capacity of an instrument to predict an event or behavior in a particular situation. For example, the SAT scores, when combined with class rank, provide a good predictor of grades at the end of the freshman year in college. Analyses of data compiled on Clemson University freshmen over a three-year period show that the multiple r for the two predictors is about 0.64, and it has been difficult to find other variables that add much to the predictive power of these measures.

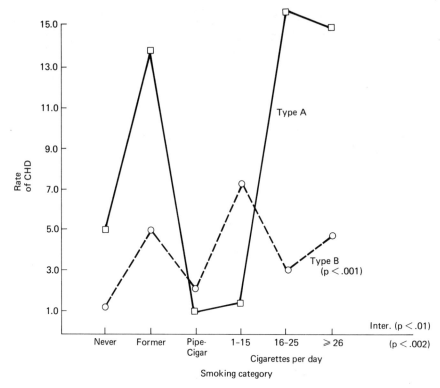

Figure 6.1   Incidence of new CHD by smoking category and behavior type for men aged 39 to 49 years (4½ years).

The predictive validity of these two measures should remind us to attempt to cross-classify other variables with the behavior pattern to enhance its validity. Predictive validity may be difficult to establish, especially in the case of CHD, since the illness event might occur many years after the original assessment. While the Type A pattern has been shown to be fairly stable over time, the correlations are not so high as to preclude some changes in behavioral style. In spite of this, the behavior pattern is as valid a predictor of CHD as most other risk factors. This type of validity might also be called "descriptive" (or "concurrent") validity if it is used to correctly identify existing groups. Studies that use prevalence rates of illness fall in this category.

Content validity refers to the degree to which the interview or inventory samples the relevant domain of behaviors. Frequently, an interview is called Type A without it being clear that the content is identical to that used by Rosenman and Friedman. The JAS is good in this regard, since the items were constructed by Jenkins in collaboration with Rosenman and Friedman. Other scales do not always reflect the universe of behaviors that describe the behavior pattern.[8]

Construct validity refers to the "reality" of the trait that is being measured. A construct is an idea that has direct reference to the physical world. Intelligence is a construct assessed by a number of measuring instruments; anxiety is another construct valuable in the understanding of human behavior. Is the Type A behavior pattern a construct? As with any concept that is operationalized and quantified, I would need to say that it is indeed a construct. Whether or not it exists at a more concrete level and could be labeled a "trait" is another question. The behavior pattern is a *consistent syndrome* of behaviors (traits) that can be specified and quantified. It is theoretically more sound to refer to it as a "behavior type" than as a "personality type." Personality is a construct that implies something more extensive than the overt behavior pattern known as Type A. Traditionally, the term "type" is used to refer to a more inclusive concept than a "trait," so it seems to be in keeping with that tradition to use the term "type" in this context.

One of the principal problems related to construct validity is the specification of what a construct is by determining what it is *not*. Although a number of correlational studies have been conducted, more research might be useful in exploring further the relation of the Type A pattern to anxiety, need patterns (achievement, affiliation, and power), intelligence, neuroticism, extraversion, life satisfaction, self-concept scales, and a host of other personality dimensions. One factor analysis of the interview and 16-PF personality inventory scales produced four factors: Type A, responsibility, extraversion, and neurotic anxiety.[4,5] Factor analyses of the interview and of the JAS have shown that these are not unidimensional. Factorial validity is a form of construct validity, and more such studies need to be reported before we can draw firm conclusions about the behavior pattern. We call it a "behavior type" and it is probably best to leave it at that for the time being. Perhaps the expression "coronary-prone behavior pattern" is best.

Those who design research should make a checklist of these five criteria and make every effort to plan, execute, and analyze their research with a view to satisfying their demands. There is little chance for redeeming a study that grossly violates even one of these standards. Most of the reports published in journals adhere pretty well to them, but sometimes there are studies that do not make it clear how they met the criteria. Those of us who have worked with the assessment of the Type A behavior pattern have a pretty good record in this respect, but as more and more people begin to use the procedures we should make every effort to maintain consistently high standards in our research programs. It should be thought of as a matter of quality control.

References

1. Matheson, D.W., Bruce, R.L., Beauchamp, K.L.: Introduction to Experimental Psychology. New York: Holt, 1974, p. 50.
2. Sherwitz, L., Berton, K., Leventhal, H.: Type A assessment and interaction in the behavior pattern interview. *Psychosom Med* **39**:229–240, 1977.
3. Schucker, B., Jacobs, D.R.: Assessment of behavioral risks for coronary disease by voice characteristics. *Psychosom Med* **39**:219–228, 1977.

4. Caffrey, B.: Reliability and validity of personality and behavioral measures in a study of coronary heart disease. *J Chronic Dis* **21**:191–204, 1968.
5. Caffrey, B.: A multivariate analysis of sociopsychological factors in monks with myocardial infarctions. *Am J Public Health* **60**:452–458, 1970.
6. Glass, D.C.: Stress, behavior patterns, and coronary disease. *Am Sci* **65**:177–187, 1977.
7. Jenkins, D.C., Rosenman, R.H., Zyzanski, S.J.: Cigarette smoking: its relationship to coronary heart disease and related risks factors in the Western Collaborative Group Study. *Circulation* **38**:1140–1155, 1968.
8. Vickers, R.: A short measure of the Type A personality. University of Michigan, personal communication, 1973.

Chapter 7

Reliability and Validity of Methods Used to Assess Coronary-Prone Behavior

Theodore M. Dembroski

The purpose of this chapter is to present an overview of the reliability and validity of the Structured Interview and the Jenkins Activity Survey, which were developed to assess the Type A coronary-prone behavior pattern. Evidence supporting the construct validity of the Type A pattern is reviewed including recent findings on the relationship between Type A behavior and physiological reactions. A schematic model is presented which integrates for hueristic purposes the interrelationships between behavioral and physiological processes that may lead to coronary heart disease.

Structured Interview Reliability

Reliability refers to the degree to which an assessment procedure consistently measures an attribute. The reliability of the Structured Interview has been explored by examining the extent of agreement produced by (1) assessing subjects at different points in time, and (2) different persons assessing subjects at the same point in time.

Reliability of the interview procedure appears comparable to many routinely used psychological and medical assessment instruments. Interjudge agreement of classification usually ranges between 75 and 90%.[1-3] Test-retest with the interview procedure of over 1,000 subjects in the Western Collaborative Group Study (WCGS) showed about 80% agreement in the dichotomous A-B classification over periods that ranged from 12 to 20 months (tetrachloric correlation coefficient = .82).[2] Reliability using the four-point scale (A_1, A_2, B_3, B_4) was somewhat lower for both test-retest and interjudge agreement, but it is noted that the dichotomous rating is the one usually used as the estimate of risk. Acceptable reliability estimates also have been reported elsewhere.[3]

As more objective methods of scoring the interview are developed,[4] it will be possible to investigate how use of these scoring techniques affects reliability. In addition, recent reanalyses of taped interviews from the WCGS showed that some components of the behavior pattern (e.g., competitive drive, potential for hostility, and impatience) are more predictive of CHD than others.[4] Thus, reliability of subcomponents of the behavior pattern will need to be established. Fortunately, this can be readily accomplished by reinspection of tapes from the WCGS.

Efforts are under way to explore the use of the interview technique in assessing Type A behavior in subjects who differ in sex, age, socioeconomic status, etc. Attention might be devoted to developing an alternate form of the interview for use in establishing reliability of the interview in these populations. Also, as more people are formally trained in the interview technique, it will be necessary to examine other factors that can affect reliability. For example, typically, mature lay females have been used to administer the Structured Interview. It would be important to know how respondents are influenced by age, sex, status, etc., of the interviewer and vice versa. It would also be useful to know how consistent interviewers are in the manner in which they administer the Interview to different subjects. Directly related is the need for information on how certain interviewer mannerisms affect the responses of subjects and *vice versa*.[6]

Jenkins Activity Survey (JAS) Reliability

The JAS shows about 65 to 70% classification agreement with the Structured Interview. Extreme groups, i.e., plus or minus one standard deviation from the mean, show about 90% agreement with the Interview.[5] The JAS was administered to more than 2,800 subjects participating in the WCGS. Test-retest reliability was determined at one- and four-year intervals, respectively.[7] The results showed about a .65 correlation between testing occasions for the Type A scale and the "Speed-Impatience" and "Job Involvement" components of the JAS. The "Hard-driving" component showed a slightly lower (approximately .58) test-retest correlation than the other components. Comparison of the correlations between one-year and four-year intervals were not appreciably different. Reliability coefficients were probably affected by changes in items and scoring procedures initiated with the aim of improving agreement with the Interview between testing intervals, although at present, it is not known what effect these changes had on reliability. Thus, when a standard version of the JAS is made available, it will be useful to reexamine its reliability, and an alternate form of the JAS would be useful to this effort.

Validity

In general, an instrument is considered valid if it can be demonstrated that it measures what it was designed to measure. Both the Structured Interview and the JAS were designed to measure attributes included in the Type A pattern, such as potential for displaying hostility, hard-driving, and achievement behaviors, impatience, and competitiveness. In establishing the validity of an instrument, it is useful to determine whether it is measuring attributes other than those intended.

A number of psychological tests have been administered to various samples in efforts to determine whether the Type A pattern is related to standard measures of personality. Measures used in these efforts included such scales as the Thurstone Temperament Schedule, Gough Adjective Check list, California Psychological Inventory, MMPI, Cattell 16-PF Questionnaire, Rotter's I-E scale, Test Anxiety Questionnaire, etc. Details on the results of these correlational studies may be found in Glass.[8] Briefly, the results showed that the Type A pattern, in general, reflects characteristics independent of those assessed by traditional measures of personality. In fact, the significant correlations obtained in this line of research usually supported the validity of the Type A pattern. For example, subscales of the various psychological instruments that assessed such dimensions as activity level, speed, achievement, aggression, dominance, and related characteristics correlated significantly with measures of the Type A pattern, while other dimensions (e.g., neurotic anxiety, defensiveness, "Thrill-Seeking" Scale, etc.) did not. Thus, it appears that the Type A pattern does not reflect any distinguishing personality or psychopathologic characteristic as measured by traditional psychological inventories. Important relationships probably exist between the Type A pattern and other psychological attributes, but it appears that these relationships will need to be established by use of means other than traditional psychological tests. The late Dr. R. W. Bortner alertly recognized this and began work on the development of a performance test battery in which actual behaviors could be used (e.g., writing speed) as criteria to distinguish interview defined Type A and B subjects.[8a] Preliminary results were encouraging, but, unfortunately, illness interrupted Dr. Bortner's work.

Currently, social psychological laboratory and field research have been helpful in supporting the validity of the Type A concept and the currently used assessment procedures, and in identifying additional psychological attributes of the Type A pattern. The definition of Type A emphasizes that the enhanced aggressiveness, impatience, and hard-driving behaviors that characterize the pattern most readily occur when appropriate social and/or physical environmental challenges are salient. Social psychological experiments have provided empirical support for the validity of this assumption. (Details on the experiments reported in this paragraph can be found in Glass.[8] For most of his studies, Glass used extreme groups assessed by the JAS to maximize classification agreement with the Interview.) For example, a study with college students was arranged so that the cooperative task performance of Type A's was deliberately slowed by another person. Pattern A subjects compared to their counterparts responded to the person with significantly more behavioral signs of impatience and irritation. In another experiment, Type A's relative to Type B's actually responded with greater behavioral aggression towards a person who interfered with their performance on an important task. Another study showed that Type A's performed worse than B's in a Differential Rein- forcement of Low Rates (DRL) task, a paradigm in which subjects are required to learn to inhibit responding until appropriate passage of time to obtain a reward.

Differences between Type A's and B's in rate of response was illustrated in a study in which Type A's worked at near maximum capacity on a task whether or not there was a deadline, while Type B's increased their effort only in response to the presence of a deadline. The same program of research showed that Type A's physically exerted themselves (as measured by aerobic consump- tion) more than B's on a treadmill, but reported significantly less feelings of exhaustion than B's. In sum, the series of studies conducted by Glass and associates support the validity of the three major components of the Type A pattern: aggressiveness, impatience, and hard-driving. Interestingly, additional attributes of Pattern A behavior can be uncovered by research of this kind. For example, Glass found that Type A's responded more vigorously than Type B's when threat of failure on an important task was made salient, but gave up trying to solve the problem sooner than B's. The behavioral and physiological impli- cations of this apparent heightened concern with control of the environment, which gives way to helplessness-prone tendencies in Type A's, are discussed in more detail by Glass elsewhere in this volume.

Systematic investigations of differences between Type A's and Type B's in naturalistic, day-to-day behavior have not yet been reported. However, a recent study of 236 managers in 12 different companies disclosed that interview-determined Type A's compared to B's reported on a job tension questionnaire greater self-confidence, more dissatisfaction with having respon- sibility for supervising others, and more complaints about conflicting work demands and heavy workloads.[9] In another study of working men (N = 943), JAS scores were correlated positively and significantly with a variety of indices of job status and success.[10]

The results of these studies suggest that the work environment may be instrumental in inducing Type A behavior. On the other hand, research by Glass et al. suggests that hard-driving behavior in the work situation may be self-imposed by Type A's in the service of needs to control their environment. Findings from a recent experiment conducted with college students in our laboratory are consistent with this interpretation.[11] The results of this experi- ment showed that Type A's significantly more than B's preferred to work alone rather than with others when under stress. Subsequent correlational studies also showed that preference for working in solitude when under pressure was associated with subjects with coronary disease and the Type A pattern.[11]

In sum, the studies reported above appear to support the concurrent, predictive, and construct validity of the Type A concept and the testing procedures used to assess it. However, more research is needed to replicate and confirm the findings reported thus far. For example, it would be of interest to explore the relationship between the Type A pattern and the need for achievement.[12] If a strong relationship is found, the wealth of information extant on achievement motivation could be used to better understand the Type A pattern. In addition, most of the validity data derived from laboratory studies used college students as subjects. Other populations of subjects should be included in future research. Moreover, systematic study of the naturalistic behavior of Type A and Type B subjects is needed to provide information on the frequency of Type A behavior and the situations that evoke it in everyday life. Directly related is the need to know the distribution and stability of Type A behavior in the general population. In addition, future research should continue attempts to identify additional important attributes of the Type A pattern to provide information useful to intervention strategies and attempts to improve the measurement of the Type A pattern.

Relationship between Behavioral and Physiological Reactions

The validity of the Type A concept has been discussed above from a psychological or behavioral standpoint. The validity of the Type A pattern as a risk factor for CHD has been discussed elsewhere in this volume. The validity of the Type A concept from a physiological perspective has not yet been discussed, but will receive attention later in the Mechanisms Section where the question of how the pattern translates itself into CHD is examined. However, research aimed at identifying the situations under which differential physiological arousal is induced between Types A and B is relevant to the validity question from multiple perspectives.

Unfortunately, there is a dearth of research that has investigated physiological arousal in Type A's and B's in response to social challenge. This is surprising, since the definition of Type A underlines the importance of environmental stimuli in evoking pattern A behavior, and it has been demonstrated that Type A's evidence a variety of biochemical derangements indicative of elevated autonomic nervous system activation.[13] A notable exception is a study by Friedman in which Type A's and B's were subjected to a competitive problem-solving task.[14] Type A's relative to B's responded with significantly greater levels of plasma norepinephrine despite the fact that no difference in this substance was observed between the Types in baseline. The situationally evoked difference in catecholamine levels between the Types suggests different levels of cardiovascular reaction.

To test this issue, a recent study conducted in our laboratory subjected Type A and Type B college students to a reaction time task in which the instructions emphasized the need for rapid and accurate performance.[15,16] Although no significant differences were observed between the Types during baseline, Type A's compared to B's responded with significantly greater increases in both heart rate and systolic blood pressure indicative of greater sympathetic arousal.[15] The implications of the type of reaction exhibited by Type A's to social challenge for CHD are discussed elsewhere in this volume.

Our research into the cardiovascular reactivity of Type A and B subjects has revealed interesting consistencies with epidemiological findings. For example, we have found that the Rosenman and Friedman structured interview was a better predictor of sympathetic arousal than the Jenkins Activity Survey, which parallels the findings obtained in the WCGS (see Chapter 4 by Rosenman).[16] Our research also has permitted the opportunity of exploring specific components of the Type A pattern that appear worthy of more extensive examination. (Details on measuring components in the Type A interview, which we have adapted for college students, can be found in the appendix of this chapter.) For example, as mentioned earlier and in the Section Summary of the Assessment Section, Matthews et al.[4] found that potential for hostility, competitiveness, irritability, impatience, and vigorous voice stylistics derived from the structured interview were the attributes most predictive of CHD. We have found that these stylistic and behavioral components of the Type A pattern (derived from the SI) were also the best predictors of challenge-induced cardiovascular arousal in our laboratory paradigm.[16]

If it can be established that certain behavioral reactions are associated with enhanced and potentially damaging physiologic arousal, then a potential link is established in the pathogenic process through which these behaviors translate into CHD. If such behaviors can be identified, refinements in their measurement and alteration can be pursued. Important to this effort is the identification of the types, range, and frequency of environmental situations that evoke these behavioral and/or physiological reactions. For example, ongoing work in our laboratory suggests that Type A and B subjects only differ in mild elevations of cardiovascular function under conditions of low explicit social challenge, but show pronounced differences in physiological arousal under conditions of high challenge. These results underline the importance of situational variables in evoking Type A behaviors and associated physiologic reactions. Of interest also is our observation that some Type B subjects respond to challenges with enhanced arousal and some Type A subjects do not, just as some Type B subjects develop CHD and some Type A subjects do not. Such findings suggest that it may be possible to develop a paradigm in which a direct measure of physiological response to social and/or physical challenge can be examined as a predictor of coronary heart disease.

A Psychosocial-Physiological Model

In discussing the validity of measurements designed to assess coronary-prone behavior, the following variables were emphasized: (1) environmental events, (2) psychological processes, (3) behavioral processes, and (4) physiological processes. For heuristic purposes, these variables have been organized into a model, which attempts to show how these processes may interrelate in everyday life (Figure 7.1). It is assumed that investigation of these interrelationships and how they may differ in those designated as Type A and Type B will, among

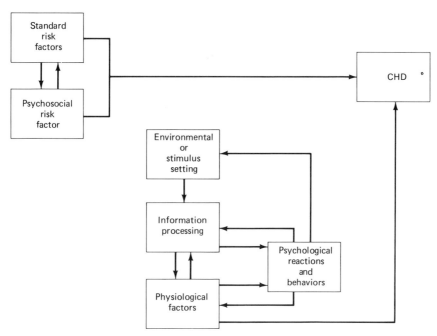

Figure 7.1   Model of the relationship between psychosocial-physiological variables and coronary heart disease.

other things, provide information useful to improving the measurement of coronary-prone behavior as a psychosocial risk factor in CHD.

Given that a relationship has been established between the psychosocial risk factor, standard risk factors, and CHD, the following questions are suggested by the model: (1) Do those high (Type A) and low (Type B) in the psychosocial risk factor differ with regard to the environment in which they work and live? (2) Do they differ in the manner in which they interpret or process information in response to the occurrence of the same or similar environmental events? (3) Is the manner in which they process information differentially affecting and/or affected by certain physiological factors? (4) Is the manner in which they process information differentially affecting and/or affected by particular psychological reactions (e.g., anger, impatience, etc.) and behaviors (e.g., aggression, avoidance, etc.)? (5) Do they differ in psychological reactions and behaviors that affect and/or are affected by particular physiological processes? (6) Is their behavior differentially influencing the environment in a manner that tends to perpetuate or exacerbate particular psychological and physiological processes? (7) Can differential physiological processes be identified and directly related to the development of CHD?

The research thus reviewed has already suggested differences between Type A and Type B subjects with regard to some of the questions advanced above. The results of future research can be expected to further elucidate psychological and physiological differences between those who are and are not relatively prone to develop CHD. Obviously such research is intimately related to basic biomedical, developmental, and intervention considerations, but as

more of these differences become known, it will be possible to further refine
existing measures of coronary-prone behavior and perhaps to develop new and
more effective measures.

References

1. Friedman, E.H., Hellerstein, H.K., et al.: Behavior patterns and serum cholesterol in two
   groups of normal males. *Circulation* (Supplement II) **32**:89, 1965.
2. Jenkins, C.D., Rosenman, R.H., Friedman, M.: Replicability of rating the coronary-prone
   behavior pattern. *Br J Prev Soc Med* **22**:16–22, 1968.
3. Caffrey, B.: Reliability and validity of personality and behavioral measures in a study of
   coronary heart disease. *J Chronic Dis* **21**:191–204, 1968.
4. Matthews, K.A., Glass, D.C., Rosenman, R.H., Bortner, R.W.: Competitive drive, Pattern A,
   and coronary heart disease: a further analysis of some data from the Western Collaborative
   Group Study. *J Chronic Dis* **30**:489–498, 1977.
5. Jenkins, C.D., Rosenman, R.H., Friedman, M.: Development of an objective psychological
   test for the determination of the coronary-prone behavior pattern in employed men. *J Chronic
   Dis* **20**:371–379, 1967.
6. Sherwitz, L., Berton, K., Leventhal, H.: Type A assessment in the behavior pattern interview.
   Psychosom Med **39**:229–240, 1977.
7. Jenkins, C.D., Rosenman, R.H., Zyzanski, S.J.: Prediction of clinical coronary heart disease
   by a test for the coronary-prone behavior pattern. *N Engl J Med* **290**:1271–1275, 1974.
8. Glass, D.C.: Behavior Patterns, Stress, and Coronary Disease. Hillsdale, N.J.: Lawrence
   Erlbaum Associates, 1977.
8a. Bortner, R.W., Rosenman, R.H.: The measurements of pattern A behavior. *J Chronic Dis*
   20:525–533, 1967.
9. Howard, J., Cunningham, D., Rechnitzer, P.: Work patterns associated with Type A behavior:
   a managerial population. Human Relations, (in press).
10. Mettlin, C.: Occupational careers and the prevention of coronary-prone behavior. *Soc Sci Med*
   10:367–372, 1976.
11. Dembroski, T.M., MacDougall, J.M.: Stress effect on affiliation preferences among subjects
   possessing the Type A coronary-prone behavior pattern. *J Pers Soc Psychol*, **35**:23–33, 1978.
12. McClelland, D.C.: The Achieving Society. Princeton: Van Nostrand, 1961.
13. Friedman, M.: Type A behavior pattern: some of its pathophysiological components. *Bull NY
   Acad Med*, **53**:593–604, 1977.
14. Friedman, M., Byers, S.O., Diamant, J., Rosenman, R.H.: Plasma catecholamine response of
   coronary-prone subjects (Type A) to a specific challenge. *Metabolism* **24**:205–210, 1975.
15. Dembroski, T.M., MacDougall, J.M., Shields, J.L.: Physiologic reactions to social challenge in
   persons evidencing the Type A coronary-prone behavior pattern. *J Human Stress* **3**:2–10,
   1977.
16. Dembroski, T.M., MacDougall, J.M., Shields, J.L., Petitto, J., Lushene, R.: Components of
   the coronary-prone behavior pattern and cardiovascular responses to psychomotor performance challenge. *J Behav Med* **1**:159–176, 1978.

Appendix 1: Component Quantitative Scoring Key for the Structured Interview

Stylistics

Each stylistic dimension is scored on a 1 to 5 scale, anchored as indicated
below.

    1. *Loud and Explosive Speech*—The subject shows louder than average

voice with vigorous emphasis on some words or sentences, particularly simple declarative statements ("Never!") or emphatic adjectives ("I'm *always* on time"). It is often the challenges by the interviewer that will trigger marked increases in loudness or explosiveness. This is a key point to remember: Look for abrupt, single word answers.

1 = Consistently *soft* voice without particular emphasis on key words.
3 = Average loudness with occasional increased emphasis on words or abrupt declarations.
5 = Consistently *loud voice* with frequent *explosive* declarations, often consisting of single words.

2. *Rapid and Accelerated Speech*—The subject shows rapid word production with or without an acceleration of speech at the end of a long sentence. In the extreme, this may be accompanied by "word clipping" (failure to pronounce the ending sounds of words), word repetition ("yes, yes"), or word omission ("No!" [I] "Never do that"). Accelerated speech is often observed during attempts at self-justification in response to interview challenges.

1 = Consistently slow, measured word production, often accompanied by pauses, "ahs," or breaks at the end of sentences.
3 = About average production rate with instances of both slow, deliberate speech and rapid word production.
5 = Extreme tendency toward high rate of speech, accelerated endings, word clipping, word repetition, and omission.

3. *Response Latency*—Responses are given with very short latencies and in the extreme occur prior to completion of the question. Also included is "hurrying" in which the subject attempts to speed up the question by saying "yes, yes" or "mm, mm", or some other verbal device.

1 = Consistently long latencies (one or more seconds) between the end of the question and the beginning of the answer.
3 = About a 50–50 mixture of long and short latency responses with *few* interrupting answers and no more than one or two "hurryings."
5 = Consistently short latencies with several interruptions and "hurryings."

4. *Hostility*—This is a difficult dimension to score; pay attention to both stylistics and content. Responses are argumentative ("*Nobody* always does anything!"), repeatedly and unnecessarily qualified ("It depends."), pointlessly challenging of the interviewer ("What do you mean by *that*?"). The voice characteristics suggest boredom, condescension, or surliness. Subject's answers to specific questions suggest impatience and irritability when faced with obstacles (. . . "Car going too slowly . . . ", " . . . wait in lines . . . ") and the tendency to make harsh generalizations ("The students here are all narrow-minded."). Extreme levels of hostility may be accompanied by *obscenity* or use of emotion laden words ("I *hate* it here!").

1 = None or very few statements with possible hostile content or structure, and no hostile voice stylistics.

3 = Some potentially hostile statements and some suggestion of hostility in voice stylistics.

5 = Frequent hostility expressed in content, form, and stylistics.

5. *Competition for Control of Interview*—Subject attempts to gain control of the interview by interrupting interviewer with lengthy responses, engaging in verbal duets, or offering extraneous (and often hostile) comments or questions that divert the direction of the interview. Distinguish simple hostility (negativism) from hostility directed toward intimidating the interviewer and thus gaining control. Excessive qualification without hostile or competitive intent occurs occasionally. Frequently, Type Bs will show such behavior especially those who appear nervous.

1 = No tendency to compete; subject passively responds to questions.

3 = Occasional attempts to compete.

5 = Repeated attempts to gain control. Score a five only if you perceive an ongoing struggle for control of the interview.

Content

Each question is scored on a 1 to 5 scale, with 1 indicating the complete absence of the trait ("No, I never get impatient.") and 5 indicating that the trait is always present ("I'm always impatient in lines." "I hate lines."). Use the 1 and 5 scores only when there is absolutely no doubt about the extreme character of the response. A score of 3 indicates an "average" level of the trait. A mean rating value is computed for all questions making up each dimension. This score is then multiplied by 10 to eliminate the decimal point.

STRUCTURED INTERVIEW COMPONENT SCORING SHEET

SUBJECT NAME AND CODE NUMBER _____

SCORED BY _____

DATE SCORED _____

I. STYLISTICS
   LOUD AND EXPLOSIVE   _____

   RAPID AND ACCELERATED   _____

   RESPONSE LATENCY   _____

   HOSTILITY   _____

   COMPETITION   _____

COMMENTS:

II. CONTENT ANALYSIS

Competitive Drive	Hostility	Speed	Impatience
#3 _____	#6 _____	#15 _____	#12_____
#4 _____	#14a_____	#15a_____	#14_____
#5 _____	#14b_____	#17a_____	#18_____
#5b _____	#16 _____	#17b_____	#19_____
#7 _____		#17c_____	
#8 _____		#20 _____	
#9a _____		#22 _____	
#10 _____			
#11 _____			
#11a_____			
#21 _____			

Appendix 2: Behavior Pattern Interview (Student Form)

INTRODUCTION: Most of the questions are concerned with your superficial habits and none of them will embarrass you. I would appreciate it if you would answer the questions to the best of your ability. Your answers will be kept in the strictest confidence. (Begin taping; emphasize italicized words)

Your code number is _____ .

1. May I ask your age, *please*?
2. What is your student classification?
   a. How long have you been at this college?
3. Are you *satisfied* with your school work thus far? (Why not?)
4. Do you feel that college carries *heavy* responsibility?
   a. Is there any time when you feel particularly *rushed* or under *pressure*?
   b. When you are under *pressure* does it bother you?
5. Would you describe yourself as a *hard-driving, ambitious* type of person in accomplishing the things you want, getting things done as *quickly* as possible, *or* would you describe yourself as a relatively *relaxed* and *easy-going person*?
   a. Do you have a boyfriend/girlfriend? (Close friend?)
   b. How would he/she describe you . . . as *hard-driving* and *ambitious* or as relaxed and easy-going?
   c. Has he/she ever asked you to slow down in your work? *Never*? How would he/she put it . . . in *his/her own* words?

6. When you get *angry* or *upset*, do people around you know it? How do you show it?

7. Do you think you drive *harder* to *accomplish* things than most of your associates?

8. Do you complete homework assignments before they are due? How often?

9. Do you know any children between the ages of 6 and 8? Did you *ever* play competitive games with them, like cards, checkers, Monopoly?
   a. Did you *always* allow them to *win* on *purpose*?
   b. *Why*? (*Why not*?)

10. When you play games with people your own age, do you play for the fun of it, or are you really in there to *win*?

11. Is there a lot of *competition* in school? Do you enjoy this?
    a. Are you competitive in other areas . . . sports for example?

12. When you are in your automobile, and there is a car in your lane going *far too slowly* for you, what do you do about it? Would you *mutter* and *complain* to yourself? Would anyone riding with you know that you were *annoyed*?

13. Most people who go to school have to get up fairly early in the morning . . . in your particular case . . . . what . . . time . . . do you . . . ordinarily . . . get up?

14. If you make a *date* with someone for, oh, two o'clock in the afternoon, for example, would you *be there* on *time*?
    a. If you are kept waiting, do you *resent* it?
    b. Would you *say* anything about it?

15. If you see someone doing a job rather *slowly* and you *know* that you could do it faster and better yourself, does it make you *restless* to watch?
    a. Would you be tempted to *step in and do it* yourself?

16. What *irritates* you most about this college, or the students here?

17. Do you *eat rapidly*? Do you *walk* rapidly? After you've *finished* eating, do you like to sit around the table and chat, or do you like to *get up and get going*?

18. When you go out in the evening to a restaurant and you find eight or ten people *waiting ahead of you* for a table, will you wait? What will you do while you are waiting?

19. How do you feel about waiting in lines: *bank lines, supermarket lines, cafeteria lines, post office lines* . . .?

20. Do you *always* feel anxious to *get going* and *finish* whatever you have to do?

21. Do you have the feeling that *time* is passing too *rapidly* for you to *accomplish* all the things you'd like to *get done* in one day?
    a. Do you *often* feel a sense of *time urgency*? *Time pressure*?

22. Do you *hurry* in doing most things?

All right, that completes the interview. Thank you very much.

Chapter 8

Multi-Dimensional Analysis of Coronary-Prone Behavior

Donald L. Tasto, Margaret A. Chesney, Joseph H. Chadwick

Introduction

Various aspects of psychological stress and behavior in response to stress have been implicated in the etiology of chronic mental and physical disease. A set of relationships of particular interest are those among psychological stress, personality factors, and coronary heart disease (CHD). This subject area is currently receiving considerable attention, and might well become an important *model* problem in the larger context of stress and health.

The association between behavioral characteristics and coronary heart disease was first noted in the literature by Osler,[1] who described the coronary-prone individual as a "keen and ambitious man, the indicator of whose engines are set at full speed ahead." Fifty to sixty years later, a more general interest in this subject began to emerge, and attributes such as compulsive, restless, hard-working, striving, needful of authority, and passively hostile were added to Osler's description of the coronary-prone individual by Dungar,[2] Gildea,[3] Miles et al.,[4] Arlow,[5] and Kemple.[6]

More recently, Rosenman and Friedman formulated a hypothesis concerning the link between CHD and certain emotional factors. In a representative example of their early research, these investigators studied two groups of males matched on age, diet, and exercise. They found a greater prevalence of clinical CHD in the group that exhibited a particular overt behavior pattern than in the other group without such characteristics.[7,8] The coronary-prone behavior pattern of the first group was referred to as Type A and described as a constellation of overt behaviors that include expressive facial and body gestures, rapidity and explosiveness of speech, hyperalertness, and general restlessness. These behaviors were also related to psychological characteristics of the coronary-prone group, who were described as hard-driving, ambitious, competitive, hostile, impatient, and time urgent. The behavior pattern of the subjects lacking these traits was referred to as Type B.

The most significant support for the role of the Type A-B behavior pattern in CHD comes from the Western Collaborative Group Study (WCGS). Over 3,500 men were examined and followed for about 10 years in this longitudinal study, to determine whether the Type A pattern had a causal or a merely associative relationship to CHD. The results of this prospective study clearly confirmed that Type A is a precursor to CHD. Specifically, this study revealed that the Type A factor is not only related to established CHD risk factors including smoking, blood pressure, and serum cholesterol, but is also related to suspected, but not yet established, risk factors such as catecholamines.[9,10] The CHD risk ratio revealed by the WCGS between Type A's and Type B's is approximately 2:1. The bulk of the risk carried by the A-B factor is independent of its correlations with other known CHD risk factors.

The relationship between the Type A behavior pattern and CHD has not only been supported by actual incidence of CHD in prospective studies, but also by autopsy findings[11] and by at least three angiographic studies from different facilities.[12] Furthermore, Rosenman and Friedman's findings have received considerable confirmation by other investigators in the field.[13] The sum total of evidence leaves the Type A behavior pattern as the most established and important constellation of psychological factors in the etiology of CHD.

In light of the ability of the Type A behavior pattern to predict CHD, its measurement is an important issue. Currently, the only available technique that is fully satisfactory with respect to discriminating between Type A and B is a structured psychological interview. Persons being interviewed are asked a number of questions dealing with job orientation, time urgency, competitiveness, etc. The interviewer records the answers to the questions and also notes the speech characteristics and mannerisms of the subject. To identify the subject as Type A or B, the interview is subjectively rated on a global basis. Approximately 15 minutes of interviewer time is required to carry out and rate each interview.

The interview rating procedure has a number of strengths and weaknesses. Its most important strength is the fact that it successfully discriminates between Type A and B in relation to CHD. The primary weakness is the fact that great care must be taken in the training and standardization of interviewers to maintain reliability and reproducibility. The interview is therefore not as readily exportable as would be desired. A second weakness is that the interview, with its holistic approach, does not lend itself well to further investigation of the meaning or underlying structure of the Type A risk factor.

These weaknesses are significant in light of the interest developing within medicine and psychology to study interventions directed toward altering the Type A behavior pattern in an attempt to prevent coronary heart disease. Prior to, or at least concurrent with, the exploration of interventions, it is most important that more detailed and objective measures of the Type A-B behavior pattern be developed.

For example, it is possible that Type A behavior is actually a number of independent risk factors. If this is the case, then interventions may have positive effects on only some of the elements of Type A behavior, but the interview, by its global nature, could erroneously overlook these effects; or, if Type A behavior and the risk it creates are viewed as a process, the interview and the intervention may deal with different points in the process. Measures of Type A and B behavior patterns that are more dimensional and objective should help to clarify these issues.

Our concept of how to attack this problem is what might be termed multidimensional analysis of the Type A-B behavior pattern. One manner in which this analysis might be accomplished is to individually examine each of the known elements of the Type A-B behavior pattern. This strategy will not only introduce more dimensions into the measurement, but will increase the probability of identifying the underlying nature of the Type A risk process. Drs. Friedman and Rosenman have described several behavioral and emotional elements within the Type A constellation including:

1. Self-report of attitudes and behaviors
2. Speech characteristics
3. Motor behavior characteristics
4. Physiological response characteristics
5. Psychological response characteristics

Elements of the Type A Behavior Pattern

Self-report of Attitudes and Behavior

The development of a self-report questionnaire to assess the same habits and activities as the interview appeared at the beginning to be a straight-forward task—given the interview's demonstrated effectiveness. Despite a substantial effort for over 10 years[14,15] to develop a questionnaire that would be equivalent to the interview, questionnaires remain considerably weaker than the interview—explaining approximately one-quarter of the variance in CHD rates that is explained by the interview.

The failure of the questionnaire to approach the strength of the interview in assessing Type A risk is paradoxical since most persons familiar with the field believe that the questions themselves have substantial face validity. The fact remains that questionnaires are only modestly predictive, and this is a primary reason why further study is required. The most thoroughly analyzed of the questionnaires, the Jenkins Activity Survey,[14] makes an independent, albeit small, contribution to CHD prediction. It is possible that this scale is measuring only one dimension of the Type A pattern and that by supplementing self-report questionnaires with measure of other Type A dimensions, useful predictive power will be achieved.

In a current project at the Stanford Research Institute we are exploring four different self-report questionnaires: the Jenkins Activity Survey, the scale developed by Vickers at Michigan, a scale from the Thurstone Activity Scale, and a scale developed from the Adjective Checklist.[16] In addition, approximately 20 other psychological subscales are being explored in this study, and any scale or item that shows especially strong correlations to the Type A-B interview rating will be included in the analysis of questionnaires.

One problem with the questionnaire may be that it creates response bias by being too transparent. It might be desirable to develop a set of questionnaires representing alternative forms and using items that are substantially more opaque than the items that have been emphasized to date. Such items could be found by searching the Type A predictive scales of conventional personality inventories.

Speech Characteristics

Drs. Rosenman and Friedman have consistently stated that speech stylistics play an important role in the assessment of Type A. Specifically, certain voice and speech patterns are believed to be associated with the Type A factor, such as explosively accentuating various words, hastening the pace of speech toward the end of sentences, and hurrying the speech of others. This theory has received substantial support recently by Shucker and Jacobs[17] working at the Laboratory of Physiological Hygiene, University of Minnesota. These investigators have found very strong correlations between a multivariate index formed from a number of fairly simple voice characteristics and Type A assessments by the standard interview. On a preliminary basis, it appears that speech stylistics may correlate with the interview almost as strongly as the interview correlates with itself. It therefore seems desirable to further explore the contributions speech characteristics make in the measurement of Type A behavior. This exploration might proceed by identifying perceptual and acoustical speech parameters that predict the subject classifications achieved by standard Type A-B interviews. Once these speech parameters are identified, alternative, less transparent scenarios could be constructed to elicit them, and, in doing so, provide a measure of Type A behavior.

Motor Behavior Characteristics

Type A-B behavior, as a concept, includes observation of motor behavior. During the standard interview, the interviewer takes note of overt behavior and makes a global personal estimate of the general behavior of the person being assessed. Specifically, certain behaviors are believed to be indicative of the coronary-prone behavior pattern including rapid body movements, tense facial and body musculature, hand and teeth clenching, and excessive unconscious gesturing. In addition to these behaviors, Dr. Rosenman[10] has asserted that *handwriting behavior* exhibits factors that may contribute to the Type A-B assessment. A recent pilot study using people primarily classified Type A or Type B in Friedman and Rosenman's Western Collaborative Group Study indicates that there exist some quantifiable differences between handwriting dynamics of Type A and Type B individuals.

One approach to this type analysis would be to videotape a sample of the Type A-B interviews and directly measure the subject's motor activity during sample time segments of the interview. A second approach to this analysis would be to obtain handwriting samples (signature and standardized material) from the subjects using a pen such as the one developed by SRI's Information Sciences Division. This pen converts the three-dimensional forces generated in handwriting into electrical signals, which are then analyzed by computer. By this means, a variety of features can be derived from handwriting characteristics that can be correlated with the Type A-B interview and other measures.

There is a range of potential physiological and behavioral measures that to date have been shown to bear a relationship to Type A-B, but that have not been used for assessment. Possibilities in these areas will be discussed in the next two sections.

Physiological Response Characteristics

A fourth element of the Type A-B behavior pattern is the response of individuals when under situational stress. While the standard interview is successful at characterizing a person as Type A or Type B, it does not explain whether disease is the result of individuals being *exposed to different levels* of environmental stress or the result of individuals *responding differently to the same* environmental stress. Friedman et al.[18] explored this issue and found that in a stress situation (competitive puzzle task) Type A subjects exhibited an elevated biochemical response (plasma norepinephrine) while Type B subjects did not. In another study examining the effect of an impending computer shutdown on Type A and B subjects, Caplan and Jones[19] found evidence that the effect of this stress situation was greater for Type A than Type B persons.

Physiological response to situational stress needs to be explored in a multidimensional study of Type A behavior. Several situations could be used as simulated stressors, including the cold pressor test,[20] physical exercise, challenging mental tasks, and competitive tasks. While subjects identified as either Type A or Type B are performing these tasks, physiological response measures can be taken including the ECG, heart rate, blood pressure, vasoconstriction (e.g., by blood flow to the forearm), and catecholamines in the blood. In addition, self-report measures could be given to assess perceived discomfort of the specific simulated stressors as well as general somatization and perceived discomfort during hypothetical stressful situations.[21]

Psychological Response Characteristics

The preceding element has focused on *physiological* responses under different conditions. There is evidence that Type A's and B's also show different *psychological* responses under different conditions. A relatively new approach to research in this area would be to experimentally explore cognitive styles and learning acquisition associated with the Type A-B dimension. For example, experimental studies by Glass and colleagues[22] have examined the Type A characteristic of "time urgency" by presenting to Type A and Type B subjects a task that required a delay before responding to a signal. Subjects identified as Type A's performed this task less well, reflecting what the experimenters suggested was an impatience with delay or time urgency. Glass and his co-workers have also studied the psychological response to stressors, demonstrating, for example, what they have termed a "hyper-responsiveness" of Type A's to salient stressors that could not be avoided or escaped.

The measurement of Type A-B to date is an assessment of behaviors, reactions, performance, etc., under different sets of circumstances. What is not directly measured by the traditional interview of self-assessment procedures, however, is the learning acquisition process itself. Glass[22] has pointed the way to this possibility by demonstrating clear differences between Type A's and Type B's in the mastery of tasks under varying stimulus conditions. These differences were group differences (correlations between task performance and JAS scores were not presented) and were primarily in the form of interactions rather than main effects, meaning that Type A's performed better on some tasks and Type B's performed better on others.

These factors suggest that the power of learning tasks to differentiate Type A's from Type B's may be enhanced by doing intrasubject comparisons on different types of tasks, i.e., comparing Type A's performance on one kind of task with performance on another type of task and deriving a difference score that could be compared to Type B's difference score on the same tasks. For example, a Type A may learn to perform better on a task after threatened by loss of environmental control than he would on the same type of task when it did not involve such a threat. The Type B, on the other hand, may show just the reverse pattern. The difference in scores among subjects within each type of behavior could then be compared. This would have the advantage of minimizing variance in error due to individual differences in overall learning rates.

In a multidimensional study of Type A-B behavior, it would be of interest to study differential learning rates in Type A's and Type B's under varying experimental conditions. The parameters of optimal A-B differentiation, however, need to be refined by exploring a variety of learning tasks and conditions under which they are administered.

Functions of Type A-B Measurement

The five approaches described above should be considered in light of the functions of Type A-B measurement. There are several purposes that the measurement of Type A-B can serve.

Epidemiology

The measurement of Type A-B has primarily been focused on its predictive characteristics for CHD. In addition to CHD, however, some attempt should be made to relate the Type A-B dimension to other illnesses such as cancer, ulcers, psychological disturbances, etc.

The value of measuring Type A-B by the interviewer, within the context of epidemiology, is primarily linited to its use as a univariate predictor of future events. We should like to suggest that the Questionnaires, Voice Characteristics, and Motor Behavior components of the multidimensional analysis be viewed as extending the epidemiological capabilities of Type A-B by increasing the reliability and exportability of the measures and by making Type A-B a multivariate predictor of future events.

Etiology

The interview, while epidemiologically predictive of CHD, does not tell us anything directly about the etiology of CHD. If behavioral factors are predictive of CHD, the two major questions that arise are: (1) How did these behaviors come about? (2) What are the underlying physiological mechanisms that tie the behaviors to CHD?

In regard to the first question, we would recommend that the *Psychological Response Characteristics* component of the multidimensional analysis be considered within the scope of understanding the etiology of Type A-B behavior. If clear differences emerge between Type A's and Type B's in learning processes, such differences may give clues, albeit retrospective in the initial studies, as to how Type A or Type B behaviors are acquired.

In regard to the mechanisms that mediate Type A behavior and CHD, it would be desirable to measure the components of Type A-B, and to relate these to measures of physiological functions[23,24] that could be monitored on a continuous basis over time. Most of the literature relating Type A-B to physiological risk factors, such as blood pressure, etc., has used static single-point measures. The dynamics of physiological functioning, assessed by continuous monitoring, may well uncover relationships between Type A-B and physiological risk factors that are not apparent from the static measurement of the latter.

Factors Maintaining Type A Behavior

The multidimensional assessment of Type A-B under varying situational stresses will allow for the determination of any lability associated with the manifestation of Type A behavior. This line of research could provide insight into environmental factors that maintain Type A behavior. The focus has traditionally been on measuring Type A behavior, and to define Type B behavior as the absence of Type A. The implicit assumption that follows is that persons classified Type A have acquired or learned something that persons classified Type B have not. While this assumption may be correct, it is also plausible that the development of Type B behavior involves as much learning—both operant and respondent—as the development of Type A.

Targets for Behavioral Change

The reliable and multidimensional measurement of Type A behavior will provide targets for behavioral interventions. It may well be that interventions need to be directed at several behavioral phenonena that characterize the coronary-prone personality, and that the interventions need to be tailored to individuals based on differences in the various levels of Type A manifestations. The multidimensional approach to measurement would help decipher which behaviors are important targets for interventions and which are not.

Effects of Interventions

The measurement of Type A in a quantifiable form is critical to the assessment of intervention effects. It may be that certain behavioral phenonomena are more susceptible to the effects of interventions than are others. It may also be that beneficial changes in certain behavioral modes carry greater CHD risk reduction than changes in other behavioral modes. Assessment in relationship to interventions is critical for determining the effectiveness of the interventions; and a precisely quantifiable, multidimensional approach to measurement holds the greatest promise for detecting what may be rather subtle behavioral changes that result from interventions.

Reliability

Reliability is important because it places a ceiling on validity. Validity in this case refers to the predictive power of Type A-B for future events, either epidemiologically or as an index of change following interventions. It is generally true that the validity of a measure cannot exceed the square root of its reliability. If the global Type A-B rating is broken into component parts, the reliability of each of these parts must be assessed. The two most important types of reliability to be considered in this context are test-retest reliability and interrater reliability.

Test-Retest Reliability

If an assessment is made at multiple points in time under constant conditions, the quantitative relationships among these points are an index of test-retest reliability and are usually expressed as correlational coefficients between any two points in time. If a high test-retest reliability is consistently found, it can be concluded that, under the conditions of assessment, the measuring instrument itself is reliable and the trait it is measuring is stable. If the test-retest reliability is low, this can be because the measuring instrument is less than adequate or because the trait itself is not stable. However, the balance of these two factors leads to a depressed test-retest reliability, and the depression places limits on the predictive power of the trait.

It would appear that this first step in assessing the reliability of the components of the Type A-B dimension would be to develop test-retest reliabilities from heterogeneous samples under constant conditions.

Interrater Reliability

Interrater reliability refers to the concordance among judges when subjective judgments are the basis for quantifying a variable. High interrater reliabilities ensure agreement among the raters but say nothing about the stability of a trait. Low interrater reliabilities, like test-retest reliabilities, will place a celing on predictive power. If the trait measured has an inadquate interrater reliability and an inadequate test-retest reliability, these two problems will compound themselves in the limitations they place on validity.

The interview for Type A-B requires subjective quantification, and interrater agreements have been reported at 74%.[25] Although this percentage may be enhanced by bifurcating the ratings into A or B (rather than A_1, A_2, B_3, B_4), the fact still remains that factors that lower agreement among raters to less than perfect are not related to the characteristics of the trait but are strictly a reflection of the measuring instrument itself, which in this case is the interviewer making quantitative assessments.

The component analysis we are proposing would essentially eliminate problems with interrater reliability. The outcone measures in each case are objective and scoring would produce near unanimous agreement whether it be done by computer or by human. Type A behavior is clearly a real phenomenon with laudatory predictive power for CHD. It would be unfortunate if the predictive power it does have is suppressed because of nonconcordance among raters. Whether we can enhance predictability by reducing the subjectivity of raters' judgments is an empirical question at this point since the process of increasing the objectivity of human judgments may eliminate a certain amount of information. The extent to which such information is critical to the predictive power of the Type A-B dimension remains to be clarified, ultimately in prospective studies.

Validity

Following a satisfactory resolution of the reliability issues, which primarily revolve around enhancing consistency of what is measured over multiple points in time, the next issue is to establish the validity of these measures.

Concurrent Validity

Establishing concurrent validity refers to correlating the new measure being developed with another measure that presumably has validity in its own right. In this case, that would be a matter of simultaneously administering the interview and obtaining measures of each of the components to correlate the components with the interview, which is known to have predictive validity. This should be the first step in establishing the validity of the components since it can be done at one point in time, and it is relatively cost and time efficient.

The correlations to be expected between the components and the interview is a point for discussion. The hope is to find correlations of moderate magnitude. If the correlations are not significant, it would not be worth pursuing this line of research. On the other hand, there are two reasons why the correlations cannot and should not be too high:

1. The correlations between the components and the interview cannot be expected to exceed the reliabilities of the interview, i.e., the degree to which the interview correlates with itself.
2. The extent to which the components have predictive power beyond that of the interview for future coronary events is the extent to which the correlations between the components and the interviews will be moderated. Viewed in another way, if the components correlated perfectly with the interview, there would be no possibility of the components showing better predictive capabilities than the interview, nor any possibility of the components enhancing the predictive power of the interview.

Whether moderate correlations between the components and the interview are an indication of higher predictive power for the components or whether moderate correlations occur because the component measures have too severely truncated the information from the interview, resulting in lower predictive power for the components, is an empirical question that requires a prospective study to answer definitively.

A second step in the process of establishing concurrent validity would be the development of alternate forms that correlate highly with each other and to an acceptable degree with the interview. To the extent that multiple measures over time will be used to track Type A behavior, it would be desirable to have alternate forms for each component measure so as to eliminate, as much as possible, the problems associated with adaptation of subjects to repeated administrations of identical forms of an instrument.

A third step in establishing concurrent validity would be to cross-sectionally relate the components as well as the interview to the degree of atherosclerosis in a heterogeneous sample of subjects who have not had myocardial infarctions. Since many patients these days are having angiograms for a variety of reasons, it would be possible to obtain Type A-B measures on a sample of these people and relate the findings to the degree of atherosclerosis.

Some light may be shed on the issue, however, by cross-sectionally assessing the relationship between the prevalence of coronary heart disease and the component measures of Type A-B. Once acceptable concurrent validities are established between the interview and the components, a study could be conducted to assess Type A with the interview and with the components on a sample of persons who have had coronary heart disease and on a sample of persons, matched for age and other relevant variables, who have not. The results of comparing these two groups may give some preliminary indications as to the relative power of the component and the interview assessments of Type A-B; however, there is one major drawback to this approach. Once a patient has had a coronary, this fact alone may change behavior, including response on Type A-B measures. Such a phenomenon could be a confounding factor when using postcoronary patients.

Predictive Validity

After it has been determined which components have acceptable concurrent validity and the degree to which they are able to discriminate persons who have had CHD from those who have not, a prospective epidemiological study will be in order. To really test the predictive validity of the components, a study on the order of the Western Collaborative Group Study would be appropriate. Such an undertaking would be time-consuming and costly, and should not be embarked upon until the measurement technology for the multiple components of Type A-B has been highly refined.

What may be equally germane to the concept of a quantifiable component analysis of Type A-B, however, is a prospective study on the predictive power of changes in Type A-B following interventions. If interventions produce changes, to what extent are these changes predictive of later CHD, and to what extent is the predictive power of the changes dependent upon the level of preintervention Type A behavior?

On the basis of the interview, people are usually placed in four categories at most. This nosology clearly has predictive power for CHD when determined epidemiologically. However, these categories may not be sufficiently sensitive to detect changes in the Type A pattern that may occur as a result of behavioral interventions. The multidimensional analysis of Type A-B will allow a finer quantification of multiple behavioral measures used (1) to detect behavioral changes as a result of interventions, and (2) to precisely correlate the degree of responsiveness to interventions with later CHD. To ultimately test the predictive validity of the multidimensional analysis, it is evident that prospective studies on both epidemiology and interventions, with heart attacks or deaths as the main endpoints, will be necessary.

References

1. Osler, W.: The Principles and Practice of Medicine. Edinburgh: Young, J. Reutland, 1892.
2. Dunbar, F.: Psychosomatic Diagnosis. New York: Paul B. Hoeber, 1943.
3. Gildea, E.G.: Special features of personality which are common to certain psychosomatic disorders. *Psychosom Med* **11**:273, 1949.
4. Miles, H.H.W., Waldfogel, S., Barrabee, E.J., Cobb, S.: Psychosomatic study of 46 young men with coronary artery disease. *Psychosom Med* **16**:455, 1954.
5. Arlow, J.A.: Identification of mechanisms in coronary occlusion. *Psychosom Med* **7**:195–209, 1945.
6. Kemple, C.: Rorschach method and psychosomatic diagnosis: personality traits of patients with rheumatic desease, hypertensive, cardiovascular disease, coronary occlusions, and fracture. *Psychosom Med* **7**:85, 1945.
7. Friedman, M., Rosenman, R.H.: Association of specific overt behavior pattern with blood and cardiovascular findings—blood cholesterol level, blood clotting time, incidence of arcus senilis, and clinical coronary artery disease. *JAMA* **169**(12):1286–1296, 1959.
8. Rosenman, R.H., Friedman, M.: The possible relationship of the emotions to clinical coronary heart disease. *In* Hormones and Atherosclerosis (Pincus, G., ed.). New York: Academic Press, 1959, pp. 283–300.
9. Rosenman, R.H., Friedman, M., Straus, R., Wurm, M., Kositcheck, R., Hahn, W., Werthessen, N.T.: A predictive study of coronary heart disease. *JAMA* **189**:103–110, 1964.

10. Rosenman, R.H., Brand, R.J., Jenkins, D., Friedman, M., Straus, R., Wurm, M.: Coronary heart disease in the Western Collaborative Group Study. Final follow-up experience of 8-½ years. *JAMA* **233**:872–877, 1975.
11. Friedman, M., Rosenman, R.H., Straus, R., Wurm, M., Kosticheck, R.: The relationship of behavioral pattern A to the state of coronary vasculature: a study of 51 autopsy subjects. *Am J Med* **44**:525–537, 1968.
12. Zyzanski, S.J., Jenkins, C.D., Ryan, T.J., Flessas, A., Everist, M.: Psychological correlates of coronary angiographic findings. *Arch Intern Med* **136**: 1234–1237, 1976.
13. Jenkins, C.D.: Recent evidence supporting psychologic and social risk factors for coronary disease. *N Engl J Med* **294**(18):987–994, 1976.
14. Jenkins, C.D., Rosenman, R.H., Zyzanski, S.J.: Prediction of clinical coronary heart disease by a test for the coronary-prone behavior pattern. *N Engl J Med* **290**(23):1271–1275, 1974.
15. Bortner, R.W.: A short rating scale as a potential measure of pattern A behavior. *J Chronic Dis* **22**:87–91, 1969.
16. Gough, H.G., Heilbrun, A.B.: The Adjective Checklist. Palo Alto, Ca.: Consulting Psychologists Press, 1965.
17. Schucker, B., Jacobs, D.R.: Assessment of behavior pattern by voice characteristics. *Psychosom Med* **39**:219–228, 1977.
18. Friedman, M., Byers, S.O., Diamant, J., Rosenman, R.H.: Plasma catecholamine response of coronary-prone subjects (Type A) to a specific challenge. *Metabolism* **24**:205–210, 1975.
19. Caplan, R.D., Jones, K.W.: Effects of work load, role ambiguity, and Type A personality on anxiety, depression, and heart rate. *J Appl Psych* **60**:713–719, 1975.
20. Lovallo, W.: The cold pressor test and automatic function: a review and integration. *Psychophysiology* **12**:268–282, 1975.
21. Farr, J.L., Seaver, W.B.: Stress and discomfort in psychological research: subject perceptions of experimental procedures. *Am Psychol* **30**:770–773, 1975.
22. Glass, D.C.: Stress, behavior patterns and coronary disease. *Am Sc* **65**:177–187, 1977.
23. Williams, R.B., Jr., Bittker, T.E., Buchsbaum, M.S., Wynne, L.C.: Cardiovascular and neurophysiologic correlates of sensory intake and rejection. I. Effect of cognitive tasks. *Psychophysiology* **12**:427–433, 1975.
24. Bittker, T.E., Buchsbaum, M.S., Williams, R.B., Jr., Wynne, L.C.: Cardiovascular and neurophysiologic correlates of sensory intake and rejection. II. Interview behavior. *Psychophysiology* **12**:434–438, 1975.
25. Keith, R.A., Lown, B., Stare, F.J.: Coronary heart disease and behavior patterns. *Psychosom Med* **27**:424–434, 1965.

SECTION III

MECHANISMS

Section Summary: Mechanisms Linking Behavioral and Pathophysiological Processes

Redford B. Williams, Jr., Meyer Friedman, David C. Glass, J. Alan Herd, Neil Schneiderman

Attempts to elucidate and describe specific mechanisms that link adaptive physiological processes with subtle and overt behavioral expressions must proceed experimentally. Much of the current thinking remains in the realm of the theoretical, but certain physiological response patterns are more or less fixed and predictable. Lessons learned from other well-described studies of long-term adaptive physiological responses to perturbations of neutral or relaxed states can be valuable in seeking explanations to the question of coronary-prone behavior. The chapter by Dr. Herd will point out valuable examples from the fields of thermoregulation, exercise, reproduction, and others involving links between behavioral phenomena and internal homeostatic mechanisms. From existing knowledge of these mechanistic links, we should be able to design experimental studies to test reasonable hypotheses framed to explore emerging theories regarding coronary-prone behavior.

The association between specific patterns of behavior and various manifestations of coronary heart disease suggest the existence of mechanisms whereby behavioral phenomena are linked, presumably, via central nervous system effects, with those processes involved in atherogenesis and the precipitation of acute clinical events. Results of clinical, epidemiological, and laboratory studies indicate that behavior patterns seen in certain individuals under natural circumstances can be elicited in laboratory situations and can be elicited in experimental animals. On the basis of these studies, a hypothesis concerning these mechanisms has been formulated. Our approach towards this hypothesis includes a consideration of (1) neuroendocrine and metabolic responses associated with such observable behavioral phenomena, (2) qualitatively distinct patterns of cardiovascular responses observed in association with varying organism-environmental interactions, (3) laboratory studies of individual differences observed in psychomotor responses to situational variables, and (4) behavioral-physiological studies in experimental animals that suggest that these interactions have pathophysiological consequences.

Biochemical and Neuroendocrine Mechanisms

There are several pathophysiological processes that may accelerate the onset of coronary heart disease in Type A subjects. The most extensive evidence concerning such processes is related to certain biochemical and neuroendo-crine responses to physiological and behavioral challenges that have been iden-tified in middle-aged male subjects. The data presented below were derived primarily from comparisons of Type A-1 (extreme Type A) subjects with Type B subjects.

First, most Type A-1 subjects exhibit an increased serum level of cortico-tropin.[1] This presupposes both an increased secretion of hypothalamic cortico-tropin releasing factor and of pituitary melanocyte stimulating hormone. The latter's presumed excess secretion probably is the reason for the increased occurrence of periorbital pigmentation in many Type A-1 subjects. Second, despite this increased serum level of ACTH, most Type A-1 subjects respond subnormally (in respect to cortical secretion) following the injection of *exoge-nous* ACTH.[2] Third, most Type A-1 subjects appear to exhibit a reduced serum level of growth hormone both prior to and after arginine challenge.[3] This abnormality, however, was usually observed while subjects were studied in their typical working milieu. Fourth, most Type A-1 subjects, while not show-ing an abnormal glucose tolerance, nevertheless do exhibit an hyperinsulinemic response to a glucose challenge.[4] Fifth, most Type A-1 subjects, when studied in their *usual working milieu* or when engaged in a *competitive contest* that challenges them, both excrete increased norepinephrine[5] and exhibit a higher serum level of this same hormone when compared to Type B subjects.[6] In addition, there is evidence of accelerated clotting in Type A-1 subjects.[8] Sixth, compared to Type B subjects, Type A-1 subjects exhibit an increased serum triglyceride prior to and for many hours following the ingestion of a fat meal.[7] Such persons typically show increased sludging of erythrocytes during their postprandial hypertriglyceridemic cycle.[2,7] Seventh, most Type A-1 subjects exhibit hypercholesterolemia.[4] Their hyperlipoproteinemia is usually of the Type III or IV variety (Lees-Frederickson classification).

Specific Patterns of Behavioral-Cardiovascular Response

It must be noted at the outset that there are very few published studies documenting a difference between Type A and Type B subjects in psy-chophysiological response to environmental stimulation. This state of affairs is in contrast to the area of neuroendocrine response, where the work of Friedman, Rosenman, and colleagues, as noted above, has shown clear differences between the types, particularly with regard to responses of biochemical indices of sympathetic nervous system function. These differences in sympathetic nervous responses suggest that careful studies should prove successful in documenting psychophysiological response characteristics that differentiate Type A from Type B individuals. Preliminary investigations by Dembroski et al.[9] and Manuck[10] suggest that heart rate and blood pressure responses are more marked in young Type A males during challenging perceptual-motor and cognitive tasks.

Whereas little is known regarding how Type A and Type B subjects might differ in terms of psychophysiological responses, there is a great deal of evidence suggesting that behavioral stimulation can exert a potent influence upon various aspects of cardiovascular function. Recent advances in knowledge of the central nervous control of the circulation have led Hilton[11] to advance the proposition that the brain is organized not to produce isolated behavioral or physiological responses, but rather to integrate patterned responses of both behavioral and physiological functions.

An example of one such centrally mediated response system is seen when "fight/flight" behavior is engendered by a variety of experimental situations. In such situations (e.g. solution of difficult mental arithmetic problems), there are observed concomitant increases in motor activity, cardiac output, and muscle blood flow, while there is an active vasoconstriction in the skin and visceral circulations.[12]

In contrast to the cardiac output/muscle vasodilator response observed in "emergency" situations, there has been described in both the animal and human literature a qualitatively different pattern of behavioral/physiological response that is observed under circumstances other than those eliciting fight/flight behavior. When required to attentively observe sensory stimuli in the environment, humans show a decrease in heart rate[13] and motor activity,[14] and an active vasoconstriction in skeletal muscle.[15] A similar response pattern, with an active vasoconstriction in muscle, decrease in cardiac output, and increased total peripheral resistance, has also been described in the cat during attentive observation of another cat.[16]

Thus, it would appear that differing behavioral interactions of the organism with the environment are associated with quite distinct patterns of cardiovascular response. Both the cardiac output/muscle vasodilation response pattern observed during emergency situations and in association with "mental work" and the total peripheral resistance/muscle vasoconstriction pattern observed during attentive observation of the environment could prove to be important contributors to the endothelial "injury" that Ross and Glomset[17] have proposed as the initiating event in atherogenesis. Furthermore, activation of such sympathetically mediated physiological response patterns could also be playing a role in the precipitation of acute clinical CHD events, via effects to increase myocardial oxygen consumption beyond the capacity of an atherosclerotic coronary system or via precipitation of potentially fatal arrhythmia.

The association of Type A behavior with both increased levels of arteriographically-documented coronary atherosclerosis and increased incidence of acute CHD clinical events[18] suggests that both the above "pathopsychophysiological" mechanisms could be operative in Type A individuals. As noted at the beginning of this section, there are few studies where physiological responses to environmental stimulation have been compared in Type A and Type B subjects; moreover, there are no studies in which such mechanisms have been assessed and related to such indices of CHD as coronary atherosclerosis.

Behavioral Responses to Situational Variables

The concept of perceived control may help us to understand the circumstances under which Type A subjects are more likely than Type B subjects to demonstrate potentially damaging physiological reactions. If the Type A individual is, indeed, more concerned than his Type B counterpart with controlling the physical and social environment, then he should show greater increments in sympathetic cardiovascular activity in response to threats to that control, and should increase his efforts at mastery. However, he should become even more distressed and give up efforts at control when the threat is, in fact, beyond his control; so try as he may, there is nothing he can do to master the situation.

Preliminary support for these notions comes from a retrospective study in which Glass et al. compared coronary patients, noncoronary patients, and healthy, nonhospitalized controls[19] (see also Chapter 12). Not surprisingly, the cardiac patients had higher Jenkins Activity Survey (JAS) scores than the other two groups. Of greater interest were scores on a so-called Loss Index, a 10-item scale from the Holmes-Rahe Schedule of Recent Experience[20] that asked a person to describe the incidence during the last year of stressful life events over which he had minimal control, e.g., "death of a loved one" or "being fired." Both patient groups experienced such losses to a greater extent than the nonhospitalized controls.

Such losses have been implicated in the arousal of feelings of helplessness,[21,22] and some research suggests that such a psychic state is a precursor of sudden death.[23] Recent findings suggest that helplessness-inducing stressful life events (i.e., losses) specifically discriminate individuals with illness from those without disease.[19] Since the coronary patients in this study also had higher JAS scores, it appears that the interaction between helplessness and Pattern A may be prodromal to coronary disease events. This conclusion must be viewed with caution for a number of methodological reasons, including the retrospective nature of the study.

Subsequent research by Glass and associates[19] on reaction to controllable versus uncontrollable stress seems to indicate that the Type A individual at first tries harder than the Type B individual to control highly stressful situations. Extended stress exposure, however, may lead to a greater certainty of lack of control, hence to feelings of helplessness and a decline in efforts at mastery.

This pattern of reaction to uncontrollable stress by Type A's might be described as initial *hyper-responsiveness* (such as heightened psychomotor activity) followed by subsequent *hypo-responsiveness.* Pattern A behavior might, then, be conceptualized as a style of response elicited in susceptible individuals by appropriate environmental circumstances, some of which may be uncontrollable, stressful events. It is conceivable that other types of environmental events might elicit Type A behavior (e.g., challenges, or events that signify the potential for reward rather than harm), but such issues have received little empirical attention. Equally important is the need for research into the possible attributional mechanisms that may mediate the reaction of Type A's to environmental stressors including physiological correlates of such reactions.

Research in this area to date has been limited to an analysis of the relationship between behavior Pattern A and controllable versus uncontrollable environmental stressors. However, the long-range goal should be to show how the interplay of these variables influences the development of coronary disease, and ultimately, how it helps to precipitate an acute coronary event. Pursuit of such goals necessarily involves systematic examination of physiological and biochemical processes such as the rise and fall of catecholamines (e.g., norepinephrine) as a function of the hyper- and hypo-responsiveness of Type A's to stressful stimulation.

Pathophysiological Processes in Animal Models

A variety of experimental paradigms have linked prolonged, severe behavioral stress with the development of cardiovascular pathology. The literature also suggests that at least two diverse sets of experimental contingencies may lead to separate modes of biochemical and physiological response, which in turn may lead to different pathological consequences.

In terms of experimental contingencies, a tentative distinction can be made between predictability, control, and dominance on the one hand, and unpredictability, helplessness, and a submissive posture on the other.

In the face of severe or prolonged aversive stimulation, dominant animals, who possess an appropriate coping response and a predictable schedule, will ordinarily exhibit a broad range of neuroendocrine, metabolic, and cardiovascular phenomena, including an increased cholesterol level,[8] elevated arterial pressure,[24-26] decreased clotting times,[8] and myofibrillar degeneration.[28]

In contrast to the pattern of cardiovascular responses that occur when an animal is able to exert control over its environment, a different pattern of cardiovascular changes seems to occur when an animal lacks control. Thus, during a procedure in which irregularly scheduled electric shocks are presented,[28] after inescapable water stress,[29] or when a submissive animal has no escape from a victor,[30] a pattern is seen in which bradycardia may be followed by death, but evidence of structural pathology is not apparent.

The physiological mechanisms leading to pathological states remain speculative. However, active coping during predictable aversive situations is usually associated with increases in heart rate, cardiac output, blood pressure, and blood flow to muscle. The central nervous system mechanisms involved include attenuation of the baroreceptor reflex,[31] shunting of blood to skeletal muscle,[32] and active sympathetic vasodilation in the muscle. Activation of the sympathetic nervous system leads to the release of catecholamines, which directly affect the heart and vasculature, and also lead to increased cholesterol levels and platelet aggregation as well as to decreased clotting time. Effects of diet, including fats and salt, interact with the neurogenic factors[32] in mediating long-term effects. Future experiments should be directed towards monitoring cardiovascular dynamics, catecholamines, cholesterol, and the renin-angiotensin system during acute and chronic aversive situations in which a behavioral coping mechanism is present, absent, or intermittently available.

The physiological mechanisms that occur in animals revealing bradycardia in the face of an unavoidable stressor are even more speculative than those associated with coping. If the aversive situation also occurs suddenly and unpredictably, the animal may show a pronounced increase in plasma epinephrine as well as norepinephrine.[34] In the absence of movement, animals reflexively respond to a pronounced increase in blood pressure with a profound bradycardia. Such a situation leads to a relatively large secretion of norepinephrine and acetylcholine at the heart, a condition promoting arrhythmias.[35] In the presence of marked adrenergic activity, decreased cardiac output associated with bradycardia and increased afterload could lead to a decrease in myocardial oxygenation, another condition facilitating arrhythmias, as well as myocardial infarction.

Future research should be directed towards comprehensively monitoring cardiovascular dynamics and myocardial oxygenation during experiments in which unavoidable stressors are likely to lead to bradycardia. Research is also needed to determine the manner in which hypertension, atherosclerosis, and a long history of having to cope under aversive circumstances might precipitate cardiovascular dysfunction in association with severe unavoidable stressors.

Although bradycardia is characteristic of animals that do not have a coping mechanism and who are undergoing an acute severe stress, it is also seen in both acute and chronic situations involving anticipatory or attentional behaviors such as those that occur immediately preceding fighting in cats[36] or when dogs are placed in a harness one hour prior to avoidance conditioning.[37] In these instances, the bradycardia response is accompanied by an increase in systemic arterial pressures due to an increase in total peripheral resistance. It is conceivable that over a prolonged period, such effects could contribute to cardiovascular pathology.

The data suggest that the responses of animals attempting to cope during aversive stimulation may have implications for our understanding of coronary-prone behavior in humans. Studies of the physiological response of animals to severe unavoidable stress after a history of successful coping behavior might also shed light on the disproportionate number of deaths that occur among Pattern A individuals suffering unavoidable aversive stimulation such as job loss, retirement, or death of a spouse.[19]

Conclusions

1. Paralleling behaviors displayed by Type A subjects during both daily activity and during specific laboratory manipulations, differences have been noted in both lipid metabolism and neuroendocrine responses of Type A as compared to Type B subjects.

2. Just as varying environmental circumstances give rise to varying behavioral adjustments, there is also evidence of qualitatively distinct patterns of cardiovascular response in association with specific organism-environmental interactions. Among these are pressor responses associated with increased cardiac output, and active muscle vasodilatation during defense behavior on the one hand, and increased total peripheral resistance and active muscle vasoconstriction during vigilant observation of the environment on the other hand.

3. Laboratory studies indicate the existence of measurable differences in psychomotor performance between Type A and Type B subjects. Experimental manipulation of relevant situational variables (e.g., uncontrollable aversive stimulation) have altered psychomotor performance in predictable ways. The behavioral distinctions thus made between Type A and Type B subjects suggest that reliable biological differences can also be identified.

4. There are data from animal experimentation suggesting that both short- and long-term environmental manipulations give rise to different patterns of neuroendocrine and cardiovascular response with consequences for such outcomes as sustained blood pressure increases and myocardial fibrosis, as well as such acute effects as sudden death in association with arrhythmias.

5. A hypothesis concerning mechanisms linking behavioral patterns and pathophysiological processes can now be formulated. Specific behaviors exhibited to an extreme degree by certain individuals are associated with neuroendocrine, metabolic, and cardiovascular phenomena. These may have a role in atherogenesis through (1) endothelial damage from hemodynamic disturbances, circulating lipid substances, and platelet aggregation; (2) smooth muscle proliferation and lesion progression through continuous endothelial injury, accumulated lipid substances, and local effects of hormonal and humoral factors; and (3) complications from endothelial rupture and thrombosis through hemodynamic disturbances, platelet aggregation, and thrombosis. Vascular limitations imposed by arterial disease decrease supply of oxygen and substrates to the myocardium in the presence of increased requirements for cardiac work. Short-term demands for myocardial performance are accentuated by elevations in blood pressure, cardiac output, and heart rate that may not be met by increases in coronary blood flow. The immediate consequences may be myocardial infarction, cardiac arrhythmias, and possibly, sudden death.

6. Given the above hypothesis whereby specific patterns of behavioral response might initiate a series of neuroendocrine/physiological events playing an important role in the pathogenesis of coronary heart disease, the following types of research questions deserve high priority:

Are the specific behaviors that are exhibited to an extreme degree by certain individuals reliably associated with concomitant extremes of neuroendocrine and physiological response?

Can central nervous system mechanisms be identified whereby the behavioral, neuroendocrine, and physiological responses described above are integrated?

Are such extremes of neuroendocrine and physiological responding, which may be characteristic of certain individuals, reliably associated with increased prevalence of the various manifestations of coronary heart disease, including arteriographically-documented coronary atherosclerosis, myocardial infarction, and sudden death?

References

1. Friedman, M., Byers, S.O., Rosenman, R.H.: Plasma ACTH and cortisol concentration of coronary-prone subjects. *Proc Soc Exp Biol Med* **140**:681–684, 1972.
2. Friedman, M.: The Pathogenesis of Coronary Artery Disease. New York: McGraw-Hill, 1969.
3. Friedman, M., Byers, S.O., Rosenman, R.H., Neuman, R.: Coronary-prone individuals (Type A behavior pattern) growth hormone responses. *JAMA* **217**:929–932, 1971.
4. Friedman, M., Byers, S.O., Rosenman, R.H., Elevitch, F.R.: Coronary-prone individuals (Type A behavior pattern). Some biochemical characteristics. *JAMA* **212**:1030–1037, 1970.
5. Friedman, M., St. George, S., Byers, S.O.: Excretion of catecholamines, 17-ketosteroids, 17-hydroxy-corticoids and 6-hydroxy-indole in men exhibiting a particular behavior pattern (A) associated with high incidence of clinical coronary artery disease. *J Clin Invest* **39**:758–764, 1960.
6. Friedman, M., Byers, S.O., Diamant, J., Rosenman, R.H.: Plasma catecholamine response of coronary-prone subjects (Type A) to a specific challenge. *Metabolism* **24**:205–210, 1975.
7. Friedman, M., Rosenman, R.H., Byers, S.O.: Serum lipids and conjunctival circulation after fat ingestion in men exhibiting Type A behavior pattern. *Circulation* **29**:874–886, 1964.
8. Friedman, M., Rosenman, R.H.: Association of specific overt behavior pattern with blood and cardiovascular findings. *JAMA* **169**:1286–1296, 1959.
9. Dembroski, T.M., MacDougall, J.M., Shields, J.L.: Physiologic reactions to social challenge in persons evidencing the Type A coronary-prone behavior pattern. *J Human Stress* **3**:2, 1977.
10. Manuck, J., Craft, R., Gold, K.: Coronary-Prone Behavior Pattern and Cardiovascular Response. *Psychophysiology* (in press).
11. Hilton, S.M.: Ways of viewing the central nervous control of the circulation—old and new. *Brain Research* **87**:213–219, 1975.
12. Brod, J., Fencl, V.Z., Hejl, Z., Jirka, J.: Circulatory changes underlying blood pressure elevation during acute emotional stress (mental arithmetic) in normotensive and hypertensive subjects. *Clin Sci Mol Med* **18**:269–279, 1959.
13. Lacey, J.I., Lacey, B.C.: On heart rate responses and behavior: a reply to Elliott. *J Pers Soc Psychol* **30**:1–18, 1974.
14. Obrist, P.A.: The cardiovascular-behavioral interaction—as it appears today. *Psychophysiology* **13**:95–107, 1976.
15. Williams, R.B., Bittker, T.E., Buchsbaum, M.S., Wynne, L.C.: Cardiovascular and neurophysiologic correlates of sensory intake and rejection. I. Effect of cognitive tasks. *Psychophysiology* **12**:427–433, 1975.
16. Adams, D.B., Baccelli, B., Mancia, B., Zanchetti, A.: Relation of cardiovascular changes in fighting to emotion and exercise. *J Physiol* **212**:321–336, 1971.
17. Ross, R., Glomset, J.A.: The pathogenesis of atherosclerosis. *N Engl J Med* **295**:369–420, 1976.
18. See Association section of the present volume.

19. Glass, D.C.: Behavior Patterns, Stress, and Coronary Disease. Hillsdale, N.J.: Lawrence Erlbaum Associates, 1977.

20. Holmes, T.H., Rahe, R.H.: The social readjustment rating scale. *J Psychosom Res* **11**:213–218, 1967.

21. Engel, G.L.: A life setting conducive to illness: the giving-up—given-up complex. *Ann Intern Med* **69**:293–300, 1968.

22. Engel, G.L.: Sudden death and the "medical model" in psychiatry. *Can Psychiatr Assoc J* **15**:527–538, 1970.

23. Greene, W.A., Goldstein, S., Moss, A.J.: Psychosocial aspects of sudden death: a preliminary report. *Arch Intern Med* **129**:725–731, 1972.

24. Forsyth, R.P.: Regional blood flow changes during 72-hour avoidance schedules in the monkey. *Science* **173**:546–548, 1971.

25. Henry, J.P., Ely, D.L., Stephens, P.M.: Changes in catecholamine-controlling enzymes in response to psychosocial activation of defence and alarm reactions. *In* Physiology, Emotion, and Psychosomatic Illness. Amsterdam, CIBA Foundation, 1972.

26. Herd, J.A., Morse, W.H., Kelleher, R.J., Jones, L.G.: Arterial hypertension in the squirrel monkey during behavioral experiments. *Am J Physiol* **217**:24–29, 1969.

27. Henry, J.P., Stephens, P.M., Axelrod, J., Mueller, R.A.: Effect of psychosocial stimulation on the enzymes involved in the biosynthesis and metabolism of noradrenaline and adrenaline. *Psychosom Med* **33**:227–237, 1971.

28. Corley, K.C., Mauck, H.P., Shiel, F.O'M.: Cardiac-responses associated with "yoked-chair" shock avoidance in squirrel monkeys. *Psychophysiology* **12**:439–444, 1975.

29. Richter, C.P.: On phenomenon of sudden death in animals and man. *Psychosom Med* **19**:191–198, 1957.

30. Von Holst, D.: Renal failure as the cause of death in *Tupaia belangeri* (tree shrews) exposed to persistent social stress. *J Comp Physiol* **78**:236–273, 1972.

31. Adair, J.R., Manning, J.W.: Hypothalamic modulation of baroreceptor afferent unit activity. *Am J Physiol* **229**:1357–1364, 1975.

32. Djojosugito, A.M., Folkow, B., Kylstra, P., Lisander, B., Tuttle, R.S.: Differentiated interaction between the hypothalamic defense reaction and baroreceptor reflexes. I. Effects on heart rate and regional flow resistance. *Acta Physiol Scand* **78**:376–383, 1970.

33. Friedman, R., Dahl, L.: The effect of chronic conflict on the blood pressure of rats with a genetic susceptibility to experimental hypertension. *Psychosom Med* **37**:402–416, 1975.

34. Mason, J.W., Mangan, G.F., Brady, J.V., Conrad, D., Rioch, D.M.: Concurrent plasma epinephrine, norepinephrine, and 17-hydroxy-cortico-steroid levels during conditioned emotional disturbances in monkeys. *Psychosom Med* **23**:344–353, 1961.

35. Manning, J.W., Cotten, M.deV.: Mechanism of cardiac arrhythmias induced by diencephalic stimulation. *Am J Physiol* **203**:1120–1123, 1962.

36. Adams, D.B., Baccelli, B., Mancia, G., Zanchetti, A.: Cardiovascular changes during naturally elicited fighting behavior in the cat. *Am J Physiol* **216**:1226–1235, 1969.

37. Anderson, D.E., Tosheff, J.G.: Cardiac output and total peripheral resistance changes during preavoidance periods in the dog. *J Appl Physiol* **34**:650–654, 1973.

Chapter 9

Physiological Correlates of Coronary-Prone Behavior

J. Alan Herd

The link between behavioral phenomena and coronary heart disease must include many physiological processes. Distinctive behavior patterns occur repeatedly in certain individuals over a long period of time and lead eventually to clinical manifestations of coronary heart disease. Many physiological systems participate in behavioral phenomena and many pathophysiological processes contribute to atherogenesis. Ultimately, the clinical complications of coronary heart disease occur when other pathophysiological processes operate in the presence of coronary artery disease. The challenge for behavioral physiologists is to utilize the theories and facts from modern physiology in determining the link between behavior, atherogenesis, and coronary heart disease.

A great deal of attention has been given to the behavioral characteristics of individuals prone to coronary heart disease. Less attention has been given to their physiological characteristics. If we are to discover the mechanisms whereby behavioral phenomena contribute to atherogenesis and coronary heart disease, we must identify what alterations in physiological processes are associated with those behaviors. Some may be altered transiently during acute responses to specific stimuli, but in addition, some may be altered continuously by some chronic adaptive process. Therefore, behavioral physiologists must attend to those physiological characteristics that persist beyond momentary responses to behavioral events in subjects who display coronary-prone behavior patterns.

In most physiological studies, behavior is considered an integral part of specific responses to environmental situations. Thermoregulation, exercise, reproduction, aggression, and other functions involving the whole animal include behavioral phenomena, as well as internal homeostatic mechanisms. We have come to recognize that a variety of stimuli elicit specific complex patterns of behavioral, metabolic, visceromotor, and hormonal adjustments that aid the organism in adjusting to its environment. We should expect that individuals displaying coronary-prone behavior have more than just a set of skeletal muscle movements, facial appearances, and vocal expressions. They also must have a set of physiological functions that produce some persistent effects on atherogenesis and the development of coronary heart disease.

The association between autonomic nervous system activity and behavioral phenomena was established by Walter B. Cannon.[1] His studies of adrenal medullary secretion demonstrated its association with emotional displays in experimental animals. Following Cannon's lead, classical physiology developed a functional scheme in which sympathetic nervous system activity increased in association with situations evoking fight or flight responses. Parasympathetic nervous system activity was perceived as associated with situations of rest when restorative or vegetative functions occurred. Typically, fight or flight situations were found to elicit increases in blood pressure, heart rate, cardiac output, and a redistribution of blood flow from splanchnic beds to skeletal muscles, myocardium, and brain.[2] We now know we must consider many different neuroendocrine responses and metabolic consequences, as well as autonomic nervous system regulation accompanying specific behavioral-physiological patterns of response.

These specific patterns are initiated, elaborated, modulated, sustained, and eventually terminated by the central nervous system acting through neural and hormonal mechanisms. All of these processes have been well-studied. Neurophysiological processes are concerned in sensory systems, learning and conditioning processes, and in motor systems that affect the responses. Behavior of an animal is formed by skeletal muscle activity and emotional displays that accompany that activity. Skeletal muscle activity also has metabolic, hormonal, and cardiovascular consequences according to the type and intensity of the skeletal muscle activity. Autonomic nervous system activity has direct effects on cardiovascular function, on lipid mobilization, on glycogen mobilization, on renin secretion, and on the secretion of epinephrine. It also affects muscle tone and shivering mechanisms. Neuroendocrine responses may include not only sympathoadrenomedullary secretions, but also the elaboration of hypothalamic-hypophysial releasing factors and secretion of glucagon.

Metabolic consequences of skeletal muscle activity include heat production, extraction and utilization of substrates from blood, and alterations in acid-base balance. Cardiovascular responses are influenced by autonomic nervous system activity, by local metabolic effects in skeletal muscle, by hormonal influences, and by mechanical effects of posture and skeletal muscle activity. Other hormonal effects of integrative responses include influences on insulin secretion and activity, renin-angiotensin system activity, and the secretion of aldosterone.

Long-term adaptive effects may follow on from influences occurring over a long period of time. Prolonged exposure to a cold environment affects lipid metabolism, heat production, and autonomic nervous system activity. Regular intermittent bouts of strenuous physical activity affect lipid metabolism, skeletal muscle composition, cardiac function, and autonomic nervous system activity. Prolonged exposure to low partial pressure of oxygen at high altitude induces alterations in respiratory function, renal function, and acid-base balance. Integrative physiology is concerned with these long-term adaptive alterations as well as short-term transient responses to environmental stimuli.

Behavioral physiologists have given most attention to the short-term physiological correlates of behavioral phenomena. The most attention of all has been given to the short-term cardiovascular correlates. Although marked changes in heart rate and blood pressure can occur, we must not ignore the neuroendocrine responses and metabolic concomitants of behavioral phenomena. Effects of these other physiological functions can be seen in subjects exposed to low ambient temperatures and in subjects undertaking strenuous physical activity. Thermoregulatory responses demonstrate the importance of neuroendocrine function in physiological adaptation to the environment. Strenuous exercise demonstrates the importance of increased substrate utilization in behavioral-physiological responses.

Thermoregulatory responses are elicited naturally by high or low ambient temperatures. They also can be elicited by local changes in the temperature of the preoptic anterior hypothalamus[3]. In low ambient temperature, or when the preoptic anterior hypothalamus is cooled artificially, the specific thermoregulatory response includes behavioral as well as physiological components. Subjects seek to escape the cold and conserve body heat by complex behavioral responses[4]. In addition, the sympathetic nervous system stimulates vasoconstriction of skin blood vessels[5], enhances muscle tone, facilitates shivering[6], mobilizes lipid from adipose tissue[7], promotes renal secretion of renin, and secretes epinephrine from the adrenal medulla into the circulation[8]. Other neuroendocrine responses also occur[8].

Thermal receptors in the preoptic anterior hypothalamus influence secretion of hypothalamic-hypophysial releasing hormones, which in turn influence secretion of adrenocorticotrophic hormone, thyroid-stimulating hormone, and growth hormone. The end result of all these specific responses is an increase in heat production and a decrease in heat loss. Lipid substances are mobilized into the circulation as triglycerides and free fatty acids, but then are utilized by skeletal muscles, heart, and adipose tissues in production of heat[7]. Initially, heat is produced almost entirely by skeletal muscles through shivering, but eventually, other mechanisms take over the majority of heat production. Adaptive changes in the mitochondria of skeletal muscle and adipose tissue enable those cells to generate heat through increased active transport of $Na+$ and $K+$ under the influence of $Na+K+-ATPase$[9]. Both the immediate thermoregulatory responses and the chronic adaptive changes are more prominent in small animals, such as rodents, than in large animals, such as humans. However, the basic pattern of thermoregulatory responses is the same in all species studied.

Strenuous physical activity produces a set of physiological responses in association with the activity of skeletal muscles. The mechanical and metabolic effects of skeletal muscle affect cardiovacular function, which is influenced still further by the autonomic nervous system. Heart rate, cardiac output, and systolic blood pressure rise[10] and blood is redistributed from splanchnic vascular beds to active skeletal muscle, myocardium, and brain.[11] Sympathetic nervous system activity also mobilizes lipid from adipose tissue,[12] suppresses insulin secretion,[13] and enhances the effects of glucagon on carbohydrate metabolism.[14]

As sympathetic nervous system activity increases, it causes renal secretion of renin and raises levels of epinephrine and norepinephrine in the circulating blood.[15] The majority of energy derived from metabolic substrates in skeletal muscle and myocardium comes from the utilization of lipids.[16] Stores of lipid in skeletal muscle and myocardium are utilized and replenished from free fatty acids and triglycerides circulating in the blood flowing through the active muscles.[16]

Initially, strenuous physical activity has little lasting effect on physiological functions, but eventually, repeated episodes of strenuous physical activity produce cardiovascular and metabolic adjustments that persist beyond the period of exercise. These are associated with a reduction in heart rate and blood pressure[17] at rest and during exercise, a reduction in serum concentrations of triglycerides[18] and very low density lipoproteins, an increase in mitochondrial enzymes[19] and myoglobin[20] in skeletal muscle cells, and cardiac hypertrophy.[21] These physiological adaptations are retained so long as the subject regularly undergoes strenuous physical activity.

Both thermoregulation and exercise serve to illustrate the influence of neuroendocrine responses and metabolic activities on lipid metabolism. Since lipid metabolism is altered in humans with coronary-prone behavior patterns, it is possible that similar mechanisms may be operating in thermoregulation, exercise, and coronary-prone behavior patterns. In each of these behavioral-physiological patterns of response, the sympathetic nervous system is activated above normal basal levels.

Catecholamines are probably the most important factors promoting lipid mobilization.[22] They are effective in mobilizing lipid from adipose tissue[23] both by their liberation from noradrenergic nerve terminals in adipose tissue and by their secretion from the adrenal medulla into the blood and arrival in adipose tissue through the circulation.[22] Also, glucocorticoids promote lipid mobilization[22] and insulin opposes it.[24] Thus, lipid mobilization is promoted by sympathoadrenomedullary stimulation of adipose tissue, especially when levels of glucorticoids in the blood are rising and levels of insulin are falling. Cold environments and strenuous exercise[25] both increase rates of lipid mobilization by increased sympathetic nervous system stimulation. Increased rates of lipid mobilization also may occur in individuals with coronary-prone behavior patterns.

When triglyceride stores in adipose tissue are mobilized, they are hydrolyzed to free fatty acids and glycerol.[22] These free fatty acids are utilized by skeletal muscles and myocardium in the production of energy.[25] They both are stored in these tissues as triglycerides and are used directly. The free fatty acids not stored or utilized in the production of energy are eventually taken up by the adipose tissues or by the liver.[26] Free fatty acids taken up by the liver are formed into triglycerides and secreted as a component of very low density lipoproteins (VLDL).[27]

The rate at which the liver secretes VLDL is determined partly by the rate it synthesizes free fatty acids from carbohydrates and partly by the rate it receives free fatty acids in the blood. In the fasting state, the secretion of VLDL by the liver is determined principally by the levels of free fatty acids in the blood.[28] These levels, in turn, are determined principally by the effects of catecholamines on adipose tissue and rates of energy production.

The effects of neuroendocrine function on blood lipids appear to depend on the balance between lipid mobilization and the utilization of free fatty acids for production of energy. Physiological responses to cold environments and to strenuous exercise include not only high rates of lipid mobilization but also high rates of free fatty acid extraction and utilization for energy. If increased rates of lipid mobilization occur in individuals with coronary-prone behavior patterns that are not matched by high rates of extraction and utilization, the result may be increased rates at which the liver synthesizes and secretes VLDL.

Pathophysiological mechanisms leading to atherosclerosis include damage to vascular endothelium and proliferation of vascular smooth muscle cells.[29] Damage to vascular endothelium may be the result of hemodynamic factors such as high levels of arterial blood pressure or turbulence at bifurcations in large arteries. It also may be the result of chemical factors such as high blood levels of very low density lipoproteins or other circulating substances.[30] Proliferation of vascular smooth muscle also may be influenced by several different factors. Tissue cultures of vascular smooth muscle cells proliferate most readily in the presence of very low density lipoproteins.[31] Proliferation *in vitro* also is enhanced by the presence of insulin in the culture medium.[32] These results from laboratory studies of atherogenic factors suggest mechanisms whereby physiological processes associated with neuroendocrine and metabolic factors may influence atherogenesis in humans and experimental animals.

The clinical manifestations of coronary heart disease may occur through several mechanisms. These include the processes of thrombosis and embolism, increases in oxygen and substrate requirements of the myocardium, increases in cardiac rate, and disorders of cardiac rhythm. Each of these complicating mechanisms has been studied extensively. Results of these studies show that sympathoadrenomedullary function may contribute to several different mechanisms that may cause clinical complications.

One mechanism whereby sympathoadrenomedullary function may contribute to clinical manifestations of coronary heart disease is in production of ventricular arrhythmias and sudden death. The underlying disease responsible for sudden death is usually coronary atherosclerosis[33] and it is probable that most individuals dying suddenly suffered ventricular fibrillation that was triggered by a ventricular premature beat falling in the ventricular vulnerable period.[34] Some investigators have reported that sudden death may occur even without evidence of coronary thrombosis, suggesting that ventricular arrhythmias may themselves precipitate ventricular fibrillation in the absence of acute myocardial infarction.[35] Cardiac arrhythmias have been found in association with exercise and behavioral activities. Exercise testing often will expose arrhythmias not observed while monitoring the electrocardiogram during normal daily activities.[36] Behavioral activities such as public speaking,[37] automobile driving,[38] and emotional stress[39] have also been reported to produce ventricular arrhythmias. In contrast, ventricular arrhythmias have been reported to occur much less frequently when subjects were asleep than when they were awake.[40]

Increased levels of circulating catecholamines may predispose an individual to ventricular arrhythmias. These arrhythmias frequently occur during infusions of epinephrine or isoproterenol.[41] Levels of exercise sufficient to provoke ventricular arrhythmias are associated with increased levels of catecholamines circulating in the blood.[15] Levels of catecholamines in the blood also are elevated during behavioral activities such as public speaking[37] or driving a racing car.[42] As in physical activity, it is possible that at least part of the effects of behavioral activities on ventricular irritability are mediated by circulating catecholamines. Whatever the mechanism might be, prospective epidemiological studies have shown that ventricular arrhythmias were significantly associated with the presence of coronary heart disease and its complications[43] including a high risk of sudden death.[44]

Further studies should improve our understanding of the basic mechanisms linking behavioral-physiological response patterns to coronary heart disease. In particular, we need information concerning neuroendocrine responses associated with coronary-prone behavior patterns. We also need information concerning long-term adaptive changes occurring in individuals with coronary-prone behavior patterns. At the present time, it seems most likely that neuroendocrine responses and alterations in lipid metabolism promote atherogenesis, and sympathoadrenomedullary activity precipitates clinical complications of coronary artery disease such as myocardial infarction and sudden death.

References

1. Cannon, W.B., de la Paz, D.: Emotional stimulation of adrenal secretion. *Am J Physiol* **28**:64–70, 1911.
2. Caraffa-Braga, E., Granata, L., Pinotti, O.: Changes in blood-flow distribution during acute emotional stress in dogs. *Pfluegers Arch* **339**:203–216, 1973.
3. Baldwin, B.A., Ingram, D.L., LeBlanc, J.A.: The effects of environmental temperature and hypothalamic temperature on excretion of catecholamines in the urine of the pig. *Brain Res* **16**:511–515, 1969.
4. Adair, E.R.: Evaluation of some controller inputs to behavioral temperature regulation. *Int J Biometeorol* **15**:121–125, 1971.
5. Nagasaka, T., Carlson, L.D.: Effects of blood temperature and perfused norepinephrine on vascular responses of rabbit ear. *Am J Physiol* **220**:289–292, 1971.

6. Tanche, M., Therminarias, A.: Thyroxine and catecholamines during cold exposure in dogs. *Fed Proc* **28**:1257–1261, 1969.
7. Himms-Hagen, J.: Lipid metabolism during cold exposure and during cold-acclimation. *Lipids* **7**:310–323, 1972.
8. Gale, C.C., Jobin, M., Proppe, D.W., Notter, D., Fox, H.: Endocrine thermoregulatory responses to local hypothalamic cooling in unanesthetized baboons. *Am J Physiol* **219**:193–201, 1970.
9. Edelman, I.S.: Thyroid thermogenesis. *N Engl J Med* **290**:1303–1308, 1974.
10. Astrand, P.O., Ekblom, B., Messin, R., Saltin, B., Stenberg, J.: Intra-arterial blood pressure during exercise with different muscle groups. *J Appl Physiol* **20**:253–256, 1965.
11. Van Citters, R.L., Franklin, D.L.: Cardiovascular performance of Alaska sled dogs during exercise. *Circ Res* **24**:33–42, 1969.
12. Young, D.R., Shapira, J., Forrest, R., Adachi, R.R., Lim, R., Peligra, R.: Model for evaluation of fatty acid metabolism for man during prolonged exercise. *J Appl Physiol* **23**:716–725, 1967.
13. Hunter, W.M., Sukkar, M.Y.: Changes in plasma insulin levels during muscular exercise. *J Physiol* (London) **196**:110P–112P, 1968.
14. Gerich, J.E., Langlois, M., Noacco, C., Schneider, V., Forsham, P.H.: Adrenergic modulation of pancreatic glucagon secretion in man. *J Clin Invest* **53**:1441–1446, 1974.
15. Kotchen, T.A., Hartley, L.H., Rice, T.W., Mougey, E.H., Jones, L.G., Mason, J.W.: Renin, norepinephrine, and epinephrine response to graded exercise. *J Appl Physiol* **31**:178–184, 1971.
16. Hagenfeldt, L., Wahren, J.: Human forearm muscle metabolism during exercise. II. *Scand J Clin Lab Invest* **21**:263–276, 1968.
17. Choquette, G., Ferguson, R.J.: Blood pressure reduction in "border-line" hypertensives following physical training. *Can Med Assoc J* **108**:699–703, 1973.
18. Holloszy, J.O., Skinner, J.S., Toro, G., Cureton, T.K.: Effects of a six-month program of endurance exercise on the serum lipids of middle-aged men. *Am J Cardiol* **14**:753–760, 1964.
19. Mole, P.A., Oscai, L.B., Holloszy, J.O.: Adaptation of muscle to exercise. Increase in levels of palmityl CoA synthetase, carnitine palmityltransferase and palmityl CoA dehydrogenase and in the capacity to oxidize fatty acids. *J Clin Invest* **50**:2323–2330, 1971.
20. Pattengale, P.K., Holloszy, J.O.: Augmentation of skeletal muscle myoglobin by a program of treadmill running. *Am J Physiol* **213**:783–785, 1967.
21. Oscai, L.B., Mole, P.A., Holloszy, J.O.: Effects of exercise on cardiac weight and mitochondria in male and female rats. *Am J Physiol* **220**:1944–1948, 1971.
22. Heindel, J.J., Orci, L., Jeanrenaud, B.: Fat mobilization and its regulation by hormones and drugs in white adipose tissue. *In* International Encyclopedia of Pharmacology and Therapeutics. Pharmacology of Lipid Transport and Atherosclerotic Processes. (Masoro, E.J., ed.). **24**,1:175–373. Oxford: Pergamon, 1975.
23. Rosell, S., Belfrage, E.: Adrenergic receptors in adipose tissue and their relation to adrenergic innervation. *Nature* **253**:738–739, 1975.
24. Butcher, R.W., Baird, C.E., Sutherland, E.W.: Effects of lipolytic and antilipolytic substances on adenosine 3′,5′-monophosphate levels in isolated fat cells. *J Biol Chem* **243**:1705–1712, 1968.
25. Zierler, K.L., Maseri, A., Klassen, D., Rabinowitz, D., Burgess, J.: Muscle metabolism during exercise in man. *Trans Assoc Am Physicians* **81**:266–273, 1968.
26. Shapiro, B.: Triglyceride metabolism. *In* Handbook of Physiology. Sect. 5. Adipose Tissue. (Renold, A.E., Cahill, G.F., Jr., eds.) Washington, D.C.: American Physiology Society, 1965, pp. 217–223.
27. Schonfeld, G., Pfleger, B.: Utilization of exogenous free fatty acids for the production of very low density lipoprotein triglyceride by livers of carbohydrate-fed rats. *J Lipid Res* **12**:614–621, 1971.
28. Basso, L.V., Havel, R.J.: Hepatic metabolism of free fatty acids in normal and diabetic dogs. *J Clin Invest* **49**:537–547, 1970.
29. Ross, R., Glomset, J.A.: The pathogenesis of atherosclerosis. *N Engl J Med* **295**:369–377, 420–425, 1976.
30. Ross, R., Harker, L.: Hyperlipidemia and atherosclerosis. *Science* **193**:1094–1100, 1976.

31. Ross, R., Glomset, J.A.: Atherosclerosis and the arterial smooth muscle cell. *Science* **180**:1332–1339, 1973.
32. Stout, R.W., Bierman, E.L., Ross, R.: Effect of insulin on the proliferation of cultured primate arterial smooth muscle cells. *Circulation Res* **36**:319–327, 1975.
33. Kuller, L., Lilienfield, A., Fisher, R.: Epidemiological study of sudden and unexpected deaths due to arteriosclerotic heart disease. *Circulation* **34**:1056–1068, 1966.
34. Smirk, F.N., Palmer, D.G.: A myocardial syndrome with particular reference to the occurrence of sudden death and of premature systoles interrupting the antecedent T waves. *Am J Cardiol* **6**:620–629, 1960.
35. Adelson, L., Hoffman, W.: Sudden death from coronary disease related to a lethal mechanism arising independently of vascular occlusion or myocardial damage. *JAMA* **176**:129–135, 1961.
36. Kosowsky, B.D., Lown, B., Whiting, R., Guiney, T.: Occurrence of ventricular arrhythmia with exercise as compared to monitoring. *Circulation* **44**:826–832, 1971.
37. Taggart, P., Carruthers, M., Somerville, W.: Electrocardiogram, plasma catecholamines, lipids and their modification by oxprenolol when speaking before an audience. *Lancet* **2**:341–346, 1973.
38. Taggart, R., Gibbons, D., Somerville, W.: Some effects of motor-car driving on the normal and abnormal heart. *Br Med J* **4**:130–134, 1969.
39. Sigler, L.H.: Emotion and arteriosclerotic heart disease. I. Electrocardiographic changes observed on the recall of past emotional disturbances. *Br J Med Psychol* **40**:55–64, 1967.
40. Lown, B., Tykocinski, M., Garfein, A., Brooks, P.: Sleep and ventricular premature beats. *Circulation* **48**:691–701, 1973.
41. Lockett, M.: Dangerous effects of isoprenaline in myocardial failure. *Lancet* **2**:104–106, 1965.
42. Taggart, P., Carruthers, M.: Endogenous hyperlipidaemia induced by emotional stress of racing driving. *Lancet* **1**:363–366, 1971.
43. Hinkle, L.E., Jr., Carver, S.T., Stevens, M.: The frequency of asymptomatic disturbances of cardiac rhythm and conduction in middle-aged men. *Am J Cardiol* **24**:629–650, 1969.
44. Fisher, F.D., Tyroler, H.A.: Relationship between ventricular premature contractions on routine electrocardiography and subsequent sudden death from coronary heart disease. *Circulation* **47**:712–719, 1973.

Chapter 10

Type A Behavior: Its Possible Relationship to Pathogenetic Processes Responsible for Coronary Heart Disease (a Preliminary Enquiry)

Meyer Friedman

The data so far accumulated that suggest that the behavior pattern we have described as Type A* may play a role in the pathogenesis of clinical coronary heart disease (CHD) fall into five categories.

Historically considered, the first body of evidence suggesting the possible involvement of a particular behavior pattern in the causation of clinical CHD, while never published, nevertheless first drew our attention to the possibility that some kind of an emotional disturbance might be at play in the initiation or intensification of this disease. This evidence consisted of the observation of certain relatively *specific* psychomotor manifestations shown by almost every coronary patient under the age of 60 to 65 years. Thus, we were able to detect various identifying characteristics in speech patterns and in the response reactions to external stimuli of almost all our coronary patients.[1-4] It was the detection of these peculiarly similar stereotype psychomotor manifestations in successive coronary patients in the 1950s that first made us suspect and commence to investigate the possible role of the central nervous system in the occurrence of clinical CHD.

The second body of evidence we obtained suggesting the possibly important role of Type A behavior in the pathogenesis of clinical CHD was our observation of the markedly increased prevalence of clinical CHD in a group of severely afflicted middle-aged Type A subjects as compared to a group of Type B subjects.[5] We felt that if Type A behavior could be used as a differentiating

* Type A behavior is a relatively specific type of *continuous* emotional disquiet that is initiated and sustained in an individual by (1) his abnormally intense, chronic struggle to achieve more and more objectives or to participate in more and more events in less and less time, or (2) his exaggerated hostile reactions to various activities of other human beings. Usually, but not always, subjects exhibiting Type A behavior possess and suffer from both these traits. Type B behavior lacks both these behavioral components.

index, allowing us to segregate seven times as many coronary patients in a group of subjects exhibiting this behavior as in a group of subjects exactly the same in their eating, exercise, and work habits, but who exhibited a converse type of behavior (Type B), we were absolutely forced to investigate the role of such behavior in heart disease.

The third body of evidence we obtained suggesting a possibly close pathogenetic relationship of Type A behavior to the early onset of clinical CHD was a series of clinical observations indicating that some of the commonly accepted risk factors for clinical CHD were preferentially exhibited or possessed by Type A subjects long before they suffered from or exhibited signs of clinical CHD. Thus, *severely* afflicted Type A subjects as a group exhibited a higher serum cholesterol,[1,5] an elevated pre- and postprandial serum triglyceride,[6] increased sludging,[6] a faster clotting time,[5] a higher excretion of norepinephrine,[7] and more recently, a higher serum level of this hormone during an emotional challenge,[8] than a group of Type B subjects. In addition, the majority of Type A subjects exhibited a higher average serum level of corticotropin,[9] a greater insulinemic response to glucose,[10] and a decreased growth hormone response to arginine.[11]

Besides the increased prevalence of these risk factors, the prevalence of excess smoking of cigarettes and hypertension is far greater in Type A subjects than in Type B subjects.

From these observations, it perhaps can be understood why we have been hesitant to indict any of these so-called risk factors as the sole pathogens of clinical CHD. From the very first, we have had to face up to the clinical reality that we observed; namely, that if a person smokes excessively, if he exhibits hypertension, if he exhibits nonfamilial hypercholesterolemia or hypertriglyceridemia, if he drinks excessive amounts of coffee, or even if he salts his food before he even savors it, he is overwhelmingly likely to possess Type A behavior. Are all these traits singly capable of inducing the same behavior pattern, or is it the behavior pattern that leads to these biochemical, physiological and, yes, psychological peculiarities? We, of course, on the grounds of common sense, believe that the latter explanation best fits the clinical situation as we have experienced it over the past four decades.

The fourth species of evidence indicating that emotional stress may play a role in coronary atherogenesis has been our series of experimental observations in which we were able to induce various biochemical and anatomical changes in experimental animals subject to certain types of emotional stress. Thus, by creating a chronic sense of expectant urgency in rats, we were able not only to hasten their clotting time[12] but also to increase their serum cholesterol level and the atherosclerosis of their coronary vasculature.[13] In more recent studies[14,15] we have been able to induce hypercholesterolemia at will in rats by interfering with their autonomic nervous system at the hypothalamic level. In the cholesterol-fed rabbit also, we had earlier observed[16] that hypothalamic derangement quickly intensified the degree of hypercholesterolemia and aggravated the degree of coronary atherosclerosis. All these data considered together, it seems quite apparent that experimentally at least, it is not difficult to effect biochemical and pathological changes of vascular relevance by setting up various types of *chronic* trauma in the central nervous system.

The fifth category of evidence we obtained suggesting the possible pathogenetic role of Type A behavior in the onset of clinical CHD consisted of the conclusions obtained from our prospective epidemiological study (The Western Collaborative Group Study) of over 3,000 initially well subjects.[2] These conclusions[17,18] clearly indicated that the incidence of new clinical CHD was significantly greater in those subjects initially diagnosed as Type A subjects.

Taken together, we believe that all these clinical, epidemiological, and now, experimental data present an extraordinarily strong case for the involvement of Type A behavior in the pathogenesis of clinical CHD. But while these observations strongly suggest such involvement, they do not inform us of the exact mechanisms by which this peculiar behavior pattern may lead to a badly diseased coronary vasculature. Thus, we do not know at this time whether Type A behavior (1) intensifies the initial growth of a coronary artery plaque; (2) enhances the chronic deposition upon and subsequent incorporation into the plaque of thromboembolic components of the blood; (3) accelerates the internal necrosis, calcification, and rupture of a plaque, thus inducing thrombosis and infarction; (4) alters the metabolism of the myocardial cell; or (5) favors the onset of life-threatening arrhythmias.

Thus, although as I have shown above, we have a surfeit of possible risk factors at play (e.g., hypercholesterolemia, sludging, excess amounts of circulating norepinephrine, or ACTH), we do not have the information to allow us to incriminate any of these factors either in the formation, the growth, or the catastrophical decay and rupture of a coronary plaque in the Type A subject. Nor will it be an easy task to determine in the future the relative pathogenetic importance of the various risk factors so often observed in Type A subjects. This will be such a difficult task for one simple reason: We really do not know for sure the mechanism whereby any heretofore commonly accepted coronary risk factor may effect arterial damage. For example, do we really know the biochemical and biophysical changes whereby cigarette smoking, hypertension, diabetes, or even hypercholesterolemia hasten the onset of angina, infarction, or sudden death (these are the usual manifestations of *clinical* CHD)?

I have brought up this last fact because it has become the mode for some epidemiologists to attempt to belittle the evidence linking Type A behavior to the pathogenesis of clinical CHD by insisting that the intrinsic metabolic processes by which this behavior hastens the onset of heart disease be elucidated. Such investigators should remember that we still have to find out what the intrinsic metabolic processes are by which the putative risk factors they have favored lead to the onset of clinical CHD. I daresay that if and when we do learn *exactly* how such risk factors as cigarette smoke, or hypertension, or a high serum cholesterol lead to coronary arterial thrombosis, infarction, and sudden death, we shall not find it too difficult to track down the precise cardiopathic mechanisms set into play by Type A behavior. It will not be difficult because this behavior so often appears to precede or give rise to these same risk factors.

References

1. Friedman, M.: The Pathogenesis of Coronary Artery Disease. New York: McGraw-Hill, 1969.
2. Rosenman, R.H., Friedman, M., Straus, R., Wurm, M., Kositchek, R., Hahn, W., Werthessen, N.T.: A predictive study of coronary heart disease. The Western Collaborative Group Study. *JAMA* **189**:15–22, 1964.
3. Friedman, M., Rosenman, R.H.: Type A behavior pattern. Its association with coronary heart disease. *Ann Clin Res* **3**:300–312, 1971.
4. Rosenman, R.H., Friedman, M.: Neurogenic factors in pathogenesis of coronary heart disease. *Med Clin North Am* **58**:269–279, 1974.
5. Friedman, M., Rosenman, R.H.: Association of specific overt behavior pattern with blood and cardiovascular findings. *JAMA* **169**:1286–1296, 1959.
6. Friedman, M., Rosenman, R.H., Byers, S.O.: Serum lipids and conjunctival circulation after fat ingestion in men exhibiting Type A behavior pattern. *Circulation* **29**:874–886, 1964.
7. Friedman, M., St. George, S., Byers, S.O.: Excretion of catecholamines, 17-ketosteroids, 17-hydroxy-corticoids and 5-hydroxyindole in men exhibiting a particular behavior pattern (A) associated with high incidence of clinical coronary artery disease. *J Clin Invest* **39**:758–764, 1960.
8. Friedman, M., Byers, S.O., Diamant, J., Rosenman, R.H.: Plasma catecholamine response of coronary-prone subjects (Type A) to a specific challenge. *Metabolism* **24**:205–210, 1975.
9. Friedman, M., Byers, S.O., Rosenman, R.H.: Plasma ACTH and cortisol concentration of coronary-prone subjects. *Proc Soc Exp Biol Med* **140**:681–684, 1972.
10. Friedman, M., Byers, S.O., Rosenman, R.H., Elevitch, F.R.: Coronary-prone individuals (Type A behavior pattern). Some biochemical characteristics. *JAMA* **212**:1030–1037, 1970.
11. Friedman, M., Byers, S.O., Rosenman, R.H., Neuman, R.: Coronary-prone individuals (Type A behavior pattern) growth hormone responses. *JAMA* **217**:929–932, 1971.
12. DeLong, E., Uhley, H.N., Friedman, M.: Change in blood clotting time of rats exposed to a particular form of stress. *Am J Physiol* **196**:429–430, 1959.
13. Uhley, H.N., Friedman, M.: Blood lipids, clotting and coronary atherosclerosis in rats exposed to a particular form of stress. *Am J Physiol* **197**:396–398, 1959.
14. Friedman, M., Byers, S.O., Elek, S.R.: The induction of neurogenic hypercholesterolemia. *Proc Soc Exp Biol Med* **131**:759–762, 1969.
15. Byers, S.O., Friedman, M.: Neurogenic hypercholesterolemia. III. Cholesterol synthesis, absorption and clearance. *Am J Physiol* **225**:1322–1326, 1973.
16. Gunn, C.G., Friedman, M., Byers, S.O.: Effect of chronic hypothalamic stimulation upon cholesterol-induced atherosclerosis in the rabbit. *J Clin Invest* **39**:1963–1972, 1960.
17. Rosenman, R.H., Friedman, M., Straus, R., Wurm, M., Jenkins, D., Messinger, H.B., Kositchek, R., Hahn, W., Werthessen, N.T.: Coronary heart disease in the Western Collaborative Group Study. A follow-up experience of two years. *JAMA* **195**:86–92, 1966.
18. Brand, R.J., Rosenman, R.H., Sholtz, R.I., Friedman, M.: Multivariate prediction of coronary heart disease in the Western Collaborative Group Study compared to the findings of the Framingham Study. *Circulation* **53**:348–355, 1976.

Chapter 11

Psychophysiological Processes, the Coronary-Prone Behavior Pattern, and Coronary Heart Disease

Redford B. Williams, Jr.

At one level of analysis, there are two avenues whereby behavior pattern might be playing a role in the etiology and course of CHD. First of all, the Type A behavior pattern might be instrumental in precipitating acute clinical events in patients with preexisting advanced coronary atherosclerosis. In addition, and perhaps in combination with this mechanism, behavior pattern might be playing a contributory role in the atherosclerotic process itself. The strongest available evidence, from the Western Collaborative Group Study[1] indicates that Type A men experience about twice the incidence of *clinical CHD events* over an 8½ year follow up compared to Type B men.

With respect to the second mechanism, contribution to the atherosclerotic process itself, Blumethanl et al.,[2] Zyzanski et al.,[3] and Kornfeld[4] have reported, on the basis of findings at coronary arteriography, greater levels of coronary atherosclerosis among Type A patients compared to Type B patients. In an earlier study, Friedman et al.[5] found greater levels of coronary atherosclerosis among Type B men studied at autopsy. Both these types of correlative studies are subject to possible selection biases. The only subjects available for autopsy study are those who suffer a fatal event, while the only subjects available for the arteriography studies are those patients who are referred to a tertiary medical center for clinical evaluation. The best evidence for an association between behavior pattern and the atherosclerotic process would be to perform coronary arteriography in healthy Type A and Type B subjects to determine whether the association held up when selection biases were thus controlled. It is doubtful that such a study in subjects without clear clinical indications for arteriography could be justified on ethical grounds.

If we may assume that the available evidence (see section on Association) indicates: (1) that the case for a role of behavior pattern in predicting subsequent clinical CHD events is nearly as strong as that for the traditional risk factors, and (2) that given the unavoidable limitations on the types of studies that can be mounted, there is some evidence supportive of a role for behavior pattern in the atherosclerotic process, thus, the question that may now be posed is, ''By what physiological mechanisms is the (putative) association between behavior pattern and clinical events and coronary atherosclerosis mediated?''

It must first be noted that there is no direct evidence concerning any possible intervening mechanism underlying the association described above. By direct evidence, I mean studies in which the proposed mechanism is assessed and then *its relationship to subsequent clinical CHD events or to coronary atherosclerosis level is determined in the same patients in which it was assessed.* On the other hand, there is considerable circumstantial evidence that psychophysiological and psychoneuroendocrine differences exist between Type A and Type B subjects, which could be important in mediating the association between behavior pattern and CHD.

Behavior Pattern and Clinical CHD Events

In Chapter 10, Dr. Friedman has described in some detail characteristics of neuroendocrine response that differentiate Type A from Type B subjects. The increased urinary norepinephrine excretion during the working day and the exaggerated plasma norepinephrine response to a challenging task observed among Type A men could be instrumental in the precipitation of acute clinical events. Eliot[6] has proposed that excess norepinephrine secretion could be responsible for the focal myocardial necrosis that is observed in association with extreme stresses. Haft et al.[7] have shown that intravascular platelet aggregation can be precipitated in the dog's heart by infusion of norepinephrine. It is interesting, therefore, that in comparison to Type B men, Type A men show increased platelet aggregation after stressful exercise.[8]

Rosenman et al.[9] have reported more rapid blood clotting times among Type A men during periods of stress. There is extensive evidence, therefore, that Type A individuals with preexisting coronary atherosclerotic involvement would be at greater risk than Type B individuals to experience an acute occlusion of the arterial lumen via effects of stress upon the blood clotting mechanism. Such effects could be mediated by changes in platelet function or by other effects of the stress upon the clotting mechanism. If such acute effects of stress upon blood clotting mechanisms are indeed acting to increase the risk of acute CHD events among Type A individuals, it is likely that these effects are mediated via the increased sympathetic nervous responses that have been described as characteristic of Type A persons.

Besides their effects upon clotting mechanisms, the increased catecholamine responses among Type A individuals are likely associated with changes in cardiovascular function, which could be key events in the precipitation of acute CHD events. Increases in cardiac output or peripheral resistance attendant upon acute stresses could impose additional workloads upon the cardiac muscle such that the blood supply available via the atherosclerotic coronary arteries becomes insufficient to meet the metabolic needs of the muscle, the result being myocardial infarction. In addition to this mechanism, that is, stresses to which the Type A person is subject that have the potential of precipitating acute CHD events, the increased sympathetic discharge could also play a role in the initiation of potentially fatal cardiac arrhythmias. Glass[10] has proposed that when the active efforts of the Type A person to control his environment (with the associated sympathetic activation) fail, there will occur a withdrawal, or giving up, with a possible shift to parasympathetic dominance. Glass cites evidence that such sympathetic-parasympathetic shifts are implicated in sudden death.

Unfortunately, there are few studies comparing Type A and Type B subjects' physiological response to behavioral stresses. There is certainly a strong need for such studies. For example, in one study, Type A and B subjects were challenged to perform well in a reaction time task. Type A's compared to B's responded with significantly greater increases in both heart rate and systolic blood pressure.[11]

In another similar study, Manuck and Craft[12] subjected Type A and Type B male and female undergraduates to a puzzle-solving task and found a larger systolic blood pressure increase during the task among Type A males compared to Type B males. There was no difference in blood pressure response between Type A and Type B females. This finding has been subsequently replicated in a different sample.[13] Such findings are encouraging to those who emphasize the need to undertake psychophysiological studies comparing Type A with Type B subjects. Support for a role in psychophysiological mechanisms in mediating the effects of stress upon CHD events is provided by the finding of Stewart Wolf that CHD patients experiencing sudden death exhibit greater levels of blood pressure lability premortem compared to surviving patients.[14]

Behavior Pattern and Coronary Atherosclerosis

Ross et al.[15] have proposed that the initiating event in the atherosclerotic process involves "injury" to the arterial endothelium. Such injury could result from hemodynamic events resulting in turbulence and shear stress, from biochemical insults, and from immunological processes. Furthermore, the response of platelets and arterial smooth muscle cells to such injury appears important, whatever the initial cause of the injury. Any effect of behavior pattern to accelerate or increase the development of atherosclerotic lesions would logically act via influences upon the arterial endothelium or the platelet and smooth muscle cell responses to injury of the endothelium. The findings cited above that Type A patients have more severe coronary atherosclerosis on arteriography provide circumstantial evidence that such influences are more active in the Type A individual. There is no direct evidence, however, that bears upon the specific nature of the physiological mechanism(s) involved. The increased platelet aggregation among Type A individuals in association with the stress cited above could be one way that behavior pattern plays a role in atherogenesis.

Despite the paucity of published evidence presently available, there is reason to postulate that hemodynamic stress may be occurring more frequently and to a greater level of intensity among Type A persons. The frequent behavioral arousals that Glass[10] postulates to occur among Type A individuals in their constant attempts to maintain their "sense of environmental control," would likely be associated with increased levels of cardiovascular response. That such is the case is strongly suggested by the cited findings of increased sympathetic nervous activity among Type A subjects when challenged.

Williams[16] has proposed two psychophysiological mechanisms whereby the interactions of the Type A individual with his environment could lead to different patterns of cardiovascular activation that, via hemodynamic effects, could play a role in endothelial injury. Where the outcome of such an interaction is the feeling that an emergency exists and that fight/flight behavior is called for, the "defense reaction" is activated. This reaction is characterized by a state of emotional arousal, increased motoric activity, and a cardiovascular response pattern characterized by an increase in cardiac output, with a shunting of this increased output away from the skin and viscera to the skeletal musculature.[17]

On the other hand, when the outcome of the interaction is a state of vigilance with attentive observation of environmental stimuli, a qualitatively different behavioral-physiological response pattern is observed: there is little emotional expression, motoric activity decreases, heart rate (and cardiac output) decrease, and there is an active vasoconstriction in skeletal muscle as well as in skin and viscera.[18] It might be postulated that Type A individuals would respond to situations calling forth either of these general behavioral-physiological response patterns to a more extreme and prolonged degree than Type B persons. It might further be postulated that extreme hemodynamic responses in association with such episodes might lead to more endothelial injury among Type A patients, accounting for the apparent increase in coronary atherosclerosis among this group.

It has to be emphasized that such a hypothesis is only inferential at the present time, and that beyond the reports by Dembroski et al.,[11] and Manuck et al.,[12] there is little direct evidence to support this otherwise attractive speculation. However, this hypothesis is testable with resources presently available. One means of testing it would be to assess cardiovascular response patterns during experimental situations giving rise to varying subject-environmental interactions as described above. If the subjects in such a study were patients free of congestive heart failure (which would modify hemodynamic function), who were going to undergo diagnostic coronary arteriography, it would be possible to relate the level of coronary atherosclerosis arteriographically to the level of cardiovascular response during psychophysiological testing. If Type A patients showed more extreme cardiovascular responses than Type B patients, and if those Type A patients with more extensive and/or severe coronary lesions also accounted for most of the extreme hemodynamic responses observed among the Type A group, then strong evidence would have been adduced in support of the above hypothesis that extreme hemodynamic responses during emergency and sensory-processing behaviors constitute the mechanism underlying the observed relationship between the Type A behavior pattern and various manifestations of CHD. Especially persuasive would be the observation that those Type A patients with extreme hemodynamic responses also accounted for most of the clinical CHD events on follow-up. Additional support would be provided if covarying the hemodynamic responses led to disappearance of the relationship between behavior pattern and CHD indices.

In conclusion, it should be noted that in no instance have any of the possible underlying psychophysiological or neuroendocrine mechanisms proposed to account for the association between behavior pattern and CHD been studied directly in conjunction with assessment of the various CHD indices to which Type A behavior pattern has been related. It is possible to formulate hypotheses based upon what we know about the psychological characteristics of the Type A person and about psychophysiological response mechanisms. Such hypotheses remain speculative at present, and there is a great need to begin the research that will subject them to direct test.

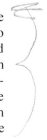

References

1. Rosenman, R.H., Brand, R.J., Jenkins, C.D., Friedman, M., Straus, R., Wurm, M.: Coronary heart disease in the Western Collaborative Group Study: final follow-up experience of 8½ years. *JAMA* **233**:872–877, 1975.
2. Blumenthal, J.A., Williams, R.B., Kong, D., Schanberg, S.M., Thompson, L.W.: Coronary-prone behavior and angiographically documented coronary disease. *Circulation* (in press).
3. Zyzanski, S.J., Jenkins, C.D., Ryan, T.J., Plessas, A., Everist, M.: Psychological correlates of coronary angiographic findings. *Arch Intern Med* **136**:1234–1237, 1976.
4. Kornfeld, D.S.: New York: Columbia University, unpublished research.
5. Friedman, M., Rosenman, R.H., Straus, R., et al.: The relationship of behavior pattern A to the state of the coronary vasculature: a study of 51 autopsied subjects. *Am J Med* **44**:525–537, 1968.
6. Eliot, R.S.: Stress-induced myocardial necrosis. *J SC Med Assoc* (Suppl.) **33**: 1976.
7. Haft, J.I., Kranz, P.D., Albert, F.J., Fani, K.: Intravascular platelet aggregation in the heart induced by norepinephrine. *Circulation* **46**:698–708, 1972.
8. Simpson, M.T., Olewine, D.A., Jenkins, C.D., Ramsey, F.H., Zyzanski, S.J., Thomas, G., Hames, C.G.: Exercise-induced catecholamines and platelet aggregation in the coronary-prone behavior pattern. *Psychosom Med* **36**:476–487, 1974.
9. Rosenman, R.H., Friedman, M.: Neurogenic factors in pathogenesis of coronary heart disease. *Med Clin North Am* **58**:269–279, 1974.
10. Glass, D.C.: Stress, behavior patterns and coronary disease. *Am Sci* **65**:177–187, 1977.
11. Dembroski, T.M., MacDougall, J.M., Shields, J.L.: Physiologic reactions to social challenge in persons evidencing the Type A coronary-prone behavior pattern. *J Human Stress* **3**:2–9, 1977.
12. Manuck, J., Craft, R., Gold, K.: Coronary-prone behavior and cardiovascular response. *Psychophysiology* (in press).
13. Manuck, J.: Department of Psychology, University of Virginia. Personal communication.
14. Wolf, S.: Psychosocial forces in myocardial infarction and sudden death. *In* Society, Stress and Disease (Levi, L., ed.). London: Oxford University Press, 1971.

15. Ross, R., Glomset, J.A.: The pathogenesis of atherosclerosis. *N Engl J Med* **295**:369–377, 420–425, 1976.
16. Williams, R.B.: Physiologic mechanisms underlying the association between psychosocial factors and coronary heart disease. *In* Psychosocial Aspects of Myocardial Infarction and Coronary Care (Gentry, W.D. and Williams, R.B., eds.). St. Louis: Mosby, 1975, pp. 37–50.
17. Brod, J., Fencl, V.Z., Hejl, Z., Jirka, J.: Circulatory changes underlying blood pressure elevation during acute emotional stress (mental arithmetic) in normotensive and hypertensive subjects. *Clin Sci Mol Med* **18**:269–279, 1959.
18. Williams, R.B., Bittker, T.E., Buchsbaum, M.S., Wynne, L.C.: Cardiovascular and neurophysiologic correlates of sensory intake and rejection. I. Effect of cognitive tasks. *Psychophysiology* **12**:427–433.

Chapter 12

Pattern A Behavior and Uncontrollable Stress

David C. Glass

Several years ago, I began a series of experiments to determine whether individuals classified as Pattern A do, indeed, exhibit excessive achievement striving, time-urgency, and hostility. The results of this research provided systematic documentation for the three components of the behavior pattern.[1,2] Moreover, a subtle consistency was revealed in the array of empirical facts. In contrast to Type B's, Type A's worked hard to succeed, suppressed subjective states (e.g., fatigue) that might interfere with task performance, exhibited rapid pacing of their activities, and expressed hostility after being harassed in their efforts at task completion—all, I would submit, in the interests of asserting control over environmental demands and requirements. I would also suggest that these demands must be at least minimally stressful, for the possibility of failure and loss of esteem was inherent in most of the experimental situations used in my research. Since there were few differences between A's and B's in how they perceived the experiments, the coronary-prone behavior pattern might be described as a characteristic style of responding to environmental stressors that threaten the individual's sense of control. Type A's are engaged in a struggle for control, whereas Type B's are free of such concerns, and hence, relatively free of characteristic Pattern A traits.

The concept of uncontrollability may be defined as follows: When an individual perceives that his responses will not determine what he gets, the outcome is considered uncontrollable. By contrast, controllability involves the subject's perception of a contingency between responding and outcomes. An uncontrollable stressor is, then, a potentially harmful stimulus that the individual can neither escape nor avoid. A controllable stressor is a harmful stimulus that can be avoided by appropriate instrumental responses.

Experimentation on Pattern A and Uncontrollable Stress

The initial reaction of Type A's to an uncontrollable stressor may be termed *hyperresponsiveness,* for it is assumed to reflect a concerted effort to assert control over the stimulus. In comparison to B's, Pattern A individuals experience increased motivation—at least initially—to master situations that they perceive as signifying lack of control. It might be expected, therefore, that A's will try harder than B's to master an experimental task administered after say, a few trials of inescapable noise stimulation. Having been exposed to a brief experience with uncontrollable stress, A's will exert compensatory efforts to reestablish a sense of control by trying to master a subsequent task. Instead of developing general expectations of uncontrollability, as Seligman's[3] learned-helplessness hypothesis might predict, Type A's actually become more motivated to assert control.

This line of thought received support in a series of laboratory experiments on the reactions of A's and B's to controllable and uncontrollable stressful events.[1,2] It appears that Pattern A behavior may, indeed, be a strategy for coping with uncontrollable stress; enhanced performance reflects an attempt to assert and maintain control after its loss has been threatened. However, enhanced responding must prove ineffective in the long run, for extended exposure to uncontrollable stress eventually leads to the perception that a noncontingency exists between responses and outcomes. The Type A individual may then be expected to give up efforts at control and show what has been called learned helplessness, or *hyporesponsiveness.*[4] While Type B's will also experience helplessness under these circumstances, nevertheless, it is the A's who should exhibit greater hyporesponsiveness because of their tendency to experience loss of control as more threatening.

The experimental data pertaining to this line of thought suggest a more complex pattern of response, however.[1,2] It appears that A's show greater helplessness than B's under *high stress* (e.g., 107-decibel inescapable noise), but not under *moderate stress* (e.g., 78-decibel inescapable noise). While I do not gainsay the possibility of an arousal interpretation of these results (after all, A's have been found to respond to stress with greater norepinephrine elevations than their Type B counterparts) the autonomic data collected in our research (e.g., phasic skin conductance) did not indicate the viability of an arousal approach to the helplessness effects.

A cognitive interpretation was, therefore, proposed.[1,2] The interpretation can be summarized as follows. Since Pattern A individuals are presumably more concerned than their Pattern B counterparts about maintaining environmental control, we might expect A's to distort cues signifying lack of control. Indeed, when uncontrollability cues do not compel attention, for example, in the case of *soft* inescapable noise, Type A's should find it relatively easy to minimize the fact that they are unable to control the situation. If, on the other hand, lack of control is a salient feature of their environment, for example, in the case of *loud* inescapable noise, A's should experience considerable difficulty in ignoring its presence and thus exert enhanced efforts at locating control-relevant cues. These efforts will eventually result in a stronger certainty that nothing can be done about terminating noise. Such expectations of uncontrollability should lead to a decrement in efforts at control, i.e., learned helplessness. A different state of affairs will occur when uncontrollability cues are low in salience. Under these conditions, A's will exert less efforts at achieving control, less effectively encode the fact of noncontingency and, hence, fail to show subsequent helplessness.

Research has been conducted that provides some support for this line of thought.[1,2] The results show that the enhanced controlling behavior of A's after brief exposure to uncontrollable stress changes to a decrement in efforts at control after prolonged exposure. However, this vulnerability of A's to learned helplessness must be qualified to take account of the prominence or salience of the cues signifying the uncontrollable nature of the stressor. Type A's exhibit helplessness only under conditions of high salience.

This latter finding must be viewed with caution, however. A number of issues remain unresolved, including the notion of cue salience itself. It appears that salience affects the way in which A's and B's respond to brief as well as extended uncontrollable stress, but future research must determine why A's have an elevated threshold for responding to signs of uncontrollability. Of equal importance is the need for additional experimentation to provide more unequivocal documentation for generalizations about salience and the hyperresponsivity and hyporesponsivity of A's. We also need to formulate a more precise conceptualization of the salience variable, along with reliable techniques for its measurement. As it now stands, we are hard pressed to give an *a priori* specification of the salience of uncontrollability, although we have been fortunate in producing manipulations that affect behavior according to our intended purposes.

More important, perhaps, than any of the preceding problems is the possibility of interpreting our behavioral results not in terms of uncontrollability and salience, but on the basis of an assumption that A's are more aroused than B's. Such an interpretation was dismissed because we were unable to detect A-B differences in autonomic arousal in several of our experiments. However, it is possible that the specific autonomic measurements used in our research were insensitive to A-B effects. It might be advisable, for example, to take continuous measurements of diastolic and systolic blood pressure, and/or precise recordings of peripheral vasoconstriction. Indeed, recent studies indicate that A's and B's may differ in these autonomic responses when both types of subjects are confronted by stressful stimulation.[5]

It should also be noted that arousal is not a unitary concept, and states of behavioral, autonomic, electrocortical, and biochemical arousal are often disassociated from one another.[6] As I noted above, there are, in fact, data suggesting that A's may be more aroused than B's as measured by biochemical indices.[7]

Additional Research on Pattern A and Uncontrollable Stress

The helplessness results observed in our laboratory studies take on added significance when viewed in the light of recent work on the relationship between disease and the magnitude of changes in an individual's life.[8] Earlier research in this area suggested that life events could be positive or negative and still lead to the onset of disease; the important factor, it was believed, was the amount of change.[9] More recent studies indicate that events may need to be negative in order to potentiate the onset of illness,[8] and there is even the suggestion that uncontrollability and helplessness induced by certain types of negative life changes may be the critical variable in facilitating the onset of some diseases.[2,10]

Consider the following array of events. Death of a close friend, a sudden financial setback, or a loss in occupational prestige, are all adverse aspects of our lives that can rarely be affected by our own actions. These losses often result in helplessness, depression, and a tendency to give up efforts to cope with the environment.[3] Engel[11] and others[12] propose that helplessness is implicated in the pathogenesis of a variety of physical diseases, ranging from the common cold to cancer. Greene, Goldstein, and Moss[13] have shown that sudden death occurs in men whose next-of-kin reported that they were depressed for a week up to several months prior to death.

While these data are certainly not conclusive, they do suggest the possibility that helplessness-inducing life events are prodromal to CHD. But why coronary disease and not some other disorder? Perhaps the Type A behavior pattern is a predisposing condition that mediates the relationship between helplessness and coronary disease. Our laboratory research indicates that extended experience with salient uncontrollable stress results in enhanced vulnerability to helplessness among Type A's. It may be, therefore, that the specific interaction of Pattern A and helplessness-inducing life events is prodromal to clinical CHD.

An ideal test of this hypothesis would require a prospective study, since consistency of results from retrospective research might conceivably reflect a tendency for some CHD cases to rationalize their illness in terms of hurrying and hard work, and/or the stress of uncontrollable life stressors. Practical considerations made it impossible for us to do longitudinal research, but it still seemed useful to conduct an exploratory retrospective project.[1,2] Therefore, hospitalized coronary patients and noncoronary controls were compared in terms of their A-B scores, as well as their recall of life events prior to disease onset. A one-year prodromal period was selected as the main focus of the study.

Three samples were used: (1) a group of 45 patients on the coronary care unit of the VA Hospital in Houston, Texas; (2) 77 patients on the general-medical and psychiatric wards—the hospitalized control group; (3) 50 building maintenance employees—the "healthy" nonhospitalized controls. Approximately 90% of this latter group were veterans, and all were free of CHD, psychiatric problems, and physical disease requiring hospitalization within the last year. All subjects were males aged 35 to 55. The three groups were frequency-matched in terms of social class, race, and religion.

The study instruments were the JAS and a modified version of the Schedule of Recent Experience. The latter measure asked the respondent to document the number of occurrences of each of 47 life events during a one-year period prior to hospitalization, or for the healthy controls, the time the questionnaire was being completed. A Loss Index was computed consisting of the percentage of cases in each sample who endorsed one or more of 10 specific events in the list of 47. These 10 items were agreed upon by three members of the research staff as reflecting stressful life events over which minimal control could be exerted; for example, "death of a close family member," "being fired," and "large decline in financial status." Selection of the items was made prior to the study. A so-called Negative Events Index was also constructed, which contained seven items designed to reflect life events that would be experienced by most individuals as stressful but not necessarily as uncontrollable or helplessness-inducing losses. Items in this index included "detention in jail" and "large increase in number of arguments with spouse."

Analysis of the JAS data revealed that coronary patients had significantly higher Pattern A scores than either the hospitalized or nonhospitalized controls. As for the Loss Index, a reliably higher percentage of each patient group (coronaries and hospitalized noncoronaries) experienced at least one loss in the one-year prodromal period compared to healthy controls. The relevant percentages were 64%, 80%, and 36%. The difference between 64 and 80 was not statistically significant. The percentages for the Negative Events Index were similar in all three samples, i.e., 49%, 57%, and 46%. None of the contrasts between these values attained even marginal levels of significance.

It would appear that helplessness-inducing life events—not just negative events—discriminate individuals with illness from those without disease. Since coronary patients have higher Pattern A scores than either hospitalized or nonhospitalized control groups, clinical CHD seems to be more likely among A's than B's, providing an excess of life events occur that are interpretable as losses of environmental control. Future research with prospective designs is obviously needed to corroborate these findings.

Conclusions

The studies cited in this paper suggest that uncontrollable stress may be a specific variable eliciting Pattern A behavior. However, it is entirely possible that a different analysis might conclude that the situations eliciting Pattern A do not constitute stress, but are more appropriately defined as challenges, that is, they signify the potential for reward rather than the threat of harm. It is conceivable, moreover, that A's respond to any type of challenge, including those that might be characterized as interpersonal and competitive. In short, Type A's may be motivated by a generalized need for social reinforcement. Future research is clearly needed to explore this and related issues, perhaps through the use of partial reinforcement designs similar to those described in Glass.[2]

The focus of this paper has been on the relationship between Pattern A and uncontrollable stress, but the major question posed to me was "What are the situational and behavioral variables that might excite physiological processes pathogenic to the cardiovascular system?" I would suggest that physiological processes mediating the association between Pattern A and uncontrollable stress may be the ones inimical to cardiovascular functioning. Although the necessary research on this issue has yet to be done—indeed, I am currently planning to conduct such experiments—preliminary specification of some of the mediating mechanisms might still be made at this time.[1,2]

A Biobehavioral Model

Evidence exists that indicates that elevated levels of adrenalin and noradrenalin may potentiate the development of coronary disease.[14,15] Since the two catecholamines are intimately related to autonomic nervous system discharge, it is not surprising that stress has been found to influence their rise and fall in the blood. It is also recognized that active coping with a stressor leads to an increased specific discharge of noradrenalin, whereas adrenalin levels remain relatively unchanged.[16-18] There are other data indicating that while adrenalin levels may rise initially in response to stressful stimulation, they decline successively as the individual increases his felt ability to master the disturbing stimuli.[19] Recent studies have also shown that severe depletion of brain noradrenalin is often associated with helplessness and giving-up responses.[20]

Consider the following integration of these biochemical results with the behavioral data reported in this paper. Once an individual perceives a threat to his sense of environmental control, he struggles, albeit with differential vigor, to reestablish and maintain control. During this period, we may expect active coping efforts and concomitant elevations in circulating noradrenalin. Adrenalin levels should remain unchanged, or perhaps, even show a decline. When the realization comes that control has been lost, the individual will become passive and give up. During this period, noradrenalin levels are likely to decline.

The alternation of control efforts followed by giving up is undoubtedly repeated over and over again during the life of an individual. It is not unreasonable to suggest that the more frequently this cycle occurs, the more the coronary arteries are likely to be affected by atherosclerotic disease. This extrapolation derives, in part, from research suggesting that excessive elevations of catecholamines over time may serve as an intermediary process whereby reactions to stressful events induce biochemical and pathogenic phenomena leading to coronary disease.[14,21] It also derives from more speculative notions implicating the rise and fall of catecholamines and rapid shifts between sympathetic and parasympathetic activity in the etiology of CHD and sudden death.[3,22,23]

Consider next how Pattern A might fit into this general picture. Studies have indicated that relative to Type B's, Type A's seem to show enhanced platelet aggregation in response to noradrenalin.[24] Moreover, at least three studies report that Type A's display elevated noradrenalin reactions to stressful stimulation, whereas Type B's fail to show this type of responsiveness.[7,24,25] Given these findings, it might be argued that the atherogenic processes described above for individuals in general apply, *a fortiori*, to Type A individuals. In other words, Pattern A subjects experience the alternation of active coping and giving up more frequently and intensely than Pattern B subjects. This assumption is not at all unreasonable if we recall that while A's vigorously engage in efforts to master their environment, nevertheless, many of these struggles end in failure and helplessness. To the extent that coronary disease is influenced by a cycle of hyperreactivity and hyporeactivity, the greater likelihood of the disease in A's *might* be explained in terms of the cumulative effects of excessive rise and fall of catecholamines released by the repetitive interplay of Pattern A and uncontrollable stress.

A first step toward testing these theoretical ideas would be to conduct experiments similar to those providing evidence for the hyper- and hyporesponsiveness of A's. These studies should involve concurrent measurements of behavioral responses and plasma catecholamines. The reactions of Type A's to brief uncontrollable stress should replicate the findings already reported in this paper. We would also expect behavioral hyperresponsiveness to be accompanied by specific elevations in plasma noradrenalin. Greater depletion of noradrenalin and, perhaps, greater increments in adrenalin might be expected to accompany the hyporesponsiveness of Type A's to prolonged uncontrollable stress. These hypotheses, if confirmed, should elucidate some of the mechanisms underlying a linkage between stress and Pattern A. To the extent that catecholamines potentiate atherogenesis, the proposed research would also shed light on processes whereby the behavior pattern and uncontrollable stress lead to cardiovascular pathology.

References

1. Glass, D.C.: Stress, behavior patterns and coronary disease. *Am Sc* **65**:177–187, 1977.
2. Glass, D.C.: Behavior Patterns, Stress, and Coronary Disease. (Chapters 4–10, 12.) Hillsdale, N.J.: Lawrence Erlbaum Associates, 1977.
3. Seligman, M.E.P.: Helplessness: On Depression, Development, and Death. San Francisco: W.H. Freeman, 1975, pp. 166–188.
4. Wortman, C.B., Brehm, J.W.: Responses to uncontrollable outcomes: an integration of reactance theory and the learned helplessness model. *In* Advances in Experimental Social Psychology (Berkowitz, L., ed.). Vol. 8. New York: Academic, 1975.
5. Dembroski, T.M., MacDougall, J.M., Shields, J.L.: Physiologic reactions to social challenge in persons evidencing the Type A coronory-prone behavior pattern. *J Human Stress* **3**:2–9, 1977.
6. Lacey, J.I.: Somatic response patterning and stress: some revisions of activation theory. *In* Psychological Stress (Appley, M.H., Trumbull, R., eds.). New York, Appleton, 1967.
7. Friedman, M., Byers, S.O., Diamant, J., Rosenman, R.H.: Plasma catecholamine response of coronary-prone subjects (Type A) to a specific challenge. *Metabolism* **24**:205–210, 1975.

8. Dohrenwend, B.S., Dohrenwend, B.P.: Stressful Life Events: Their Nature and Effects. New York: Wiley, 1974.
9. Holmes, T.H., Rahe, R.H.: The social readjustment rating scale. *J. Psychosom Res* **11**:213–218, 1967.
10. Paykel, E.S.: Life stress and psychiatric disorder: applications of the clinical approach. *In* Stressful Life Events: Their Nature and Effects (Dohrenwend, B.S., Dohrenwend, B.P., eds.). New York: Wiley, 1974.
11. Engel, G.L.: A life setting conducive to illness: the giving-up-given-up complex. *Ann Intern Med* **69**:293–300, 1968.
12. Schmale, A.H.: Giving up as a final common pathway to changes in health. *Adv Psychosom Med* **8**:18–38, 1972.
13. Greene, W.A., Goldstein, S., Moss, A.J.: Psychosocial aspects of sudden death: a preliminary report. *Arch Intern Med* **129**:725–731, 1972.
14. Raab, W., Chaplin, J.P., Bajusz, E.: Myocardial necroses produced in domesticated rats and in wild rats by sensory and emotional stresses. *Proc Soc Exp Biol Med* **116**:665–669, 1964.
15. Duguid, J.B.: Thrombosis as a factor in the pathogenesis of coronary atherosclerosis. *J Pathol* **58**:207–212, 1946.
16. Funkenstein, D.H., King, S.H., Drolette, M.E.: Mastery of Stress. Cambridge, Ma.: Harvard University Press, 1957.
17. Elmadjian, F.: Excretion and metabolism of epinephrine and norepinephrine in various emotional states. Proceedings of the 5th Pan American Congress of Endocrinology. November 1963, pp. 341–370.
18. Weiss, J.M., Stone, E.A., Harrell, N.: Coping behavior and brain norepinephrine level in rats. *J Comp Physiol Psychol* **72**:153–160, 1970.
19. Frankenhaeuser, M.: Behavior and circulating catecholamines. *Brain Res* **31**:241–262, 1971.
20. Weiss, J.M., Glazer, H.I., Pohorecky, L.A.: Coping behavior and neurochemical changes: an alternative explanation for the original "learned helplessness" experiments. *In* Psychopathology of Human Adaptation (Serban, G., ed.). New York, Plenum, 1976.
21. Rosenman, R.H., Friedman, M.: Neurogenic factors in pathogenesis of coronary heart disease. *Med Clin North Am* **58**:269–279, 1974.
22. Engel, G.L.: Sudden death and the "medical model" in psychiatry. *Can Psychiatr Assoc J* **15**:527–538, 1970.
23. Richter, C.P.: On the phenomenon of sudden death in animals and man. *Psychosom Med* **19**:191–198, 1957.
24. Simpson, M.T., Olewine, D.A., Jenkins, C.D., Ramsey, F.H., Zyzanski, S.J., Thomas, G., Hames, C.G.: Exercise-induced catecholamines and platelet aggregation in the coronary-prone behavior pattern. *Psychosom Med* **36**:476–487, 1974.
25. Friedman, M., St. George, S., Byers, S.O., Rosenman, R.H.: Excretion of catecholamines, 17-ketosteroids, 17-hydroxycorticoids, and 5-hydroxyindole in men exhibiting a particular behavior pattern associated with high incidence of clinical coronary artery disease. *J Clin Invest* **39**:758–764, 1960.

Chapter 13

Animal Models Relating Behavioral Stress and Cardiovascular Pathology

Neil Schneiderman

Introduction

At the present time there appear to be many clues, but no convincing direct evidence, specifying the exact intervening pathophysiological mechanisms that link coronary risk factors to cardiovascular disease. This is particularly true of the physiological and biochemical mechanisms that may link behavioral variables to the etiology and pathogenesis of atherosclerosis and coronary heart disease. In the face of this intransigent problem, behavioral experiments in animals offer an opportunity to study the biological mechanisms linking specific patterns of behavior with various manifestations of cardiovascular pathology.

The purpose of the present chapter is to describe the behavioral paradigms that are currently being used to study cardiovascular, neuroendocrine, and sympathoadrenomedullary changes, which may relate specific behavioral stressors to particular kinds of cardiovascular pathology. While the development of such animal models is still at an early stage, these models have furnished several interesting leads. The literature to be described in this chapter, for example, clearly indicates that prolonged, severe behavioral stress can be linked to cardiovascular pathology. More provocative are distinctions to be suggested between specific types of cardiovascular pathology and their association with alternative experimental contingencies. Some of these distinctions appear to be heuristic for understanding the behavioral contingencies that underlie coronary-prone behavior in humans. To the extent that such models are successful, they may provide a suitable vehicle for studying the pathophysiological processes that lead to coronary heart disease.

Behavioral Paradigms

Classical Conditioning

In the Pavlovian or classical conditioning experiment, a relatively neutral stimulus called the conditioned stimulus is immediately followed by another stimulus called the unconditioned stimulus. In contrast to the conditioned stimulus, the unconditioned stimulus elicits a marked response at the outset of conditioning. After repeated pairing of conditioned stimulus followed by unconditioned stimulus, the originally neutral stimulus comes to elicit a pronounced response. Most often in classical conditioning experiments concerned with cardiovascular activity, the conditioned stimulus has been a light or a tone, and the eliciting or unconditioned stimulus has been electric shock.[1-4] In some instances food,[5] a moving treadmill,[6] or intracranial electrical stimulation[7,8] have served as the unconditioned stimulus.

Changes in heart rate, myocardial contractility, cardiac output, systemic arterial blood pressure, and regional blood flow have been monitored during classical conditioning experiments. The particular cardiovascular pattern that becomes conditioned appears to be species rather than paradigm dependent. To a large extent, organisms that show a decrease in somatomotor activity during conditioning typically show one pattern of cardiovascular responses, whereas organisms that display an increase in somatomotor activity show another.[9] Cats, humans, rabbits, and rats, for example, tend to show conditioned bradycardia accompanied by decreases in somatomotor activity; whereas, dogs, monkeys, and pigeons usually show conditioned tachycardia accompanied by increases in somatomotor activity. When conditioned bradycardia occurs, it appears to be vagally mediated, but does not seem to be secondary to elevated arterial blood pressure or other responses that can modify vagal activity through baroreceptor reflexes.[10]

Changes in muscle blood flow have also been demonstrated in cats and dogs during classical conditioning. Ellison and Zanchetti,[11] for instance, conditioned cats using electric shock as the unconditioned stimulus. They observed an atropine-sensitive increase in hind-limb muscle blood flow as a conditioned response, indicative of sympathetic mediated vasodilation, which occurred only during conditioned flexion of the limb. However, when Bolme and Novotny[6] conditioned dogs using either electric shock or exercise as the unconditioned stimulus, they found that vasodilation in skeletal muscle could occur as a conditioned anticipatory response even in the absence of overt movement.

In a recent experiment, Martin et al.[12] compared cardiovascular responses in cats during situations in which a tone-conditioned stimulus was followed by either electric shock or by confrontation with a dog physically separated from the subject cat by a barrier. Vasodilation in vessels serving hind-limb skeletal muscle developed to the tone over trials in both instances, but extinguished in the confrontation situation, presumably because the cat learned that the dog could not attack it. In contrast, during a behavioral situation in which a cat's anticipation of fighting sometimes actually culminated in fighting, Adams et al.[13] observed a different cardiovascular response constellation. Adams et al. found that when an attacking cat and the subject cat were placed on opposite sides of a partitioned cage, each subject cat responded with bradycardia, decreased cardiac output, increased total peripheral resistance, mesenteric vasoconstriction, and vasoconstriction in hind-limb muscle. In contrast, once fighting began, each subject cat showed increased heart rate, cardiac output, and vasodilation in skeletal muscle, which was accompanied by a decrease in total peripheral resistance.

The magnitude of most cardiovascular changes observed during classical conditioning experiments are quite small when compared with those seen during exercise. A recent study by Gavin et al.[14] specifically compared the effects of classical conditioning and exercise upon cardiovascular responses observed in the same rhesus monkeys. It was found that during anticipation of unavoidable shock, instantaneous heart rate rose less than 20 beats per minute shortly after signal onset, then returned to baseline prior to signal offset; systolic and diastolic blood pressure increases did not exceed 10 mm Hg during the signal period. In contrast, when the same animals had to pull a T-bar (1.2 kg load) 15 times within 30 seconds to avoid shock, mean heart rate increased by more than 60 beats per minute by the end of 30 seconds, and was accompanied by monotonic increases of 40 and 29 mm Hg for systolic and diastolic pressures, respectively. Comparable results have been observed in our laboratory when lever pulling has been motivated by food reward.

Research into the classical conditioning of cardiovascular responses has typically focused upon phasic changes associated with individual trials. The effects of the conditioning procedure upon tonic cardiovascular baselines have generally been neglected. According to Dews and Herd,[15] the intrinsic rate of the heart for the rhesus monkey is approximately 150 beats per minute. In our laboratory, we have observed that when rhesus monkeys are given relatively long periods of habituation to their restraining chairs, gradual shaping of responses, and training sequences that minimize the ambiguity of stimulus cues, baseline heart rate during conditioning sessions can generally be kept near or even below the intrinsic rate. In contrast, when experimentally naive rhesus monkeys are given short periods of habituation, large numbers of trials, and/or training sequences that do not minimize ambiguity, pretrial baseline may approximate 185 beats per minute or more across daily sessions.[16,17] These findings suggest that researchers examining the effects of classical conditioning could profitably look at tonic as well as phasic cardiovascular effects induced by the conditioning procedure.

An experiment conducted by Miminoshvili, Magakian, and Kokaia[18] is suggestive. Miminoshvili et al. presented three rhesus monkeys with a number of stressful behavioral situations over a period of two years. The animals reportedly developed hypertension, coronary insufficiency, and adverse behavioral change. Although the exact experimental methods were not described in detail, the most prominent behavioral procedure seems to have been one in which aversive classical conditioning (i.e., a light signal followed by shock) was superimposed upon a bar press response for food. Miminoshvili et al. observed that during the first four months on the training schedule, blood pressure decreased from baseline. Subsequently, a sustained increase in blood pressure began to develop. The animals also developed behavioral characteristics that the investigators labeled as "neurotic." Also, in contrast to the normal diurnal pattern in which blood pressure, heart rate, and breathing rate were greater during the day than at night, Miminoshvili et al. observed that in the behaviorally disturbed state, the apogees were out of phase.

Besides examining cardiovascular changes during aversive classical conditioning, several investigators have studied psychoendocrine changes. In these experiments, as in the Miminoshvili et al.[18] study, the classical conditioning procedure has typically been superimposed upon a behavioral schedule in which the animal is required to repeatedly press a lever for food reward. After repeated pairings of conditioned and unconditioned stimuli, the animals cease responding to presentation of the conditioned stimulus. In one of these experiments, Mason et al.[19] examined concurrent plasma epinephrine, norepinephrine, and 17 hydroxycorticosteroid (17-OHCS) levels in rhesus monkeys subjected to tone-shock pairings. They found that the conditioning procedure induced marked elevations in both 17-OHCS and norepinephrine, but little or no change in epinephrine levels. Although not studied systematically, increases in epinephrine as well as norepinephrine and 17-OHCS were observed during initial aversive experiences and during complicated multiple-schedule (including classical conditioning) conditions marked by uncertainty.

Since the time of the Mason et al.[19] experiment, differential catecholamine assays have been developed, which require less than 1 ml of blood. This should facilitate more systematic and precise analyses of the conditions under which epinephrine as well as norepinephrine become elevated than was possible in the Mason et al. experiment.

Avoidance Conditioning

In the avoidance conditioning experiment, the organism is trained to avoid stimulation by making a designated response. During signalled avoidance, a warning signal warns the organism that it must make a designated response (e.g., lever pressing) to avoid being shocked. During unsignalled avoidance, the organism is required to press a level one or more times every X number of seconds to avoid or at least delay receiving a shock.

Dogs engaged in a signalled avoidance task typically reveal an increase in arterial pressure that is associated with an increase in heart rate and cardiac output accompanied by a decrease in total peripheral resistance.[20] Rhesus monkeys also show increases in blood pressure and heart rate during a signalled avoidance task, the magnitude of which is largely related to the effort the work involves.[14]

Rhesus monkeys subjected to a signalled avoidance task also show increases in plasma norepinephrine and 17-OHCS without concomitant increases in plasma epinephrine.[21] After removal of the response lever from the restraining chair during the avoidance signal, however, Mason et al. observed an increase in epinephrine level without a further increase of norepinephrine.

The effects of a signalled avoidance task upon the electrophysiological properties of the heart have also been studied.[22] Briefly, Lawler et al. measured the effective refractory period of the dog heart at different stages of a signalled avoidance experiment. This was accomplished using the addition of an extra pulse closely following a basic paced beat. The extra pulse normally induced an extrasystole. Lawler et al. then decreased the delay between the paced beat and the extra pulse until a propagated response no longer occurred. This defined the effective refractory period. It was found that the effective refractory period was decreased significantly at avoidance onset during the first five avoidance sessions, but was unaltered during the next five avoidance sessions. The changes in effective refractory period were most pronounced during the first session. These changes in refractory period were similar to those reported during stellate ganglion stimulation or catecholamine infusion in anesthetized animals.[23] Altered electrophysiological properties of the heart have previously been implicated in diverse cardiac arrhythmias, including ventricular fibrillation.[24]

In an experiment conducted upon squirrel monkeys, Herd et al.[25] found that animals trained on a signalled avoidance task for up to 200 days developed sustained increases in arterial blood pressure, both in and out of the experimental apparatus. Benson et al.[26] also observed that after prolonged training of up to four months, increases in blood pressure that occurred in the absence of lever pressing could serve as a criterion for shock avoidance.

More recently, Harris et al.[27] described the results of a series of studies with laboratory baboons in which food delivery and shock avoidance were made contingent upon specified increases in arterial pressure. They observed that pressure elevations as large as 30 to 40 mm Hg were maintained throughout repeated daily 12-hour experimental sessions over periods of at least several months. The blood pressure elevations in these baboons during the initial training sessions were accompanied by increases in heart rate and cardiac output.

Cardiovascular or biochemical changes have been examined during unsignalled as well as during signalled avoidance tasks. Dogs or monkeys engaged in unsignalled avoidance, for instance, typically reveal an increase in systemic arterial pressure that is associated with an increase in heart rate and cardiac output, but a decrease in total peripheral resistance.[28,29] Forsyth, however, observed that if his monkeys were subjected to a prolonged unsignalled avoidance session (24 to 72 hours), the increase in blood pressure became associated with an increase in total peripheral resistance.

In addition to examining the determinants of blood pressure, Forsyth[29] examined regional blood flow using a radioactive microsphere injection technique. Injections made 20 minutes after the onset of training revealed a large increase in blood flow to the heart, liver, and skeletal muscle, but a decrease in flow to the kidneys. In contrast, an injection of microspheres made after 72 successive hours of avoidance conditioning revealed increased blood flow to the heart, spleen, pancreas, and liver at the expense of the kidneys, skeletal muscle, and gastrointestinal organs. The increased resistance in skeletal muscle, which comprised more than 40% of each monkey's weight, appeared to be the predominant contributor to the observed increase in total peripheral resistance.

When rhesus monkeys were subjected to a relatively brief unsignalled avoidance session, plasma levels of norepinephrine and 17-OHCS became elevated, whereas epinephrine did not.[21] However, when monkeys were subjected to a 72-hour unsignalled avoidance session, marked elevations in urinary epinephrine occurred during the first avoidance day, then declined during the second and third avoidance days.[30]

The effects of long-term unsignalled avoidance schedules upon blood pressure have also been studied in rhesus monkeys.[31] Animals placed on a daily 12-hour avoidance schedule for 7 to 14 months ultimately became hypertensive, whereas control animals did not.

Corley et al.[32] found that EKG abnormalities and myocardial lesions, which were related to cardiovascular disease, occurred in squirrel monkeys exposed to long periods of "eight-hours on—eight-hours off" unsignalled shock avoidance. However, because no controls for shock were used, Corley et al. were unable to determine whether the myofibrillar degeneration they observed was due to the shock or to other aspects of the avoidance procedure. In a subsequent experiment, Corley et al.[33] used an "avoid-yoke" procedure to control for the effects of shock.

Avoidance-Yoke Procedure
In the "avoid-yoke" procedure the avoidance animal is trained to manipulate a lever to avoid shock.[34] Each time that the "avoidance" animal fails to meet the schedule requirement, both this animal and its "yoked" partner receive shock. Thus, both animals always receive the same number and temporal pattern of shocks, but only the "avoid" animal has control over whether shock will occur. In some experiments, other control animals are subjected to all of the experimental manipulations except shock and control over the effects of lever pressing.

In the Corley et al.[33] experiment, EKG, blood pressure, and myocardial pathology were studied in squirrel monkeys subjected to an "avoid-yoke" procedure. The animals were initially given daily one-hour sessions until fewer than ten shocks per hour were administered. Then, sessions involving eight-hour "on" avoidance periods were alternated with eight-hour "off" avoidance periods up to a limit of 96 hours per week. During each 24 hours, at least four "off" hours were spent in the home cage with food and water available. The experiment was terminated when either the "avoid" or the "yoked" animal of each pair proved to be too weak to continue.

Corley et al.[33] observed in five of six "yoked" monkeys physical deterioration and severe bradycardia with ventricular arrest, but no significant myocardial necrosis. In contrast, only one "avoid" monkey revealed the effects of stress. These findings present something of a paradox insofar as Corley et al.[32] reported that all monkeys subjected to eight hours "on-off" avoidance developed myofibrillary degeneration of the heart. The critical difference between the two studies appears to have been in the conditions for terminating the experiment. In the earlier investigation, the inability of the avoidance monkey to lever press was the criterion for termination, whereas in the later study the physical debilitation that occurred in five of six "yoked" monkeys led to earlier termination for the "avoidance" monkey. Presumably, if the "avoidance" animals in the later study had been continued in the experiment, they would have developed myofibrillary degeneration of the heart.

The observations of Corley et al.[32,33] are consistent with the results of other studies. As mentioned previously,[21,29] unsignalled avoidance can activate the sympathetic component of the autonomic nervous system. Sympathetic effects via the direct action of norepinephrine upon beta receptors in the myocardium have been demonstrated as a mechanism for myocardial necrosis.[35] The role of the central nervous system in the development of cardiac ischemia has been shown in experiments in which the hypothalamus of monkeys has been stimulated.[36] Electrical stimulation of the hypothalamus in conscious rats has also been shown to lead to sustained increases in blood pressure.[37,38]

The observations of Corley et al.[33] with regard to their "yoked" animals are also interesting in the light of other studies. Weiss,[39] for example, also showed that the "yoked" procedure can induce pathological changes. In this case, stomach ulcers were found to be more extensive in "yoked" than in "avoidance" rats. Profound bradycardia, similar to that observed by Corley et al.,[33] has also been observed in other behavioral situations. Richter,[40] for instance, found that rats that died after being subjected to severe unavoidable water stress did not drown, but instead revealed a pronounced vagally mediated bradycardia that immediately preceded death. Interestingly, Schneider[41] observed that among patients who had a past myocardial infarction, those with the greatest tendency to bradycardia in response to startle also had the poorest prognosis. In this respect, the finding by Manning and Cotten[42] that concomitant activation of sympathetic and parasympathetic inputs to the heart can facilitate severe cardiac arrhythmias is provocative. Moreover, Ebert, Allgood, and Sabiston[43] have demonstrated that the electrical instability that develops following ligation of the left anterior descending coronary artery in dogs could be prevented by cardiac denervation.

When one considers the outcomes of the two experiments by Corley et al.[32,33] together, it becomes apparent that cardiopathy, when it developed, differed between animals subjected to an unsignalled avoidance versus a "yoked" condition. Thus, squirrel monkeys subjected to unsignalled avoidance developed myofibrillar degeneration if run long enough, whereas "yoked" animals did not. In contrast, "yoked" animals ultimately revealed profound bradycardia and ventricular arrest without evidence of myofibrillar degeneration. The key difference in the experimental procedures leading to these divergent pathologies was that the animals in the "avoid" condition had control over whether they received shock, but the "yoked" animals did not. Also, the occurrence of shock was somewhat *predictable* in the "avoid," but *unpredictable* in the "yoked" condition.

Approach-Avoidance Conflict

Another paradigm that has been used to study chronic circulatory changes is the approach-avoidance conflict procedure. Friedman and Dahl[44] examined the effect of chronic conflict upon the blood pressure of rats that already had a genetic susceptibility to experimental hypertension. The strain used was originally developed by Dahl, Heine, and Tassinari[45] using selective inbreeding. Subjects of this susceptible strain develop severe, fatal hypertension from a variety of physiological insults such as excessive salt ingestion. Dahl, Heine, and Tassinari[46] have also shown that rats from the susceptible strain exhibit an exaggerated vascular reactivity to pressor agents such as norepinephrine and angiotension prior to the development of hypertension.

In the Friedman and Dahl[44] experiment, one group of rats was placed in a "conflict" condition. In this conflict condition, severely food-deprived animals were rewarded with a food pellet for the first lever press made on the average after about 50 seconds. However, every eighth bar press made by the rat also resulted in food shock. In a second condition, food-deprived rats "yoked" to the "conflict" received both food and shock unpredictably. Rats in a third condition were food deprived and received yoked-food delivery, but no experience with shock. Animals in a fourth condition were not food deprived and did not receive food on a yoked schedule, but did receive yoked-shock. A control group experienced neither food deprivation nor shock. The animals were subjected to the experimental conditions 6 hours per day, 5 days per week for at least 13 weeks. They were all maintained on a low-salt diet.

Friedman and Dahl found that the subjects exposed to conflict showed pronounced increases in systolic blood pressure. The food deprived animals that were yoked in terms of both food delivery and shock presentation showed blood pressure increases that were almost as great. These two groups were followed in descending order of degree of hypertension by the "yoked-food," "yoked-shock," and the control group.

Following the 13-week experimental period, some of the rats in each group were allowed a 13-week stress-free recovery period. The remaining animals were continued in their experimental conditions. During the recovery period, most but not all of the rats' blood pressure levels returned towards control levels.

Preavoidance Experience

Organisms subjected to repeated sessions of avoidance conditioning subsequently reveal changes from their cardiovascular baselines during the period immediately preceding these sessions.[28] In addition, the prior experience that an organism brings to an avoidance situation can influence that organism's behavioral,[47-49] physiological,[40] and biochemical[50] responses.

Anderson and Tosheff[28] studied the cardiovascular responses of dogs during daily two-hour experimental sessions consisting of a one-hour preavoidance period followed by one-hour unsignalled shock-avoidance. The results indicated that placing the animals in a restraint harness for a one-hour period immediately preceding daily sessions on the unsignalled avoidance task was associated with a preparatory cardiovascular response pattern consisting of progressive decreases in heart rate and cardiac output accompanied by a progressive increase in total peripheral resistances. This yielded a net elevation in blood pressure. As soon as the avoidance period began, cardiac output rose substantially. This further elevated blood pressure even though total peripheral resistance decreased below the level observed at the beginning of the pre-avoidance period.

The pattern of cardiovascular responses shown by dogs in the preavoidance period during the Anderson and Tosheff[28] experiment was similar to the response pattern shown by cats placed behind a glass partition shortly before episodes of fighting were to begin in the Adams et al.[13] study. In both cases, heart rate and cardiac output decreased and total peripheral resistance increased. The duration of the response pattern varied from seconds to minutes in the Adams et al. experiment and up to an hour in the Anderson and Tosheff study. The results of both investigations may be viewed as representing the conditioning of an "orienting" reflex although such a conception requires broadening the usual definition of the classical conditioning procedure.[51]

The cardiovascular responses seen in the Adams et al.[13] and Anderson and Tosheff[28] studies also bear some resemblance to the reflexive response in man to holding one's breath[52,53] and to the "diving reflex."[54] Studies of the diving reflex have shown that when a mammal submerges its head in water, marked decreases in heart rate and cardiac output occur together with a marked increase in peripheral vasoconstriction. In its purest form, it is expressed as maximal vasoconstriction to minimize peripheral oxygen loss with a similar decrease in oxygen to other systems including skeletal muscle. Such a response constellation favors circulation of the blood between the heart and the brain.

The response constellation has also been elicited by electrical stimulation of the brainstem in rats.[55] The decrease in heart rate that occurs under such circumstances is mediated by decreases in sympathetic and increases in parasympathetic activity. Wolf[56] has suggested that sudden death may result from the same physiological mechanisms controlling the diving reflex, a view that would be consistent with the pronounced bradycardia seen in the Corley et al.[33] and Richter[40] experiments.

A number of experimenters have subjected animals to severe stressors and then observed behavioral and/or biological responses when the animals were subsequently faced with an instrumental contingency. In the Richter[40] experiment, for instance, dewhiskered rats immersed in water responded with severe bradycardia followed by sudden death unless the animals were specifically shaped to come to the surface and resume swimming. According to Richter, the unshaped rats situation at death was not characterized by a fight or flight reaction, but rather by a reaction of "giving up."

A decade later, Overmier and Seligman[47] and Seligman and Maier[48] reported that dogs failed to learn to avoid or escape shock by jumping a hurdle from one side of a box to the other after being exposed to shock over which they had no control. In contrast, animals exposed to similar shocks while performing an avoidance-escape response showed no impairment in subsequent avoidance performance. Like Richter[40] before them, Seligman and his co-workers attributed the deficit in avoidance performance to the animals "giving up," or as they called it, "learned helplessness." According to the "learned helplessness" hypothesis, animals exposed to a stressor they cannot control may learn that their behavior cannot control the environment. "Learned helplessness" has subsequently been proposed as an analogue for depression.[57]

Weiss, Stone, and Harrell[58] proposed an alternative explanation for the performance deficits seen in the so-called learned helplessness experiments. They termed their alternative explanation the "motor activation deficit" hypothesis. According to this notion, animals exposed to a severe inescapable stressor develop a depletion of brain norepinephrine. As a consequence of this noradrenergic deficiency, the animals are able to mediate only a limited amount of motor activity. This amount of motor activity is insufficient for learning and performance of appropriate instrumental responses. In support of the "motor activation deficit" hypothesis, Weiss and Glazer[49] showed that rats immersed in water subsequently showed an escape-avoidance deficit if the instrumental task required considerable motor activity, but showed little deficit if the instrumental task required a small amount of motor activity.

In another study Weiss et al.[50] showed that whereas rats receiving a single exposure to cold swim or electric shock showed a large avoidance-escape deficit, subjects that received repeated exposure to the stressor for a two-week period performed similarly to a control group that received no stressor. Similarly, rats that received one session of the inescapable shock stressor showed a lower level of norepinephrine in the hypothalamus and cortex than did control rats or rats that received repeated exposure to inescapable shock.

As further support for the "motor activation deficit" hypothesis, Glazer et al.[59] found that depletion of monoamines by a single injection of tetrabenazine produced an active avoidance-escape deficit in rats when the avoidance-escape response involved a relatively high degree of motor activity, but not when a minimum of motor activity was required. These investigators also observed that by decreasing the stress-induced depletion of monoamines by the use of a monoamine oxidase (MAO) inhibitor, they could protect the animals from the effects of inescapable shock. Thus, the MAO inhibitor reduced the avoidance-escape deficit produced by the unavoidable shocks.

Although Weiss and his collaborators have not yet extended their experiments to an analysis of cardiovascular performance, the bradycardia observed in the Richter[40] experiment is consistent with the "motor activation deficit" hypothesis. Thus, studies of cardiac-somatic coupling have indicated that vagally mediated reflexive bradycardia occurs in sympathetically aroused animals when these animals inhibit their somatic activity.[60] The vagally mediated cardiac component of the baroreceptor reflex is sufficiently strong to override the concomitant sympathetic activation of the heart.[61]

Psychosocial Stress

Numerous studies have documented that the psychosocial environment in which an organism finds itself has a profound influence upon the circulation. Henry et al.[62] found that mice raised in isolation developed sustained hypertension when as adults they were exposed to frequent confrontation in an "intercommunicating" box system. In contrast, control animals reared in groups remained normotensive under such circumstances. Subsequent experiments have suggested that the pressure elevations in the socially stressed isolates were related to a pronounced increase in sympathetic nervous system activity.[63] Moreover, Henry et al. showed that at least some of these changes were apparently mediated by an increase in the adrenal enzymes, tyrosine hydroxylase and phenylethanolamine N-methyltransferase. Because it takes many hours to induce an increase in the level of these enzymes and for the increase to return to control levels, the increases observed appear to reflect a situation in which brief sympathetic discharges elicited by discontinuous emotional stimuli have become transformed into sustained sympathetic arousal. Henry et al.[64] have further indicated that mice subjected to the kind of stresses described in the companion study developed interstitial nephritis, aortic arteriosclerosis, intramural coronary artery sclerosis, and myocardial fibrosis.

Henry et al.[65] have also examined changes that occur in adrenal weight and blood pressure as a function of dominant and submissive roles assumed by mice in normally socialized colonies. During the early stages of colony differentiation, dominant mice show increased sympathetic arousal as compared with subordinates. In contrast, the subordinates reveal a relative increase in adrenocortical activity. These biochemical changes eventually vanish after about five months, but are replaced by chronic increases in blood pressure for the dominant and an increase in adrenal weight for the submissive animals. The dichotomous physiological and morphological changes observed between the dominant and submissive mice by Henry and his collaborators are reminiscent of the changes observed by Corley et al.[32,33] in the shock avoidance studies.

Psychosocial interactions have also been associated with circulatory changes in the tree shrew.[66,67] After initial fights, the subjugated tree shrew was placed in a cage that was separated only by a wire mesh from the victor. Subjugated animals hardly moved, spent almost all day lying motionless in a corner, but were obviously sympathetically aroused as evidenced by the sustained erection of the animals' tail hairs. If the dominant shrew was allowed to attack its victim, the subordinate animal did not resist. Although the attacks were not lethal, some of the defeated shrews died soon afterward, possibly from the type of cardiac arrest described by Richter.[40]

Von Holst[67] observed that subjugated animals separated from the victor by a wire mesh sank into a coma and died in uremia due to renal insufficiency. The time period varied from a couple of days to about two weeks. At autopsy, there was evidence of an acute decrease of renal blood flow with tubular necrosis and glomerular ischemia.

The effects of psychosocial changes upon circulatory performance have also

been examined in hamadryas baboons. Lapin and Cherkovitch[68] used a behavioral paradigm first developed by Miminoshvili[69] to study behavior reactions to stress. In this type of experiment, a dominant male baboon was
separated from the females and juveniles with whom he previously roamed
freely. The entire family was placed in an enclosure, but a wire mesh screen
separated the dominant male from his companions.

The large dominant male baboon initially showed considerable agitation as
evidenced, for instance, by loud, angry vocalizations. Although the agitated
behavior soon subsided, it was readily aroused by departures in routine from
the free state. Thus, for example, if the females and juveniles were fed first, the
large male would protest. When another male was put in with the females, the
subject became extremely agitated and violent. Lapin and Cherkovitch noted
that the subject male became chronically hypertensive after several months.

Physiological Mechanisms

The results of the behavioral experiments just reviewed indicate that different
behavioral situations elicit specific cardiovascular changes. When organisms
engage in behaviors that are neither too stressful nor too prolonged, the cardiovascular changes observed seem appropriate to the energy requirements of
the situation and the physical capacity of the organism. If, however, the
behavioral situation is both aversive and prolonged, or if the acute situation is
extremely stressful, adverse physiological and morphological changes may
occur. These changes may ultimately result in sudden death following pronounced bradycardia, as in the case of water stressed rats[40] and defeated tree
shrews,[66,67] or may result in hypertension, aortic arteriosclerosis, intramural
coronary artery sclerosis, and myocardial fibrosis, as in isolated mice thrown
into close group living for an extended period of time.[64]

Although a very large number of cardiovascular adjustments may be distinguished, it is possible to differentiate them into two broad categories. One of
these categories, which is associated with increased motoric activity such as
occurs during fight or flight, is characterized by increases in heart rate, cardiac
output, and vasodilation in skeletal muscle. This pattern is often seen in
socially dominant animals and/or in animals performing well-learned coping
responses requiring exertion. The second category, which is associated with
decreased motoric activity such as occurs during behavioral freezing or the
anticipation of some aversive situation is characterized by vagally-mediated
bradycardia. One exception to this pattern is that during diving, bradycardia
may persist even during the vigorous exercise of underwater swimming.[70]

The distinction between cardiovascular response patterns and their relationship to motoric activity is not limited to the realm of aversive behaviors.
Bradycardia associated with decreased motoric activity may be seen in the
orienting responses of some species (e. g., rabbits), and during vigilance tasks
such as reaction time experiments. Increases in heart rate, cardiac output, and
increased vasodilation in muscle associated with increased motoric activity

may be seen in pleasantly competitive exercise tasks, as well as in fight or flight reactions.

Even within the realm of aversive behaviors, the two broad categories of cardiovascular response may each be seen in situations ranging from those that are only mildly unpleasant to situations involving a threat to life itself. And both cardiovascular patterns may be associated with profound psychoendocrine changes. Each of the two broad categories, however, appears to be organized by the central nervous system (CNS).

Current conceptions of CNS control of the circulation emphasize that neural integration occurs at virtually every level from the cortex to the spinal cord.[71,72] It was once believed that medullary centers in the dorsal reticular formation exerted almost exclusive control over both vascular tone and reflexive cardiovascular adjustments, but this view has undergone considerable modification. The essential role of the bulbar reticular formation in the central cardiovascular regulation is still recognized, but its eminence is shared with supramedullary integrative mechanisms.

Neural Control of Bradycardia

The nerves that innervate the heart are part of the autonomic nervous system. Under most conditions, the sinoatrial node is under the tonic influence of the parasympathetic nervous system, whose postganglionic fibers liberate acetylcholine, and by the sympathetic nervous system, whose postganglionic fibers liberate norepinephrine. Parasympathetic control over the heart is exercised by the vagus nerves, which originate in the dorsal medulla. Sympathetic control over the heart is exercised by the superior, middle, and inferior cardiac nerves. The cardiac sympathetic fibers originate in the intermediolateral columns of the upper five or six segments of the thoracic cord. Provided that both the vagus and cardiac nerves are exerting tonus on the heart, bradycardia can be mediated by an increase in vagus nerve activation, a decrease in cardiac nerve activation (sympathetic inhibition), or a combination of the two.

Bradycardia responses can be initiated centrally or as reflexive changes to increases in systemic arterial pressure. This latter adjustment occurs as part of the baroreceptor reflex. Mechanoreceptors sensitive to changes in arterial pressure are known as baroreceptors. The major groups of baroreceptors lie within the walls of the carotid sinus and aortic arch although some receptors are located along the thoracic aorta as well as the subclavian, common carotid, and mesenteric arteries.[73]

Impulses from the carotid sinus and aortic arch reach the medulla via the glossopharyngeal and vagus nerves, respectively. In rabbits, the aortic nerve (containing purely baroreceptor afferent information) travels separately from the vagus nerve in the cervical neck region. In any event, section of barosensory nerves causes a rapid rise in arterial pressure indicating that the nerves are tonically active. In contrast, an increase in baroreceptor stimulation leads to a pronounced reflexive decrease in heart rate and a diminution in blood pressure unless the reflex is gated in the CNS. The bradycardia is primarily mediated by the vagus nerves. Systemic injections of atropine that block the vagus nerve and abolish the bradycardia do not eliminate the systemic hypotension. This suggests that the diminution in pressure is due largely to an inhibition of vasoconstrictor activity.[72]

The cells of origin of vagal cardioinhibitory fibers have been anatomically localized in the dorsal motor nucleus in several species such as the rabbit,[74] the pigeon,[75] and the monkey,[76] but are located in the nucleus ambiguus of cats.[77,78] Cardioinhibitory efferent cells have also been located electrophysiologically in the dorsal motor nucleus of the rabbit[79] and in the nucleus ambiguus of the cat.[80]

Recently, Kaufman et al.[81] have found a discrete area in the lateral subthalamus, which when stimulated elicits pronounced bradycardia and only a secondary fall in blood pressure. Neurons in this area receive input from more rostral areas in the brain as well as barosensory information. Kaufman et al. have also observed that single pulse stimulation of the "bradycardia" area of the lateral subthalamus is capable of activating cardioinhibitory efferent neurons in dorsal motor nucleus at short latency. An important mechanism involved in eliciting the bradycardia response from supramedullary structures is temporal summation.

Electrical stimulation of the anterior hypothalamus of the cat[82] or the rabbit[83] has also been shown to elicit bradycardia. Electrophysiological recordings from single units in the anterior hypothalamus of the cat[84] and the rabbit[85] indicate that neurons in this region receive barosensory information. In addition, studies by Klevans and Gebber[86] in the cat and by Gimpl et al.[83] in rabbits have indicated that stimulation of the anterior hypothalamus can augment or potentiate the effects of baroreceptor afferent stimulation. The bradycardia responses elicited by stimulation of the anterior hypothalamus apparently reflect descending corticofugal[87] as well as barosensory influences.

In the Brickman et al.[85] study, it was found that anterior hypothalamic units, which receive barosensory input, also are influenced by stimulation of the anterior caudate nucleus. Because the caudate is a major structure in the extrapyramidal system, which is involved in postural adjustments and gross body movements, it seems conceivable that such neurons may play some role in cardiosomatic integration.

Other structures that may be involved in the organization of the bradycardia response are the septal region, and in some species, the amygdala. Calaresu, Ciriello, and Mogenson,[88] for instance, found that electrical stimulation of histologically localized sites in the lateral septum of the rat elicited bradycardia and hypotension. Faiers, Calaresu, and Mogenson[89] have also reported that stimulation of the central, basal, and lateral nuclei of the rat's amygdala evoke bradycardia and hypotension, a finding that we have replicated in the rabbit.

Neural Control of Cardiovascular Responses Accompanying Motoric Activity

Two closely related, but distinguishable systems have been linked to sympathetic activation of the circulation. One of these systems, which is importantly involved in muscular exercise, originates in the motor cortex and descends through the hypothalamus, midbrain, and lower brain stem.[90] The other system, which appears to be activated during defensive or agonistic behavior, has its origin in the amygdala, enters the hypothalamus via the ventral amygdalofugal pathway, and reportedly descends through the brainstem in a similar fashion to the exercise system.[91,92]

One of the distinguishing characteristics of activation of the "defense" or "exercise" systems is sympathetically mediated vasodilation, that in part results from vasoconstriction of the high resistance vessels in other vascular beds such as the skin, intestines, and kidneys.[93] Other hemodynamic responses include an increase in heart rate and cardiac output. Because electrical stimulation of the posterior hypothalamus has been shown to abolish the cardiac component of the baroreceptor reflex, the increase in heart rate occurring during muscular exercise or defensive behavior has been attributed to an active inhibition of the reflexive bradycardia.[93,94] This view is supported by findings that electrical stimulation of the posterior hypothalamus of the cat inhibits barosensory neurons in the tractus solitarius in the medulla.[95,96]

Although the "defense" and "exercise" pathways appear to be closely related to one another, there seems to be considerable justification for distinguishing between them. Thus, for example, while inhibition of the cardiac component of the baroreceptor reflex has been considered to be characteristic of the defense reaction,[83,93] others have shown that electrical stimulation of the posterior hypothalamus can abolish the cardiac component of the baroreceptor reflex in conscious rabbits that are not emotionally aroused. Pribram and McGuinness[97] have also reported that lesions of the defense pathway (amygdala) abolished the visceroautonomic accompaniments of orienting, but left the somatic components intact. Previously, Abrahams et al.[98] had found that while vasodilation in muscle could be elicited by midbrain stimulation of the subcollicular region, central gray, and peduncular area, only stimulation of the subcollicular region or central gray evoked defensive behavior.

Several investigators have attempted to examine the role of the hypothalamus in sympathetic control of the heart and blood vessels. In one study Gebber et al.[99] found that electrical stimulation of the posterior hypothalamus in cats elicited a vasopressor response. Stimulation from each of these sites also elicited a compound action potential in the external carotid nerve. This nerve innervates the carotid body and bifurcation, and is composed primarily of sympathetic postganglionic vasoconstrictor fibers. Gebber et al.[99] found that the long, but not the short latency components of the postganglionic compound action potential were inhibited by baroreceptor excitation. The authors therefore suggested that the vasopressor outflow from the hypothalamus is organized into two parallel systems, each of which is related differently to the baroreceptor reflex. Presumably, the barosensory-resistant pathway may be functionally related to the sustained vasopressor responses observed during stress or exercise.

Electrophysiological evidence has also been presented; by Thomas and Calaresu[78] and Thomas et al.[100] for the existence of a sympathoexcitatory pathway, which when stimulated in the posteromedial hypothalamus projects to the lateral reticular nucleus of the medulla before relaying to the inferior cardiac nerve. This pathway appears to be separate from the one described by Gebber et al.[90] since the compound action potentials recorded by Calaresu and his co-workers were inhibited by baroreceptor activation although the latencies of some of the responses were comparable to those found in the baroreceptor resistant pathway.

One of the more intransigent problems encountered by investigators attempting to examine the neural control of the circulation has been the identification of postganglionic vasodilator fibers. Recently, Horeyseck et al.[101] found that spontaneously active postganglionic sympathetic fibers could be driven from sites in the hypothalamus that elicited vasoconstrictor responses. In contrast, spontaneously silent postganglionic sympathetic fibers could be driven from sites in the hypothalamus that evoked vasodilation in skeletal muscle.

Pathophysiology

The exact pathophysiological mechanisms that link behavioral stress to cardiovascular pathology are presently a matter of speculation, but it is likely that changes in lipid metabolism and catecholamine influences upon cardiovascular dynamics are important mediators. Evidence has been presented that the initiating lesion in coronary artery disease, which is the atheromatous plaque, develops as a result of mechanical injury to the linings of the affected artery because of increased turbulence.[102]

Studies of avoidance-schedule induced hypertension in nonhuman primates indicate that the development of sustained hypertension is preceded by a phase in which heart rate and cardiac output are both elevated.[27,103] Similarly, studies conducted upon human patients have also suggested that in the early labile stage of essential hypertension, cardiac output is elevated due to an increase in heart rate, and that total peripheral resistance is fairly normal.[104] In contrast, as the hypertension progresses to a fixed state, heart rate and cardiac output return to lower values; whereas, total peripheral resistance increases due to peripheral vasoconstriction. If the turbulence hypothesis of atherosclerosis formation is correct, it would appear that elevated arterial pressure due to increases in heart rate and cardiac output may play a role in the development of atheromatous plaques. This could occur, even if the increases in pressure occurred periodically and did not lead to sustained hypertension.

Animal as well as human research, suggests that coronary artery disease may be due to an interaction of hereditary and behavioral factors. Strains of rats, for example, have been bred which become "spontaneously" hypertensive over time.[105] This appears to be due to changes that occur in the sympathetic nervous system.[106] Increased reactivity to catecholamines has also been implicated in the developemnt of essential hypertension in humans.[107]

Although increased blood pressure may very well be an important determinant of atheroma formation, the Framingham study established that mortality risk is proportional to blood lipid as well as blood pressure level.[108] Direct experimental evidence relating the interaction of blood lipids and blood pressure upon atheroma formation has been provided by animal experiments showing that lipid-induced atherosclerosis can be accelerated by raising the blood pressure of the animal.[109] Interestingly, catecholamines are apparently the most important factors promoting lipid mobilization.[110] In general, the studies just described, support Herd's hypothesis (see Chapter 9) that neuroendocrine responses and alterations in lipid metablism promote atherogenesis, and thereby serve as predisposing factors in coronary heart disease.

The clinical manifestation of coronary heart disease may occur through several mechanisms. Thus, the precipitating event may be an embolism, thrombosis, or arrhythmia. One possible mechanism that might precipitate a coronary event is an increase in platelet aggregation that is associated with increased levels of circulating catecholamines.[111] This could lead to acute occlusion of arterial vessels during behavioral stress. Another mechanism that may precipitate the clinical manifestations of coronary heart disease may involve the production of cardiac arrythmias. These have been found to occur in predisposed individuals during exercise[112] and emotional stress[113] and can be related to increased catecholaminergic activity. So too, can the myocardial focal damage observed in squirrel monkeys that died while working on an avoidance task.[32]

Although many of the manifestations of coronary heart disease may be related to neuroendocrine and sympathoadrenal responses, other factors may also be operative. Thus, the arrythmias associated with profound bradycardia in animals lacking control over highly aversive situations[33,40] may be related to either (1) concomitant release of norepinephrine and acetylcholine at the heart[42] during an exaggerated baroreceptor reflex response,[61] (2) myocardial ischemia related to increased oxygen demands due to sympathetic arousal coupled with decreased cardiac output, which might be related to an exaggerated breath withholding or baroreceptor reflex, or (3) the inducement of abberant phase relationships between vagal firing and the cardiac cycle.[114] Concerning this last possibility, studies by Levy and his colleagues have indicated that the phase of the cardiac cycle at which the vagus nerves are stimulated is a critical determinant of both heart rate and AV conduction time. Moreover, vagal stimulation can make the SA node unstable, or depress the SA node, and prevent an AV junctional escape rhythm from emerging during periods of asystole by concomitant vagal suppression of the junctional pacemakers. Interestingly, Schneider[41] has observed that among patients who had a past myocardial infarction, those with the greatest tendency to bradycardia in response to startle also had the poorest prognosis.

Discussion

The most salient finding to be derived from the present review of the animal literature is that a variety of experimental paradigms have incontrovertably linked prolonged, severe behavioral stress with the development of cardiovascular pathology. More provocative are distinctions to be made between specific types of pathology and their association with alternative experimental contingencies. One obvious distinction that can be made is in terms of control over the environment.

In general, animals confronted with severe or prolonged aversive situations tend to reveal one pattern of cardiovascular performance if a coping response is available, but another pattern of cardiovascular performance in the absence of a coping response. During avoidance conditioning, for example, when the animal's response controls the delivery of shock, the animal's cardiovascular responses tend to include increases in heart rate, cardiac output, systemic arterial pressure, and vasodilation in skeletal muscle.[28,29] Similar cardiovascular changes have been observed during attack behavior.[13] In contrast to the pattern of cardiovascular responses that occur when an animal is able to exert control over its environment, different cardiovascular changes seem to occur when an animal lacks control over its environment. Thus, during a pre-avoidance session,[28] anticipation of fighting,[13] a "yoked" procedure,[33] and after inescapable water stress[40] animals showed pronounced bradycardia.

When the animals that have a coping response in their repertoire develop cardiovascular symptoms, they can occur in the form of hypertension[25,27,31] and myofibrillar degeneration. In contrast, animals that do not have a coping response in their repertoire may reveal profound bradycardia and ventricular arrest without evidence of myofibrillar degeneration if confronted with severe stress.[33,40]

If one assumes that a dominant animal is one that usually attempts to assert control over its environment, the findings of Henry and his co-workers can also be integrated within the coping-noncoping framework. Recall that Henry et al.[65] found that dominant mice showed increased sympathetic arousal as compared with subordinates. Henry et al. also found that the dominant mice developed chronic increases in blood pressure, whereas the subordinate mice did not. Moreover, Henry et al.[64] have shown that mice who become hypertensive also developed interstitial nephritis, aortic arteriosclerosis, intramural coronary artery sclerosis, and myocardial fibrosis.

Although one pattern of cardiovascular response in typically associated with the presence of a coping response and another with its absence, the generalization is not invariable. In aversive classical conditioning, during which the animal does not have a coping response available, cats, humans, rabbits, and rats tend to show conditioned bradycardia; whereas, dogs, monkeys, and pigeons usually show conditioned tachycardia.[9] The cardiovascular pattern that becomes conditioned seems to be related to whether or not the species typically engages in skeletal motor activity during the preshock signal. Gavin et al.[14] among others have noted that the tachycardia response in rhesus monkeys occurs at the onset of the signal and then recedes to the baseline before the shock occurs. In addition, we have observed that the rhesus monkey shows the same heart rate and blood pressure changes during appetitive as during aversive classical conditioning. It would therefore seem that in most instances of classical conditioning—unless a severe shock is used—a conditioned "orienting" rather than a conditioned "defensive" reaction is being monitored. Interestingly, when Yehle et al.[115] used a 20 mA paraorbital shock during classical conditioning of the rabbit, the conditioned responses consisted of a vasopressor response and bradycardia. In contrast, during subsequent studies[116] which a 3–5 mA shock was used, the conditioned response always consisted of bradycardia in the absence of a pressor response.

Thus far the discussion has centered upon situations in which a coping response is either present or absent, and differential cardiovascular responses have been related to this variable. In situations in which a coping response is present, aversive consequences are predictable. However, in situations during which a coping response is not present, an aversive consequence may or may not be predictable. Thus, during classical conditioning, in which a coping response is not available, shock may be predictable; whereas, in an avoidance-yoke experiment, the yoked animal also has no coping response, but the shock would be unpredictable. In the Richter experiment,[40] dewhiskered rats showed bradycardia and sudden death if suddenly immersed in water and not subsequently "shaped" to swim. For the animals that were "shaped" to swim, swimming may have become a coping response, but immersion in water also became a more predictable occurrence. It would therefore appear that further research is needed to separate out cardiovascular effects associated with the presence or absence of a coping response from those associated with predictability versus nonpredictability.

The possible mechanisms mediating stress-induced cardiovascular pathology are largely a matter of speculation although some interesting clues exist. In highly aversive, predictable situations, rhesus monkeys appear to respond with an increase in plasma norepinephrine and 17-OHCS, whereas the level of epinephrine does not increase.[21] However, when rhesus monkeys were given protracted training sessions, the level of urinary epinephrine increased during the first 24 hours and then gradually declined. In rats, sympathetic responses during prolonged stress seem to have been at least partially mediated by an increase in the adrenal enzymes, tyrosine hydroxylase, and phenylethanolamine N-methyltransferase.[63]

Further evidence that animals who receive predictable shocks and also possess a coping response respond to prolonged stress with sympathetic arousal, was presented in the Corley et al. experiments.[32,33] In these studies, squirrel monkeys subjected to a prolonged shock-avoidance schedule suffered myofibrillary degeneration of the heart similar to that seen after infusion of norepinephrine.[35]

During highly aversive unpredictable situations, plasma epinephrine as well as norepinephrine and 17-OHCS become elevated. Also, when rats receive a highly aversive, unpredictable stress experience they tend to show a depletion in brain catecholamine that is associated with a "motor activation deficit."[50] This deficit is compatible with the initiation of a baroreceptor response resulting in profound bradycardia. The animal data therefore seem to suggest that dominant animals, and animals that possess coping responses will respond to predictable stressful situations by generalized sympathetic arousal. In contrast, subjugated animals and animals that do not possess coping responses may respond to stressful situations by an inhibition of motor activity and bradycardia. Even to the casual observer, these latter animals may seem to be severely depressed.

In the literature on humans, individuals who exhibit excessive achievement striving, time urgency, and hostility have been classified as Type A.[117] This behavior pattern has been linked in humans to the occurrence of coronary heart disease. One study, for example, showed that Type A men had more than twice the rate of heart disease during an eight and one-half year prospective study, than did men not showing this pattern.[118] It was also found that a higher incidence in Type A men still prevailed when adjustments were made for traditional risk factors such as cigarette smoking, serum cholesterol, and hypertension.

Several years ago Glass[119] began a series of studies to determine whether individuals classified as Type A exhibit excessive achievement striving, time urgency, and hostility when placed in stressful experimental situations. Briefly, Glass found that Type A students in contrast to non-Type A college students, worked hard to succeed, suppressed feelings of fatigue that might interfere with task performance, and exhibited rapid pacing of their activities. Glass argued that Type A individuals adhered to this pattern in the interest of asserting control over an environment that they perceived as threatening.

In Glass's experiments, the initial reaction of Type A college students was one of hyperresponsiveness, which appeared to reflect a concerted effort to assert control over the environment. This pattern even extended itself to uncontrollable situations where non-Type A individuals would readily give up.

The responses of Glass's Type A individuals seem reminiscent of the animals previously described, who were either dominant or who possessed a coping mechanism. Such animals tended to respond to aversive situations by becoming sympathetically aroused and increasing motor activity. If this was the case, however, and if we could generalize from the literature on animals to humans, we might expect that these individuals would develop essential hypertension rather than coronary heart disease.

Faced with the above dilemma, it becomes necessary to invoke other assumptions and hypotheses to at least speculatively tie the two literatures together. At the outset, it should be noted that most Type A men do not die of coronary heart disease. Moreover, it is not known how Type A men respond to a severe, uncontrollable, real-life stressor. While Glass's student subjects did not develop general expectations of uncontrollability, and indeed, became more motivated to assert control, it is conceivable that when faced with a severe, truly uncontrollable, unpredictable situation (e.g., spouse's death, job loss), some Type A individuals might be left without an adequate coping mechanism. In fact, it might even follow from Glass's findings that Type A individuals faced with a severe stressor might exhibit greater hyporesponsiveness than non-Type A individuals, because of their tendency to experience loss of control as more threatening.

Several studies conducted upon humans have suggested that helplessness-inducing life events may be prodromal to coronary heart disease. Greene et al.[120] for instance, have shown that sudden death due to coronary heart disease has been associated disproportionately often by reports from next-of-kin that the deceased was severely depressed in the period preceding death. In another study, Glass[121] found that coronary patients had reliably higher Type A scores than nonhospitalized controls matched for sex, age, social class, race, and religion. He also found that a significantly higher percentage of helplessness-inducing losses occurred in the one-year prodromal period for the coronary patients compared to healthy control subjects.

These findings are also consistent with those of Rahe,[122] who found that coronary heart disease was associated with high scores on a questionnaire that assessed significant life changes of recent origin, such as job loss or death of a spouse. These results therefore help to resolve the apparent discrepancies between animal and human research findings.

Conclusions

The studies cited in this paper link prolonged, severe behavioral stress with the development of cardiovascular pathology. A distinction was made between predictability, control, and dominance on the one hand, and unpredictability, helplessness, and a submissive posture on the other. In the face of severe or prolonged aversive stimulation, dominant animals, who possess an appropriate coping response and a predictable schedule, will respond to the situation with sympathetic arousal until the stressor is removed. If stress becomes too protracted, the animal may develop hypertension, structural vascular damage, and myofibrillar degeneration. In contrast to dominant animals, and those possessing an effective coping mechanism, submissive animals and animals lacking control or predictability over aversive situations may respond with an inhibition of motor activity, depression, profound bradycardia, and ultimately, ventricular fibrillation.

Although the distinction just drawn is supported by experimental evidence, programmatic research is needed to determine the exact behavioral and physiological mechanisms involved. Interestingly, both the animal and clinical human literature describe similar progressive changes in the course of some cardiovascular diseases. Thus, for example, studies conducted upon rhesus monkeys[29,31] and upon humans[123] suggest that the early stages leading to essential hypertension may be characterized by increased heart rate and cardiac output; whereas, later stages of hypertension are associated with normal cardiac output, but increased peripheral resistance. The biological mechanisms underlying these changes are not well understood. Consequently, developmental models are needed to elucidate these changes. Such models need to comprehensively monitor cardiovascular performance, the renin-angiotensin system, psychoendocrine changes, and responses to sympathetic challenge over prolonged periods of time.

While the animal literature has provided provocative clues concerning sudden death and coronary heart disease, neither the underlying physiological mechanisms nor the exact behavioral contingencies have been adequately defined. The CNS pathways and neuronal mechanisms involved also need clarification. So, too, do the biochemical changes involved in stress-induced coronary heart disease.

One of the most difficult problems yet to be faced by those investigating animal models of coronary heart disease is the interaction of other risk factors with stress. Thus, for example, it would be interesting to examine the interaction between stress and salt concentration in the diets of rats genetically susceptible to experimental hypertension.[124] The report by Friedman and Rosenman[125] that Type A individuals have higher serum cholesterol levels than non-Type A individuals suggests that relationships among specific stressors, diet, and serum cholesterol could profitably be studied in behaving animals. Interestingly, Gunn et al.[126] have already shown that chronic stimulation of the ventromedial hypothalamus of the rabbit accelerated the process of atherosclerosis induced by a diet high in cholesterol.

Another area of investigation that needs study is the effect of stress upon already damaged hearts and/or circulatory systems. Most animal models of stress have concerned themselves with the effects of stress upon healthy individuals. Animal models need to be developed to study the effects of stress upon circulatory systems that more closely approximate the conditions of middle-aged persons, who have already begun to suffer debilitation of bodily systems. Thus, for example, Raab[127] has suggested that anginal attacks correlated with acute stress-induced increases in plasma catecholamine levels are explicable when one considers that both epinephrine and norepinephrine cause an increase in the consumption of oxygen by the heart.

One of the hypotheses presented in the present paper is that dominant animals facing predictable stressors for which coping mechanisms exist, may characteristically respond to the environment with fairly sustained sympathetic arousal. The sympathetic arousal could lead to an increased cholesterol level,[125] hypertension,[25,29,65] decreased clotting time,[125] atherosclerosis,[64] and myofibrillary degeneration.[33] If indeed the person showing Type A behavior is an assertive individual constantly striving to achieve mastery over a threatening environment, then it is likely that such a person might acquire some of the symptoms just described over a prolonged period of time. This inevitably leads to the question of whether the person who chronically displays Type A behavior becomes increasingly vulnerable to the adverse consequences evoked by a profound unavoidable stressor such as divorce, a spouse's death, job loss, or retirement.

In view of this possibility, programmatic research is needed in which organisms are subjected to prolonged, intensive avoidance training or psychosocial stress, and then subjected to a severe unavoidable stressor. Cardiovascular performance and myocardial oxygenation as well as psychoendocrine changes should be carefully monitored to determine the exact mechanisms that are operative when animals respond to severe unavoidable stress with profound bradycardia. If such animal models can be developed, it will help clarify the mechanisms relating behavioral stress and specific cardiovascular pathologies.

References

1. Cohen, D.H., Durkovic, R.G.: Cardiac and respiratory conditioning, differentiation, and extinction in the pigeon. *J. Exp Anal Behav* **9**:681–688, 1966.
2. Dykman, R.A., Gantt, W.H., Whitehorn, J.C.: Conditioning as emotional sensitization and differentiation. *Psychol Monographs* **79**:1–17, 1956.
3. Obrist, P.A., Webb, R.A.: Heart rate during conditioning in dogs: relationship to somatic-motor activity. *Psychophysiology* **4**:7–34, 1967.
4. Schneiderman, N., VanDercar, D.H., Yehle, A.L., Manning, A.A., Golden, T., Schneiderman, E.: Vagal compensatory adjustment: relationship to heart-rate classical conditioning in rabbits. *J Comp Physiol Psychol* **68**:176–183, 1969.
5. Randall, D.C., Brady, J.V., Martin, K.H.: Cardiovascular dynamics during classical appetitive and aversive conditioning in laboratory primates. *Pavlov J Biol Sc* **10**:66–75, 1975.
6. Bolme, P., Novotny, J.: Conditional reflex activation of the sympathetic cholinergic vasodilator nerves in the dog. *Acta Physiol Scand* **77**:58–67, 1969.
7. Brickman, A., Schneiderman, N.: Classical conditioning of cardiovascular changes in rabbits using stimulation of posterior hypothalamus as the US. *Psychophysiology* **14**:287–292, 1977.
8. VanDercar, D.H., Elster, A.S., Schneiderman, N.: Heart rate classical conditioning in rabbits to hypothalamic or septal US stimulation. *J Comp Physiol Psychol* **72**:145–152, 1970
9. Cohen, D.H., Obrist, P.A.: Interactions between behavior and the cardiovascular system. *Circ Res* **31**: 693–706, 1975.
10. Fredericks, A., Moore, J.W., Metcalf, F.U., Schwaber, J.S., Schneiderman, N.: Selective autonomic blockade of conditioned and unconditioned heart rate changes in rabbits. *Pharmacol Biochem Behav* 493–501, 1974.
11. Ellison, G.D., Zanchetti, A.: Sympathetic cholinergic vasodilation in muscles. Specific appearance during conditioned movement. *Nature* (London) **232**:124–125, 1971.
12. Martin, J., Sutherland, C.J., Zbrozyna, A.W.: Habituation and conditioning of the defense reactions and their cardiovascular components in cats and dogs. *Pfluegers Arch* **365**:37–47, 1976.
13. Adams, D.B., Baccelli, G., Mancia, G., Zanchetti, A.: Cardiovascular changes during naturally elicited fighting behavior in the cat. *Am J Physiol* **216**:1226–1235, 1968.
14. Gavin, W.P., Silbret, M., Gaide, M.S., Klose, K.J., Schneiderman, N., Smith, J., Augenstein, J.S.: Heart rate and blood pressure changes during signal avoidance and aversive classical conditioning in rhesus monkeys. Submitted for publication.
15. Dews, P.B., Herd, J.A.: Behavioral activities and cardiovascular functions: effects of hexamethonium on cardiovascular changes during strong sustained static work in rhesus monkeys. *J Pharmacol Exp Ther* **189**:12–23, 1974.
16. Klose, K.J., Augenstein, J.S., Schneiderman, N., Manas, K., Abrams, B., Bloom, L.J.: Selective autonomic blockade of conditioned and unconditioned cardiovascular changes in rhesus monkeys. *J Comp Physiol Psychol* **89**: 810–818, 1975.
17. Ramsay, D.A.: Form and characteristics of the cardiovascular conditioned response in rhesus monkeys. *Conditional Reflex* **5**:36–51, 1970.
18. Miminoshvili, D.I., Magakian, G.O., Kokaia, G.I.: Attempts to obtain a model of hypertension and coronary insufficiency in monkeys. *In* Theoretical and Practical Problems of Medicine and Biology in Experiments on Monkeys (Utikin, I.A., ed.). New York: Pergamon, 1960.
19. Mason, J.W., Mangan, G.F., Brady, J.V., Conrad, D., Rioch, D.M.: Concurrent plasma epinephrine, norepinephrine, and 17-hydroxycorticosteroid levels during conditioned emotional disturbances in monkeys. *Psychosom Med* **23**:344–353, 1961.
20. Lawler, J.E., Obrist, P.A., Lawler, K.A.: Cardiovascular function during pre-avoidance, avoidance, and post-avoidance in dogs. *Psychophysiology* **12**: 4–11, 1975.
21. Mason, J.W., Brady, J.V., Tolson, W.W.: Behavioral adaptations and endocrine activity. *In* Endocrines and the Central Nervous System (Levine, R., ed.). Baltimore: Williams & Williams, 1966.
22. Lawler, J.E., Botticelli, L.J., Lown, B.: Changes in cardiac refractory period during signalled avoidance in dogs. *Psychophysiology* **13**:373–377, 1976.

23. Han, J., Moe, G.K.: Nonuniform recovery of excitability in ventricular muscle. *Circ Res* **14**:44–60, 1964.
24. Cranefield, P.F., Wit, A.L., Hoffman, B.F.: Genesis of cardiac arrhythmias. *Circulation* **47**:190–204, 1973.
25. Herd, J.A., Morse, W.H., Kelleher, R.J., Jones, L.G.: Arterial hypertension in the squirrel monkey during behavioral experiments. *Am J Physiol* **217**:24–29, 1969.
26. Benson, H., Herd, J.A., Morse, W.H., Kelleher, R.J.: Behavioral induction of arterial hypertension and its reversal. *Am J Physiol* **217**:30–34, 1969.
27. Harris, A.H., Gilliam, W., Findley, J.D., Brady, J.V.: Instrumental conditioning of large-magnitude daily 12-hour blood pressure elevations in the baboon. *Science* **182**:175–177, 1973.
28. Anderson, D.E., Tosheff, J.: Cardiac output and total peripheral resistance changes during preavoidance periods in the dog. *J Appl Physiol* **34**:650–654, 1973.
29. Forsyth, R.P.: Regional blood flow changes during 72-hour avoidance schedules in the monkey. *Science* **173**:546–548, 1971.
30. Mason, J.W., Tolson, W.W., Brady, J.V., Tolliver, G.A., Gilmore, L.I.: Urinary epinephrine and norepinephrine responses to 72-hour avoidance sessions in the monkey. *Psychosom Med* **30**:654–665, 1968.
31. Forsyth, R.P.: Blood pressure responses to long-term avoidance schedules in the restrained rhesus monkey. *Psychosom Med* **31**:300–309, 1969.
32. Corley, K.C., Shiel, F.O'M., Mauck, H.P., Greenhoot, J.: Electrocardiographic and cardiac morphological changes associated with environmental stress in squirrel monkeys. *Psychosom Med* **35**:361–364, 1973.
33. Corley, K.C., Mauck, H.P., Shiel, F.O'M.: Cardiac-responses associated with "yoked-chair" shock avoidance in squirrel monkeys. *Psychophysiology* **12**:439–444, 1975.
34. Brady, J.V., Porter, R., Conrad, D., Mason, J.: Avoidance behavior and the development of gastroduodenal ulcers. *J Exp Anal Behav* **1**:69–72, 1958.
35. Moss, A.J., Schenk, E.A.: Cardiovascular effects of sustained norepinephrine infusions in dogs. *Circ Res* **27**:1013–1022, 1970.
36. Melville, K.I., Garvey, H.L., Shister, H.E., Knaack, J.: Central nervous system stimulation and cardiac ischemic changes in monkeys. *Ann NY Acad Sci* **156**:241–260, 1969.
37. Bunag, R.D., Riley, E., Montello, M.: Sustained pressor responsiveness to prolonged hypothalamic stimulation in awake rats. *Am J Physiol* **231**:1708–1715, 1976.
38. Folkow, B., Rubenstein, E.H.: Cardiovascular effects of acute and chronic stimulation of the hypothalamic defence area in the rat. *Acta Physiol Scand* **68**:48–57, 1966.
39. Weiss, J.M.: Effects of coping behavior on development of gastroduodenal lesions in rats. Proc. 75th Ann. Convention, APA 263–264, 1968.
40. Richter, C.P.: On phenomenon of sudden death in animals and man. *Psychosom Med* **19**:191–198, 1957.
41. Schneider, R.A.: Patterns of autonomic response to startle in subjects with and without coronary artery disease. (Abstract). *Clin Res* **15**:59, 1957.
42. Manning, J.W., Cotten, M.deV.: Mechanism of cardiac arrhythmias induced by diencephalic stimulation. *Am J Physiol* **203**:1120–1123, 1962.
43. Ebert, P.A., Allgood, R.J., Sabiston, D.C.: Effect of cardiac denervation on arrhythmia following coronary artery occlusion. *Surg Forum* **18**:114–121, 1967.
44. Friedman, R., Dahl, L.: The effect of chronic conflict on the blood pressure of rats with a genetic susceptibility to experimental hypertension. *Psychosom Med* **37**:402–416, 1975.
45. Dahl, L.K., Heine, M., Tassinari, L.J.: Effects of chronic excess salt ingestion. Evidence that genetic factors play an important role in susceptibility to experimental hypertension. *J Exper Med* **115**:1173–1190, 1962.
46. Dahl, L.K., Heine, M., Tassinari, L.J.: Effects of chronic excess salt ingestion. Vascular reactivity in two strains of rats with opposite genetic susceptibility to experimental hypertension. *Circulation* **29, 30** (Suppl. II):11–22, 1964.
47. Overmier, J.B., Seligman, M.E.P.: Effects of inescapable shock upon subsequent escape and avoidance learning. *J Comp Physiol Psychol* **63**:23–33, 1967.

48. Seligman, M.E.P., Maier, S.F.: Failure to escape traumatic shock. *J Exp Psychol* **74**:1–9, 1967.
49. Weiss, J.M., Glazer, H.I.: Effects of acute exposure to stressors on subsequent avoidance-escape behavior. *Psychosom Med* **37**:499–521, 1975.
50. Weiss, J.M., Glazer, H.I., Pohorecky, L.A., Brick, J., Miller, N.E.: Effects of chronic exposure to stressors on avoidance-escape behavior and on brain norepinephrine. *Psychosom Med* **37**:522–534, 1975.
51. Sokolov, E.N.: Perception and the Conditioned Reflex. New York: Macmillan, 1963.
52. Irving, L.: Respiration in diving mammals. *Physiol Rev* **19**:112–133, 1939.
53. Schneider, E.C.: Observations on holding the breath. *Am J Physiol* **94**:464–470, 1930.
54. Herd, J.A.: Overall regulation of the circulation. *Annu Rev Physiol* **32**:289–312, 1970.
55. Feigl, E., Folkow, B.: Cardiovascular responses in "diving" and during brain stimulation in ducks. *Acta Physiol Scand* **57**:99–110, 1963.
56. Wolf, S.: Sudden death and the oxygen-conserving reflex. *Am Heart J* **71**:840–849, 1966.
57. Seligman, M.E.P.: Helplessness: On Depression, Development, and Death. San Francisco: W.H. Freeman, 1975.
58. Weiss, J.M., Stone, E.A., Harrell, N.: Coping behavior and brain norepinephrine level in rats. *J Comp Physiol Psychol* **72**:153–160, 1970.
59. Glazer, H.I., Weiss, J.M., Pohorecky, L.A., Miller, N.E.: Monoamines as mediators of avoidance-escape behavior. *Psychosom Med* **37**:535–543, 1975.
60. Obrist, P.A., Howard, J.L., Lawler, J.E., Galosy, R.A., Meyers, K.A., Gaebelein, C.J.: The cardiac somatic interaction. *In* Cardiovascular Psychophysiology (Obrist, P.A., Black, A.H., Brener, J., DiCara, L.V., eds.). Chicago: Aldine, 1974.
61. Powell, D.A., Goldberg, S.R., Dauth, G.W., Schneiderman, E., Schneiderman, N.: Adrenergic and cholinergic blockade of cardiovascular responses to subcortical electrical stimulation in unanesthetized rabbits. *Physiol Behav* **8**:927–936, 1972.
62. Henry, J.P., Meehan, J.P., Stephens, P.M.: The use of psychosocial stimuli to induce prolonged systolic hypertension in mice. *Psychosom Med* **29**: 408–432, 1967.
63. Henry, J.P., Stephens, P.M., Axelrod, J., Mueller, R.A.: Effect of psychosocial stimulation on the enzymes involved in the biosynthesis and metabolism of noradrenaline and adrenaline. *Psychosom Med* **33**: 227–237, 1971.
64. Henry, J.P., Ely, D.L., Stephens, P.M., Ratcliffe, H.L., Santisteban, G.A., Shapiro, A.P.: The role of psychosocial factors in the development of arteriosclerosis in CBA mice: observations on the heart, kidney and aorta. *Atherosclerosis* **14**:203–218, 1971.
65. Henry, J.P., Ely, D.L., Stephens, P.M.: Changes in catecholamine-controlling enzymes in response to psychosocial activation of defence and alarm reactions. *In* Physiology, Emotion and Psychosomatic Illness. Amsterdam: CIBA Foundation, 1972.
66. Von Holst, D.: Sozialer stress bei Tupujas (*Tupaia belangeri*) Die Aktivierung des sympathischen Nervensystems und ihre Beziehung zu hormonal ausgelosten, ethologischen und physiologischen Veranderungen. *Z Verg Physiol* **63**:1–58, 1969.
67. Von Holst, D.: Renal failure as the cause of death in *Tupaia belangeri* (tree shrews) exposed to persistent social stress. *J Comp Physiol* **78**: 236–273, 1972.
68. Lapin, B., Cherkovitch, G.M.: Environmental change causing the development of neuroses and corticovisceral pathology in monkeys. *In* Society, Stress and Disease: The Psychosocial Environment and Psychosomatic Diseases (Levi, L., ed.). London: Oxford University Press, 1971.
69. Miminoshvili, D.I.: Experimental neuroses in monkeys. *In* Theoretical and Practical Problems in Experiments on Monkeys (Uttan, I., ed.). Oxford, 1956.
70. Berne, R.M., Levy, M.N.: Cardiovascular Physiology, 2nd ed. St. Louis: Mosby, 1972.
71. Cohen, D.H., MacDonald, R.L.: A selective review of central neural pathways involved in cardiovascular control. *In* Cardiovascular Psychophysiology (Obrist, P.A., Black, A.H., Brener, J., DiCara, L.V., eds.). Chicago: Aldine, 1974. pp. 33–59.
72. Schneiderman, N., Francis, J.S., Sampson, L.D., Schwaber, J.S.: CNS integration of learned cardiovascular behavior. *In* The Autonomic Nervous System: Advances in Research (DiCara, L.V., ed.). New York: Plenum, 1974, pp. 277–309.

73. Green, J.H.: Physiology of baroreceptor function: mechanism of receptor stimulation. *In* Baroreceptors and Hypertension (Kezdi, P., ed.). Oxford: Pergamon, 1967.
74. Getz, B., Sirnes, T.: The localization within the dorsal motor nucleus. *J Comp Neurol* **90**:95–110, 1949.
75. Cohen, D.H., Schnall, A.M., MacDonald, R.L., Pitts, L.H.: Medullary cells of origin of vagal cardioinhibitory fibers in the pigeon. I. Anatomical studies of peripheral vagus nerve and the dorsal motor nucleus. *J Comp Neurol* **140**:299–320, 1970.
76. Mitchell, G., Warwick, R.: The dorsal vagal nucleus. *Acta Anat* **25**:376–395, 1955.
77. Kerr, F.W.L.: Preserved vagal visceromotor function following destruction of the dorsal motor nucleus. *J Physiol* **202**:755–769, 1969.
78. Thomas, M.R., Calaresu, F.R.: Localization and function of medullary sites mediating vagal bradycardia in the cat. *Am J Physiol* **226**:1344–1349, 1974.
79. Schwaber, J., Schneiderman, N.: Aortic nerve activated cardioinhibitory neurons and inter- neurons. *Am J Physiol* **229**:783–789, 1975.
80. McAllen, R.M., Spyer, K.M.: The location of cardiac vagal preganglionic motor-neurones in the medulla of the cat. *J Physiol* **258**:187–204, 1976.
81. Kaufman, M.P., Hamilton, R.B., Petrik, G.K., Schneiderman, N.: Role of subthalamus in mediation of bradycardia responses in rabbits. *Neurosci Abstr* **3**:22, 1977.
82. Hilton, S.M., Spyer, K.M.: Participation of the anterior hypothalamus in the baroreceptor reflex. *J Physiol* **218**:271–293, 1971.
83. Gimpl, M.P., Brickman, A.L., Kaufman, M.P., Schneiderman, N.: Temporal relationships during barosensory attenuation in the conscious rabbit. *Am J Physiol* **230**:1480–1486, 1976.
84. Spyer, K.M.: Baroreceptor sensitive neurons in the anterior hypothalamus of the cat. *J Physiol* **224**:245–257, 1972.
85. Brickman, A.L., Kaufman, M.P., Petrik, G.K., Schneiderman, N.: Responses of anterior hypothalamic neurons to stimulation of aortic nerve and caudate nucleus in rabbits. *Exp Neurol* **56**:622–627, 1977.
86. Klevans, L.R., Gebber, G.L.: Facilitory forebrain influence on cardiac component of baroreceptor reflexes. *Am J Physiol* **219**:1235–1241, 1970.
87. Magoun, H.W.: Excitability of the hypothalamus after degeneration of corticofugal connec- tions from the frontal lobe. *Am J Physiol* **112**:530–532, 1938.
88. Calaresu, F.R., Ciriello, J., Mogenson, G.J.: Identification of pathways mediating cardiovas- cular responses elicited by stimulation of the septum in the rat. *J Physiol* **260**:515–530, 1976.
89. Faiers, A.A., Calaresu, F.R., Mogenson, G.J.: Pathway mediating hypotension elicited by stimulation of the amygdala in the rat. *Am J Physiol* **228**:1358–1366, 1975.
90. Lindgren, P., Rosen, A., Strandberg, P., Uvnas, P.: The sympathetic vasodilator and vaso- constrictor outflow—a corticospinal autonomic pathway. *J Comp Neurol* **105**:95–104, 1956.
91. Hilton, S.M.: Hypothalamic regulation of the cardiovascular system. *Br Med Bull* **22**:243–248, 1966.
92. Hilton, S.M., Zbrozyna, A.W.: Amygdaloid region for defense reactions and its efferent pathway to the brain stem. *J Physiol* **165**:160–173, 1963.
93. Djojosugito, A.M., Folkow, B., Klystra, P., Lisander, B., Tuttle, R.S.: Differentiated interac- tion between the hypothalamic defense reaction and baroreceptor reflexes. I. Effects on heart rate and regional flow resistance. *Acta Physiol Scand* **78**:376–383, 1970.
94. Klystra, P.H., Lisander, B.: Differential interaction between the hypothalamic defense area and baroreceptor reflexes. II. Effects on aortic blood flow as related to work load on the left ventricle. *Acta Physiol Scand* **78**:386–392, 1970.
95. Adair, J.R., Manning, J.W.: Hypothalamic modulation of baroreceptor afferent unit activity. *Am J Physiol* **229**:1357–1364, 1975.
96. McAllen, R.M.: Inhibition of the baroreceptor input to the medulla by stimulation of the hypothalamic defence area. *J Physiol* **256**:45P–46P, 1976.
97. Pribram, K.H., McGuinness, D.: Arousal, activation and effort in the control of attention. *Psychol Rev* **82**:116–149, 1975.
98. Abrahams, V.C., Hilton, S.M., Zbrozyna, A.: Active vasodilation produced by stimulation of the brain stem: its significance in the defense reactions. *J Physiol* **154**:491–513, 1960.

99. Gebber, G.L., Taylor, D.G., Weaver, L.C.: Electrophysiological studies on organization of central vasopressor pathways. *Am J Physiol* 224:470–481, 1973.

100. Thomas, M.R., Ulrichsen, R.F., Calaresu, F.R.: Function of the lateral reticular nucleus in central cardiovascular regulation in the cat. *Am J Physiol* 232:H157–H166, 1977.

101. Horeyseck, G., Janig, W., Kirchner, F., Thamer, V.: Activation and inhibition of muscle and cutaneous postganglionic neurones to hindlimb during hypothalamically induced vasoconstriction and atropine-sensitive vasodilation. *Pfluegers Arch* 361:231–240, 1976.

102. Ross, R., Glomset, J.A.: The pathogenesis of atherosclerosis. *N Engl J Med* 295:369–377, 1976.

103. Forsyth, R.P., Harris, R.E.: Circulatory changes during stressful stimuli in rhesus monkeys. *Circ Res* **26, 27** (Suppl. 1):13–20, 1970.

104. Lund-Johansen, P.: Hemodynamic alterations in essential hypertension. *In* Hypertension: Mechanisms and Management (Onesti, G., Kim, K. E., Moyer, J.H., eds.) New York: Grune & Stratton, 1973.

105. Okamoto, K., & Aoki, K.: Development of a strain of spontaneously hypertensive rats. *Jpn Circ J* 27:282–288, 1963.

106. Lais, L.T., Brody, M.J.: Pathogenesis of hypertension in spontaneously hypertensive rats. *In* New Antihypertensive Drugs (Scriabine, A., Sweet, C.S., eds.) New York: Spectrum, 1977.

107. Mendlowitz, M.: Vascular reactivity in systemic arterial hypertension. *In* Hypertension: Mechanisms and Management (Onesti, G., Kim, K.E., Moyer, J.H., eds.) New York: Grune & Stratton, 1973.

108. Gordon, T., Verter, J.: Serum cholesterol, systolic blood pressure and Framingham relative weight as discriminators of cardiovascular disease. *In* The Framingham Study: An Epidemiological Investigation of Cardiovascular Disease (Kannel, W.B., Gordon, T., eds.) Washington, D.C.: U. S. Govt. Ptg. Office, 1969.

109. Bronte-Stewart, B., Heptinstahl, R.H.: The relationship between experimental hypertension and cholesterol-induced atheroma in rabbits. *J Pathol* 68:407–414, 1954.

110. Heindel, J.J., Orci, L., Jeanrenaud, B.: Fat mobilization and its regulation by hormones and drugs in white adipose tissue. *In* International Encyclopedia of Pharmacology and Therapeutics. Pharmacology of Lipid Transport and Atherosclerotic Processes. (Masoro, E.J., ed.). **24,** 1:175–373, Oxford: Pergamon, 1975.

111. Haft, J.I., Kranz, P.D., Albert, F.J., Fani, K.: Intravascular platelet aggregation in the heart induced by norepinephrine. *Circulation* 46:698–708, 1972.

112. Kosowsky, B.D., Lown, B., Whiting, R., Guiney, T.: Occurrence of ventricular arrhythmia with exercise as compared to monitoring. *Circulation* 44:826–832, 1971.

113. Sigler, L.H.: Emotion and arteriosclerotic heart disease. I. Electrocardiographic changes observed on the recall of past emotional disturbances. *Br J Med Psychol* 30:55–64, 1967.

114. Levy, M.N.: Neural mechanisms in cardiac arrythmias. *J Lab Clin Med* 90:589–591, 1977.

115. Yehle, A., Dauth, G., Schneiderman, N.: Correlates of heart-rate classical conditioning in curarized rabbits. *J Comp Physiol Psychol* 64:98–104, 1967.

116. Schneiderman, N.: Classical (Pavlovian) Conditioning. Morristown, N.J.: General Learning Press, 1973.

117. Friedman, M., Rosenman, R.H.: Type A Behavior and Your Heart. New York: Knopf, 1974.

118. Rosenman, R.H., Brand, R.J., Jenkins, C.D., Friedman, M., Straus, R., Wurm, M.: Coronary heart disease in the Western Collaborative Group Study: final follow-up experience of 8½ years. *JAMA* 233:872–877, 1975.

119. Glass, D.C.: Stress, behavior patterns and coronary disease. *Am Sci* 65:177–187, 1977.

120. Greene, W.A., Goldstein, S., Moss, A.J.: Psychosocial aspects of sudden death: a preliminary report. *Arch Intern Med* 129:725–731, 1972.

121. Glass, D.C.: Behavior Patterns, Stress, and Coronary Disease. Hillsdale, N.J., Lawrence Erlbaum Associates, 1977.

122. Rahe, R.H.: Stress and strain in coronary heart disease. *J SC Med Assoc* (Suppl.) 72:7–14, 1975.

123. Lund-Johansen, P.: Hemodynamic alterations in essential hypertension. *In* Hypertension:

Mechanisms and Management (Onesti, G., Kim, K.E., Moyer, J.H., eds.). New York: Grune & Stratton, 1973.

124. Dahl, L.K., Heine, M., Tassinari, L.J.: Role of genetic factors in susceptibility to experimental hypertension due to chronic excess salt ingestion. *Nature* **194**:480–482, 1962.

125. Friedman, M., Rosenman, R.H.: Association of specific overt behavior pattern with blood and cardiovascular findings. Blood cholesterol level, blood clotting time, incidence of arcus senilis, and clinical coronary artery disease. *JAMA* **169**:1286–1296, 1959.

126. Gunn, C.G., Friedman, M., Byers, S.D.: Effect of chronic hypothalamic stimulation upon cholesterol-induced atherosclerosis in the rabbit. *J Clin Invest* **39**:1963–1972, 1960.

127. Raab, W.: Cardiotoxic biochemical effects of emotional-environmental stressors—fundamentals of psychocardiology. *In* Society, Stress and Disease (Levi, L., ed.). London, Oxford, 1971.

SECTION IV

DEVELOPMENT

Section Summary: Coronary-Prone Behavior: Developmental and Cultural Considerations

Judith Blackfield Cohen, Karen A. Matthews, and Ingrid Waldron

Considerable research attention has been given to the identification of a coronary-prone (Type A) behavior pattern, to the development of techniques for classifying persons with respect to the presence and degree of this behavior pattern, and to establishing a "risk factor" relationship between this behavior pattern and various forms of coronary heart disease (CHD).[1-4] However, little attention has been given to issues concerning the development of this pattern of behavior, e.g., whether it is primarily a genetically determined or acquired (learned) behavior pattern, and to what extent the behavior pattern is character-istic of persons other than white, middle-class, middle-aged males in the United States. The following summary statement outlines: (1) what is currently known about sex differences and genetic influences on the Type A pattern, (2) the occurrence of Type A behavior in children, (3) cultural influences on the development of Type A behavior, and (4) suggestions for future research in these areas.

Sex Differences

Research has not yet established adequate validity of the Structured Interview (SI) and the Jenkins Activity Survey (JAS) for predicting CHD in women. A major problem in this area has been the lack of detailed studies on the adequacy of revised forms of the SI, the JAS, and other methods of assessing the behavior pattern in women, and whether these measures predict CHD in women. However, the data that are available suggest that the coronary-prone behavior pattern is correlated with the prevalence of CHD in women,[5,6] includ-ing coronary atherosclerosis. In women, as in men, most of the risk associated with the Type A pattern apparently does not act via the standard risk factors.[6-8] The coronary-prone behavior pattern has been found to be more prevalent among employed women than among housewives.[6,9]

The coronary-prone behavior pattern as measured by existing instruments appears to be more prevalent among men than among women.[6,10,11] This sex difference in behavior pattern may contribute to higher rates of CHD for men.[11] Sex differences in behavior pattern probably reflect both genetic differences in aggressiveness *and* socialization, e.g., in the encouragement of competitive achievement.[11] Sex differences in socialization might be expected, since the Type A pattern may to some extent be associated with success in the traditional male role (e.g., as reflected in high occupational status), but not with success in traditional female roles.[9]

Further research indicated by the above includes:

1. Validation of new forms of the Jenkins Activity Scale, the Structured Interview, and other methods of assessment for women who are employed and women who are not employed.
2. Studies of coronary-prone behavior pattern and the incidence of CHD in women, as is being done presently with the Framingham data.[6]
3. Longitudinal studies of women as they enter and leave the labor force, or men and women as they change jobs. This would provide a useful opportunity to test environmental effects on the behavior pattern.
4. Studies of the relationship of the coronary-prone behavior pattern to upward occupational and educational mobility, both within and between generations.
5. Replication of the findings of sex differences in coronary-prone behavior pattern and differences between housewives and employed women.
6. Studies of sex differences in socialization, e.g., in the escalation of performance standards for children described in the next section.

Genetic Contributions and Coronary-Prone Behavior in Children

At present, based on conclusions drawn from either the Structured Interview[12] or the JAS assessment of Type A characteristics,[13] there is no evidence for heritability of the coronary-prone behavior. However, factor H (hard-driving) on the JAS appears to have a modest genetic component in a sample of 56 pairs of approximately 20-year-old male and female twins.[12] In addition, several personality dimensions, such as activity level and emotionality are associated with Type A behavior and show evidence of heritability.[14] The above assertions are primarily based on twin studies and should be viewed with caution, since the twin method of study is based upon the assumption that monozygotic twins are *not* treated more alike by others than dizygotic twins. Future research should examine possible genetic determinants of coronary-prone behavior via other genetic models of research as well as the interaction of genetic influences with environmental effects.

Obviously, possible genetic contributions are relevant to our understanding of the etiology of coronary-prone behavior. The child-rearing practices associated with the development of Type A behavior may be elicited by the characteristic behavior of the children, rather than vice versa. Nonetheless, research by Matthews suggests that escalating parental standards of performance might play a role in the etiology of coronary-prone behavior, particularly in the achievement-striving component.[15] Psychological research has shown that high achievement-motivation is associated with the following parental attributes: high expectations and aspirations, frequent approval and disapproval, competitiveness, and authoritarian discipline techniques.[16,17] The pattern of maternal and paternal interactions with high need achievement children differ according to the sex of the child.[18] Achievement behavior is relatively stable over time for both boys and girls.[19]

Children exhibit aggressive behavior (1) when salient models are aggressive, (2) when aggression is rewarded by obtaining attention, esteem, or a desired resource, and (3) when aggression is allowed and returned in kind in the home.[20] Aggressive behavior is relatively stable over time for boys, but not for girls.[19]

Future research efforts might be focused on the following:

1. Development of reliable and valid instruments for measuring the coronary-prone behavior in children. Two measurement techniques show promise: (1) a children's interview for children over ten years old,[21] and (2) the MYTH,[22] a set of teacher's ratings of school-aged children's competitive achievement striving and impatience. However, reliability data and content and construct validity data are clearly needed. Certain physiological characteristics typical of adult Type A behavior and CHD patients should be related to coronary-prone behavior in children.

2. An investigation of the stability of coronary-prone behavior over time in children should be carried out. A preliminary step would be a series of two-year longitudinal studies of children at various age levels. If Type A behavior in children is relatively stable, a long-term study might be warranted and early detection of adult Type A individuals might be feasible.

3. Studies of parental modeling of specific aspects of the coronary-prone pattern would be worthwhile, with particular attention on whether behavior(s) is consistent with cultural sex role expectations. In this regard, examinations of parental behavior that promotes Type A behavior in children would be of value. Because components of the Type A behavior pattern (aggressiveness, achievement behavior, competitiveness) are relatively stable after the ages of six to ten years,[19] child-rearing practices associated with children younger than this age may play a role in the acquisition of these attributes.

4. Experiments on time-urgency in children similar to those conducted with adults should be carried out.[23] There is no developmental research on perception of time passage in Type A children. Research with adult Type A's suggests that they chronically overestimate the length of time that is

passing. Research should be conducted to explore the types of childhood experiences that affect the amount and complexity of information encoded by children. Perhaps Ornstein's work on perception of time passage might be useful.[23]

5. The effects of school and parents on the development of the coronary-prone pattern in children should be examined. The structure of the American classroom and its reward and value systems probably encourage certain components of the Type A behavior pattern in children. For example, there is evidence that the American classroom promotes social comparison and competition.[24] Similarly, the urgency of time may be reinforced in school by the use of timed tasks, discrete periods of classwork, and a value on rapid learning and performance.

Cultural Influences

At the present time, the Type A coronary-prone behavior pattern is operationally defined by what is measured or assessed by the Structured Interview and the Jenkins Activity Survey. The concept of the coronary-prone behavior pattern grew out of observations of the behavior of CHD patients who were primarily white, middle-aged men, of middle and upper management employment status.

We need to ask whether the behavior pattern is simply a reflection of a life-style produced by the typical environment of middle-aged American men, or whether it reflects a behavior pattern of high risk for CHD *independent* of the prevailing cultural environment. Comparative assessments are needed of coronary-prone behavior in a variety of cultural environments to see whether a characteristic set of behaviors associated with Type A classification and with CHD risk can be identified.

If there is a common core of behaviors making up the coronary-prone pattern that is independent of environmental influences, the question becomes: What is its prevalence in different cultural groups? There are wide differences in the incidence and prevalence of CHD among groups within a given culture and between cultures. Perhaps a more thorough understanding of the nature and universality of Type A behavior can help clarify our understanding of these differences.

It would be helpful to compare the prevalence of coronary-prone behavior in different population groups. Unfortunately, such data are only beginning to become available from studies of coronary-prone behavior among women,[8] among blacks,[10] and among men in Western European countries, such as Belgium.[25] Since these groups differ from U.S. men in degree rather than kind with regard to cultural differences, research in cultures other than those sharing Western values should be pursued. We will need information concerning the prevalence of Type A behavior in a variety of groups to determine the extent to which Type A behavior is related to CHD. In this regard, investigations of ethnically different populations within a dominant culture will also be valuable.

In one of the few cross-cultural studies of Type A behavior, Cohen et al.[26] assessed the relationship between the Type A behavior pattern and CHD among 2,437 Japanese-Americans living in Hawaii. Using the JAS, those scored as Type A were relatively rare in this group, with only 15% classified as Type A individuals.

If coronary-prone behavior is defined in terms of the total JAS score as standardized on white men in the United States, there is a modest but nonsignificant association between Type A scores and CHD among Japanese-Americans. However, if the individual factors from the scale are examined separately, the association with CHD holds for only one factor—hard-driving and competitive. Since this important aspect of the behavior pattern is not culturally compatible for the Japanese, its frequency is rare in this group. The findings from this study suggest that responses to the JAS in one cultural setting can be different from those in another setting, and thus, may be reflective of influences related to the cultural milieu. There is also support for the hypothesis that a core of culture-free items might exist that are "risk factors" for CHD in different cultural settings.

Japanese men living in Hawaii who had undergone cultural change were also more likely to develop CHD, although the magnitude of risk was small. Men who were both culturally mobile and classified as Type A, however, had two to three times the risk of developing CHD as men with either characteristic.[26] Thus, when Japanese-Americans were classified according to the most Western set of traits possible, in both individual behavior pattern and cultural environment, their risk for CHD was similar to that of white American males. However, neither behavior nor environment alone put them at the same level of risk as would be expected from prior research on these characteristics.

More research is needed on cross-cultural and subcultural variation in the expression and prevalence of coronary-prone behavior:

1. Research on the extent of Type A behavior in women, members of minority groups, and other subcultural groups in the United States would be relatively easy and would add to our knowledge in this area. The propositions are relatively straightforward: In cultural groups where politeness and cooperation are expected and rewarded, or where the expression of competitiveness and hostility are discouraged, there should be less Type A behavior. Certainly, our understanding of child-rearing practices, especially those differentially affecting boys and girls in our culture, is congruent with this expectation.
2. To more readily identify relevant dimensions of the psychosocial environment, studies should be conducted in the United States on the Type A pattern and CHD among a variety of business organizations, as well as in population groups known to be different (high or low) on relevant traits such as time-urgency or competitiveness.
3. Research analogous to that reported on Japanese-Americans should be replicated in other cultural groups, both similar and dissimilar to the United States. Priority should be given to study of groups examining the extreme ranges of CHD prevalence.

With regard to intervention, the present results point to two conclusions. First, it is possible that some aspects of a behavior pattern that are desirable but not directly related to CHD risk, can be encouraged, while those aspects of behavior that are more risk-related can be discouraged. It is possible, for example, to be hard-working and not necessarily hard-driving and competitive. In short, it is possible to be productive but not self-destructive within any given culture. Second, our evidence indicates that cultural factors strongly influence the development of the coronary-prone behavior pattern and the associated risk of coronary heart disease. Therefore, it may be useful to consider ways in which we might change our cultural institutions, such as the schools, so they may be less conducive to the development of the coronary-prone behavior pattern.

References

1. Friedman, M., Rosenman, R.H.: Type A Behavior and Your Heart. New York: Knopf, 1974.
2. Glass, D.C.: Stress, behavior patterns, and coronary disease. Am Sci 65:178–187, 1977.
3. Jenkins, C.D.: Recent evidence supporting psychologic and social risk factors for coronary disease. N Engl J Med 294:987–994, 1033–1038, 1976.
4. Zyzanski, S.J., Jenkins, C.D., Ryan, T.J., Flessas, A., Everist, M.: Psychological correlates of coronary angiographic findings. Arch Intern Med 136:1234–1237, 1976.
5. Rosenman, R.H., Friedman, M.: Association of specific behavior pattern in women with blood and cardiovascular findings. Circulation 24:1173–1184, 1961.
6. Haynes, S.G., Feinleib, M., Levine, S., Scotch, N.A., Kannel, W.B.: The relationship of psychosocial factors to coronary heart disease in the Framingham Study. II. Prevalence of coronary heart disease. Am J Epidemiol 107:384–402, 1978.
7. Blumenthal, J., Department of Psychiatry, Duke University Medical Center, personal communication, 1977.
8. Shekelle, R.B., Schoenberger, J.A., Stamler, J.: Correlates of the JAS Type A behavior pattern score. J Chronic Dis 29:318–394, 1976.
9. Waldron, I.: The coronary-prone behavior pattern, blood pressure, employment and socioeconomic status in women. J Psychosom Res, (in press).
10. Waldron, I., Zyzanski, S., Shekelle, R.B., Jenkins, C.D., Tannenbaum, S.: Type A behavior pattern in employed men and women. J Human Stress 3(4):2–18, 1977.
11. Waldron, I.: Why do women live longer than men? Part I. J Human Stress 2:2–13, 1976.
12. Rosenman, R.H., Rahe, R.H., Borhani, N.O., Feinleib, M.: Heritability of personality and behavior pattern. Paper presented at the American Psychosomatic Society, New Orleans, 1975.
13. Matthews, K.A., Krantz, D.S.: Resemblances of twins and their parents in pattern A behavior, Psychosom Med 28:140–144, 1976.
14. Buss, A., Plomin, R.: A Temperament Theory of Personality Development. New York: Wiley, 1975.
15. Matthews, K.A., Glass, D.C., Richins, M.: Behavioral interactions of mothers and children with the coronary-prone behavior pattern. In Behavior Patterns, Stress, and Coronary Disease (Glass, D.C., ed.) Hillsdale, N.J.: Lawrence Erlbaum Associates, 1977.
16. Baumrind, D.: Current patterns of parental authority, Dev Psychol Monographs 4:(1, Part 2), 1971.
17. Rosen, B.C., D'Andrade, R.: The psychological origins of achievement motivation. Sociometry 22:85–218, 1959.

18. Hoffman, L.: Early childhood experiences and women's achievement motives. *J Soc Issues* **28**:129–155, 1972.
19. Kagan, J., Moss, H.A.: Birth To Maturity: A Study of Psychological Development. New York: Wiley, 1962.
20. Cohen, S.: Social and Personality Development in Childhood. New York: Macmillan, 1976.
21. Butensky, A., Faralli, V., Heebner, D., Waldron, I.: Elements of the coronary-prone behavior pattern in children and teenagers. *J Psychosom Res* **20**:439–444, 1976.
22. Matthews, K.A.: Mother-child interaction as a determinant of Type A-Type B behavior. Unpublished doctoral dissertation, University of Texas, Austin, 1976.
23. Burnam, M.A., Pennebaker, J.W., Glass, D.C.: Time consciousness, achievement striving, and the Type A coronary-prone behavior pattern. *J Abnorm Psychol* **84**:76–79, 1975.
24. Johnson, D.W., Johnson, R.T.: Goal structures and open education. *J Res Dev Educ* **8**:30–46. 1974.
25. Zyzanski, S.J.: Coronary-Prone Behavior Pattern and Coronary Heart Disease: Epidemological Evidence. *In* Coronary-Prone Behavior (Dembroski, T.M., et. al., eds.). New York: Springer-Verlag, 1978, chapter 2 (pp. 25–40).
26. Cohen, J.B., Syme, S.L., Jenkins, C.D., Dagan, A., Zyzanski, S.J.: The cultural context of Type A behavior and the risk of CHD. *Am J Epidemiol* **102**:434, 1975.

Chapter 14

The Influence of Culture on Coronary-Prone Behavior

Judith Blackfield Cohen

Research has now demonstrated that men characterized as having a behavior style known as Type A have approximately twice the risk of developing
coronary heart disease as men not classified as Type A, independently of the
influence of other risk factors such as hypertension, cigarette smoking, and
elevated serum cholesterol.[1,2] The Type A person has been described as competitive and hard-driving, with a continuous sense of time urgency. His job is
the primary focus of his life, and he cannot devote too many hours to it. His
speed orientation and impatience are extreme, to the point of doing two things
at once when possible.

It should be emphasized, however, that such men describe themselves as
eager and challenged, rising to meet the competition. They claim to thrive on
the pace they set for themselves, and only wish that there were more time to
accomplish their job goals. In cultural terms, these men may be seen as
overdrawn but accurate images of the Western (particularly American) self-
made businessman, living to the fullest the value ideal that you can become
anything you desire if you are willing to work hard enough for it.

Beyond these descriptive details, our present understanding of Type A
behavior is limited. We do not really know what Type A behavior is (in much
the same way that we do not know what intelligence is) except that it is those
attributes assessed by the Type A behavior interview of Friedman and Rosenman,[3,4] or by the Jenkins Activity Survey (JAS) questionnaire.[5] According to
the subsequent work of Jenkins and Zyzanski,[6] there are three component
dimensions to coronary-prone behavior. They have described factor H, for
hard-driving and competitive behavior; factor J, for job involvement; and factor
S, for speed and impatience. Each of these factors is independent of the others,
but all are implicated in coronary risk.[7] Glass describes research supporting the

validity of these three behavioral components, and suggests that psy-
chodynamically, Type A persons are "hyper-responsive," reflecting their extreme concern about maintaining control over their environment.[8]

Not only do we lack a conceptually rigorous definition of Type A behavior,
we also do not know much of the etiology of Type A, except that the concept
grew from the clinical observation and insight of Doctors Friedman and
Rosenman in their work with coronary patients in San Francisco. The men
observed were white, middle-aged men, of middle or upper management employment status. Rosenman and Friedman's subsequent prospective research
in the Western Collaborative Group Study (WCGS) has included men with
essentially the same characteristics, with a somewhat wider range of occupational levels. Shekelle et al.[9] found a modest but statistically significant association between social class and Type A behavior although this association was
not uniform in all age groups.

Certainly, middle-aged employed white men in this country are at high risk
of coronary disease. However, if we identify a behavior pattern that so clearly
is compatible with the cultural setting in which they are functioning, we need to
ask whether Type A behavior is only a reflection of a life-style characteristic of
the middle-aged American male environment, or whether it reflects a behavior
pattern of high risk for coronary disease independent of the cultural environment. It is possible to envision a "core" of Type A behavior that transcends
any particular sociocultural environment and is always associated with elevated risk of CHD. Suppose that there are 40 characteristics descriptive of
Type A men in the WCGS. Let us suppose further that among these 40
characteristics, five are "true" measures of Type A behavior, and 35 are
associated with the expression of that behavior in American white middle class
culture. If enough comparative assessments were made of these 40 characteristics in a variety of cultural environments, a small set of items always associated
with the Type A rating and with CHD risk could be identified.

If there is such a common core to Type A behavior, the next question
becomes, what is its prevalence in different groups? There are wide differences
in rates of coronary disease among groups and between countries. Perhaps a
more thorough understanding of the nature and universality of Type A behavior
can help clarify our understanding of these differences. Unfortunately, such
information is only beginning to become available from studies of Type A
behavior among women,[9] and among men in other countries.[10] Since these
studies are being conducted in the United States and in Western European
countries such as Belgium, we will still be limited to information from cultural
groups who differ more in degree than in the kind of cultural environment in
comparison to United States men. Of course, we also need to know not only
how much Type A behavior there is in a group, but also the nature of the
relationship between this behavior and CHD risk.

In addition to comparative assessment, another way to shed some light on
this problem is to look for the "natural experiment" in which there is a
population where the degree of Western versus non-Western culture varies,
and where information on the Type A characteristic is also available. In such a
population, it would be possible to determine the relative independence of Type

A behavior and cultural context in relation to CHD. Thus, if we can identify cultural environments where all aspects of the "American ideal" are not present, analysis can be made of the association of Type A behavior characteristics with different cultural characteristics.

Japanese-Americans provide just such an experimental opportunity. Most Japanese migrants to the United States have come during the last 100 years and have settled permanently in Hawaii and California. They come from a cultural environment that is clearly modern and industrialized, with employment and occupational standards based on an educational achievement system similar to those of Western countries. However, the Japanese cultural orientation differs from a Western one in several major ways. For example, the highest value is placed on the well-being of the group rather than the individual.[11] Achievement and accomplishment are valued, but as reflections of credit to the family or work group. Selfish individual achievement efforts would be disruptive to the primary goal of harmony within each group. So, the Japanese value educational achievement and hard work, but cooperatively rather than competitively. In other words, the critical question for an action is not "What will this do for me?" but "What will this do for my family or company?" If the Japanese are sometimes described as being unusually flexible in their behavior, it is because they respond to the expectations of others in the particular social context, rather than to any single absolute set of behavioral standards.[12] Rewards, then, are defined in terms of working with others toward a common goal, rather than, as in Western culture, competing with others to reach a personal goal. Japanese who have migrated to the United States have achieved an enviable record of educational and occupational accomplishments, but they have done so because "they embody middle class ideals (of hard work, etc.), which are also expressions of Japanese values."[13]

As part of an international collaborative study of CHD among Japanese in Japan, Hawaii, and California,[14] 2,437 men in the Hawaii cohort were administered the JAS questionnaire during their initial examinations in 1967–68. Each man also completed questionnaire information on demographic, social, dietary, and health history items, and completed a physical examination for CHD that included an ECG. Subsequent morbidity was determined by repeat examination and hospital surveillance; mortality information has also been obtained.

One might expect that Type A behavior would be relatively rare in this group of Japanese-Americans, but the data are ambiguous. The JAS has been standardized so that approximately half of the U.S. white male population should fall into the Type A and half into the Type B range. While only 15% of the Japanese-Americans fell into the Type A range,[15] those who were the most Type A were not necessarily the most nontraditional of the group. Type A behavior was not associated with duration of residence in the United States, for example, nor with ability to read or write Japanese. There was a slight inverse gradient with age, but the gradient has been reported in U.S. whites as well.[9] With one exception (i.e., men with more education were more likely to score higher in the Type A group), Type A behavior measured by the JAS was infrequently but evenly distributed in this Japanese-American group.

Of even more importance, however, is the way in which Type A behavior was expressed among Japanese-Americans, and its relationship to CHD risk. Recall that the total Type A score, as measured in the Western Collaborative Group Study, was a combination of three independent components. Among the Japanese-Americans, however, there was significant intercorrelation and overlap among these factors. In other words, the factor groupings were methodologically as well as theoretically unsatisfactory in terms of the responses of these men to questions about their behavior. Further analysis and refactoring of answers from this population revealed new factor groupings of responses that were reflective of both the original Type A characteristics and also of a Japanese versus Western dimension.[16]

For example, the new factors separated questions about being hard-driving from those about being hard working, although both types of questions had been part of the original factor H among U.S. white male responses. The former, hard-driving and competitive, is characteristic of the Type A person, but is not congruent with Japanese cultural values. Being hard working, on the other hand, is consistent with both Type A and appropriate Japanese cultural expectations.

If Type A is defined in terms of the total JAS score as standardized on U.S. white men, there is a modest but nonsignificant association between Type A score and CHD among Japanese-Americans. However, if the new factors are considered to be more appropriate measures of Type A pattern in this group, then the association with CHD holds for only one of the new factors. This factor includes the hard-driving and competitive aspects of the behavior pattern.

The findings from this study of the Japanese in Hawaii, therefore, suggest that in another mixed cultural setting, the pattern of responses to the JAS would be different and reflective of patterns in that cultural milieu. There is also support for the hypothesis of a core of measures that would continue to be associated with CHD in this different setting. Since this core behavior is not culturally compatible for the Japanese, its frequency is rare in this group.

Another issue now emerges, and that is, whether Type A behavior has the same relationship to CHD in different cultural settings. Again, studies to date of Type A behavior and CHD have assessed this relationship within the context of a particular modern industrialized culture, namely, the American business world. Studies of modern industrialized cultures have observed, however, that this setting is itself conducive to increased disease risk. The stressful effects of the rapid social and cultural mobility found in such settings have been associated with increased CHD risk.[17] Such rapid sociocultural change in an environment is hypothesized to be stressful for two reasons: because individuals are subjected to new and unknown expectations and demands,[18,19] and because these new demands occur at the very time when prior social and cultural support systems, which might have previously been able to help meet these demands, have been lost or left behind.[20-22]

It may be that the coronary-prone behavior pattern is associated with increased risk of CHD regardless of the degree of added stress in the cultural environment, or alternatively, regardless of the degree of stress reduction potential in a supportive environment. I chose to test this question by analyzing the relationship between Type A behavior and CHD among Japanese-Americans who had remained more traditionally Japanese in their cultural orientation versus those who had become more Westernized.

Japanese men living in Hawaii who had undergone cultural change were also likely to develop CHD, although the magnitude of excess risk was small. Men who were both culturally mobile and Type A, however, had two to three times the risk of developing CHD as men with either single risk characteristic.[16] That is, when the Japanese-Americans were classified according to the most Western set of characteristics possible, in both individual behavior pattern and cultural environment, their CHD risk was similar to that of Caucasians. However, neither behavior nor environment alone put them at the same level of risk as would be expected from prior research on these characteristics.

The Japanese-Americans have been used here as a rather extended example of one cultural group whose patterns of Type A behavior can help in our general understanding of this coronary-prone behavior. Let us consider another example of a group for which there are less data, but whose cultural experience is better known to us. The Japanese cultural difference is non-Western; for U.S. white women, the analogous cultural contrast might be summarized as non-masculine. From my own experience, I would be surprised if a group of women, even if they were all working women, would rate themselves high on those JAS items that describe behavior that is not conventionally defined as appropriately feminine.

It is possible that women may be expressing this response bias in terms of cultural expectations (e.g., are uncomfortable about answering such items positively), rather than "really" scoring lower on those items. The same problems may have existed for the Japanese. Recognition of this cultural screening level in response to questions has been made by many investigators.[23,24] It does not solve the problem but it is comforting to know that these response problems are nearly universal, in regards to questions concerning physiological as well as behavioral symptoms. As long as there is no agreement on the conceptual dimensions of the coronary-prone behavior, any operational definitions will flounder on issues such as whether such response variations are concealing "true" Type A behavior with culturally appropriate responses, or whether this coronary-prone behavior really differs between groups, or is the same in all groups but more rare in some.

However, Type A patterns or their relationship to CHD among women may also vary along cultural environment dimensions. A very modest research proposal would be to inquire whether there are, say, enough women employees at the same occupational levels in the companies participating in the WCGS. Do they have sisters in other jobs or who are housewives? Regardless of whether this or another sample is used, a first step would be to identify patterns of Type A behavior characteristics among women that are similar to those among U.S. men. Those patterns that differ would be assessed in terms of cultural norms for women in this culture and would, in general, be expected to show less (or no) association with CHD risk. And again, as in the case of

Japanese-Americans, women should be studied along a range of cultural environments as discussed above. The hypothesis would again be that Type A women are at significantly elevated risk only in the more stressful environmental situations.

What are the implications of these findings for the more general issue of the relationship between culture and coronary-prone behavior? The research among Japanese-Americans was an effort to use in a new way the traditional epidemiological framework of host and environment characteristics in understanding the etiology of disease. The novelty was in using the behavioral and sociocultural characteristics of person and environment.

Prior knowledge about Type A behavior in men indicated that this behavior predisposed them to increased risk of disease. One immediate question is whether a high-risk behavior will be found in the same way in other populations. Observations from at least one natural experiment indicate that other cultural demands can crosscut behavioral inclinations, rewarding or discouraging them in ways that drastically change their distribution in the population. If we define culture as part of our environment, it is not surprising that this aspect of the human environment should affect the expression of behavior in a way analogous to other environmental impingements. On this basis, then, we should expect to find relatively fewer Type A persons in cultural settings that do not or cannot encourage Type A behavior expression.

Research on the extent of Type A behavior in women, members of other minority groups, and still other groups would be relatively easy and productive in adding to our knowledge in this area. The propositions are relatively straightforward: in cultural groups where politeness and cooperation are expected or rewarded, or where the expression of competitiveness and hostility are discouraged, there should be less Type A behavior. Certainly our understanding of child-rearing patterns, especially in differences between boys and girls in our own culture, is congruent with this expectation.

Further, it is possible that some aspects of a behavior pattern that are desirable but not as directly related to risk can be encouraged, while those aspects of behavior that are less desirable can be discouraged. It is possible to be hard working and not necessarily be hard-driving and competitive; and if the Japanese are anything, they are outstandingly successful in their adaptation to the American standard of success, whether it is measured in terms of educational, occupational, or health progress. A combination of productive but not self-destructive goals within a cultural context, which permits rewards in support and cooperation is not outside the realm of even American culture. Indeed, there are groups within this country now whose record of high accomplishment yet low disease suggests that we have much to learn from them that cannot be explained solely in terms of their other health habits.

In addition to the Japanese, we should try to identify the protective cultural environmental characteristics of Mormons, Seventh Day Adventists, and others like the Japanese-Americans. This is not to suggest that religious affiliation per se is the contributing factor to a low rate of disease, although membership in a religious community is associated with reduced risk of disease. These groups are only suggested starting points for more systematic and comparative research to serve two purposes: first, to begin assessment of cultural patterns against the same comparative standard (what works?), and second, to build more middle-range theory about the roles of cultural and behavioral factors in contributing to risk of disease (how does it all fit together?).

References

1. Rosenman, R.H., Brand, R., Jenkins, C.D., Friedman, M., Straus, R., Wurm, M.: Coronary heart disease in the WCGS: final follow-up experience of 8½ years. *JAMA* **233**:872–877, 1975.
2. Brand, R.J., Rosenman, R.H., Sholtz, R.I., Friedman, M.: Multivariate prediction of coronary heart disease in the Western Collaborative Group Study compared to the findings of the Framingham Study. *Circulation* **53**:348–355, 1976.
3. Friedman, M., Rosenman, R.H.: Association of specific overt behavior patterns with blood and cardiovascular findings. *JAMA* **169**:1286–1296, 1969.
4. Rosenman, R.H., Friedman, M., Straus, R., Wurm, M., Kositchek, R., Haan, W., Werthessen, N.T.: A predictive study of coronary heart disease. *JAMA* **189**:15–22, 1964.
5. Jenkins, C.D., Zyzanski, S.J., Rosenman, R.H.: Progress toward validation of a computer-scored test for the Type A coronary-prone behavior pattern. *Psychosom Med* **33**:193–202, 1971.
6. Zyzanski, S.J., Jenkins, C.D.: Basic dimensions within the coronary-prone behavior pattern. *J Chronic Dis* **22**:781–795, 1970.
7. Jenkins, C.D.: Recent evidence supporting psychologic and social risk factors for coronary disease. *N Engl J Med* **294**:987–994, 1033–1038, 1976.
8. Glass, D.C., Synder, M.I., Hollis, J.F.: Time urgency and the Type A coronary-prone behavior pattern. *J Appl Soc Psychol* **4**:125–140, 1974.
9. Shekelle, R.B., Schoenberger, J.A., Stamler, J.: Correlates of the JAS Type A behavior pattern score. *J Chronic Dis* **29**:381–394, 1976.
10. Zyzanski, S.J.: Coronary-Prone Behavior Pattern and Coronary Heart Disease: Epidemological Evidence. *In* Coronary-Prone Behavior (Dembroski, T.M., et al., eds.). New York: Springer-Verlag, 1978, chapter 2 (pp. 25–40).
11. DeVos, G.A.: Socialization for Achievement: Essays on the Cultural Psychology of the Japanese. Berkeley, Ca.: University of California Press, 1973.
12. Benedict, R.: The Chrysanthemum and the Sword. New York: Meridian, World Publishing Company, 1967.
13. Caudill, W., DeVos, G.A.: Achievement, culture, and personality: the case of the Japanese-Americans. *Am Anthro* **58**:1102–1126, 1956.
14. Kagan, A., Harris, B.R., Winkelstein, W., et al.: Epidemiologic studies of coronary heart disease and stroke in Japanese men living in Japan, Hawaii and California: demographic, physical, dietary and biochemical characteristics. *J Chronic Dis* **27**:345–364, 1974.
15. Cohen, J.B.: Sociocultural change and behavior patterns in disease etiology: an epidemiologic study of coronary disease among Japanese-Americans. Unpublished Ph.D Thesis. Berkeley, Ca.: University of California, 1974.
16. Cohen, J.B., Syme, S.L., Jenkins, C.D., Kagan, A., Zyzanski, S.J.: The cultural context of Type A behavior and the risk of CHD. *Am J Epidemiol* **102**:434, 1975.
17. House, J.S.: Occupational stress and coronary heart disease: a review and theoretical integration. *J Health Soc Behav* **15**:12–27, 1974.
18. Syme, S.L., Hyman, M.M., Enterline, P.E.: Some social and cultural factors associated with the occurrence of coronary heart disease. *J Chronic Dis* **17**:277–289, 1964.

19. Syme, S.L., Borhani, N.O., Buechley, R.W.: Cultural mobility and coronary heart disease in an urban area. *Am J Epidemiol* **82**:334–346, 1966.
20. Cassel, J.C.: The contributions of the social environment to host resistance. *Am J Epidemiol* **104**:107–123, 1976.
21. Kaplan, B.H., Cassel, J.C., Gore, S.: Social Support and Health. *Med Care* **15**:47–58, 1977.
22. Matsumoto, Y.S.: Social stress and coronary heart disease in Japan: a hypothesis. *Milbank Mem Fund Q* **48**:9–36, 1970.
23. Horowitz, M., Schaefer, C., Hiroto, D., Wilner, N., Levin, B.: Life event questionnaires for measuring presumptive stress. *Psychosom Med* **39**:413–431, 1977.
24. Gove, W.R.: Adult sex roles and mental illness. *Am J Sociol* **78**:812–835, 1973.

Chapter 15

Sex Differences in the Coronary-Prone Behavior Pattern

Ingrid Waldron

Available information suggests that for the half of American women who are not currently employed, the coronary-prone behavior pattern may be adequately assessed by revised forms of the Rosenman and Friedman Type A interview and the Jenkins Activity Survey, which omit questions on current employment.

In women, as in men, the coronary-prone behavior pattern is correlated with the prevalence of coronary heart disease, specifically including coronary atherosclerosis. For women, as for men, the standard risk factors apparently do not account for much of the risk associated with the coronary-prone behavior pattern.

The coronary-prone behavior pattern has been found to be more prevalent among employed women than among housewives. Women who have the hard-driving coronary-prone behavior pattern may be more likely to seek employment or less likely to leave jobs once they have begun. Also, pressures associated with employment may stimulate Type A behaviors.

Type A behavior appears to be more prevalent among men than among women. This sex difference in behavior pattern probably contributes to men's higher rates of coronary heart disease. Sex differences in behavior pattern appear to reflect both inherited sex differences in aggressiveness and sex differences in socialization, for example, in the encouragement of competitive achievement. Sex differences in socialization might be expected, since the

The unpublished data on college students referred to in this paper have been collected and analyzed with the able assistance of Ann Hickey, Cathy McPherson, Arthur Butensky, Karen Overall, Angela Schmader, and David Wohlmuth.

coronary-prone behavior pattern appears to contribute significantly to success in traditional male roles, but not to success in traditional female roles.

Problems of Assessment

The concept of Type A behavior was developed in studies of men, and includes excessive devotion to job as one key characteristic. The two standard instruments for the measurement of the pattern are the Rosenman and Friedman Type *SI* A interview and the Jenkins Activity Survey (a multiple choice questionnaire). *JAS* Both include a considerable number of questions related to employment. These employment-related questions produce the primary problem in assessment of the pattern in women, since only about half of adult women in the United States are currently employed.

Jenkins and co-workers have recently revised the Jenkins Activity Survey (JAS) and have introduced an E form for persons who are currently employed and an N form for those who are not employed, such as housewives, students, and retired persons. In the N form, the questions about behavior at work have been replaced with questions designed to tap similar behavioral dispositions in other settings. Type A scores on the N and E forms are not strictly comparable since the scores are based on somewhat different items and have not been standardized by a comparison of the scores on both forms for the same sample. However, this problem seems to be relatively minor in practice since Type A scores on the N form and the E form are both very closely related to a special Type A score, which uses identical items from the N and E forms.[1]

There is another problem, probably also minor, in comparing JAS scores between women and men. Women tend to respond to some questions in the context of child-rearing, and this may result in a lack of comparability of women's and men's responses to certain questions, such as the questions about how one responds to a person who takes too long to come to the point. One finding suggests that, at least among employed white adults, sex differences in interpretation and psychological significance of the questions may not be too great; the factor structures of responses to the JAS were very similar for employed white women and men.[2]

Problems of content are not as crucial for the interview since behavior pattern is rated to a large extent on the basis of style of response. Ratings for men and women may not be strictly comparable, since styles of speech, such as loudness and interruption, may be socialized differently in girls and boys and may therefore be related differently to the coronary-prone behavior pattern in the two sexes.

Despite the problems described, the interview and the JAS both appear to provide valid measures of Type A behavior in women. In the one sample for which scores on the revised JAS and interview ratings are both available, these measures are positively correlated, both for housewives who completed the N form and for employed women who completed the E form.[1] More importantly, at least four studies have shown that the measures of the coronary-prone behavior pattern are related to the prevalence of coronary heart disease in women.[3-6]

The Coronary-Prone Behavior Pattern and Coronary Heart Disease in Women

Positive evidence of a relationship between the coronary-prone behavior pattern and the prevalence of coronary heart disease has been found in all four studies available thus far. In the earliest study, Rosenman and Friedman[3] compared samples of extreme Type A and Type B women and found that the prevalence of clinical coronary heart disease was higher in the former. In a case-control study of patients hospitalized for coronary heart disease or for surgery and trauma, Kenigsberg et al.[4] found that the women with coronary heart disease scored higher on the Type A scale of the JAS than the controls. Recently, Haynes et al.[5,6] have used a scale composed of items that were administered in the Framingham study and were chosen by "outside experts" as representative of the coronary-prone behavior pattern. Women judged to be Type A (in the upper 50% of scores on this scale) had a significantly higher prevalence of coronary heart disease than Type B's (4.0% versus 0.5% at ages 45 to 54, 7.7% versus 2.4% at ages 55 to 64, and 20.0% versus 9.3% at ages 65 to 74). This relationship between Type A and the prevalence of coronary heart disease was observed for both housewives and working women. Finally, Blumenthal[7] found that for women undergoing coronary angiography, those rated Type A in the interview had a significantly higher prevalence of coronary atherosclerosis than those rated Type B (11 of 23 Type A women versus one of 24 Type B women).*

These studies indicate that for women, as for men, the coronary-prone behavior pattern is correlated with a higher prevalence of coronary heart disease, including coronary atherosclerosis. The findings for women parallel the findings for men in one additional respect. The coronary-prone behavior pattern does not appear to exert its primary pathological effect via the standard risk factors.[9] Haynes et al.[5] found no relationship between their Type A score and a risk score for coronary heart disease calculated on the basis of standard risk factors such as serum cholesterol, blood pressure, and cigarette smoking. Shekelle et al.[10] report that for employed women, the JAS Type A score has no significant relationship to cholesterol levels; a positive relationship with blood pressure in women aged 45 to 64, but not in younger women; and a positive, but quantitatively small, relationship with number of cigarettes smoked per day in younger women. Thus, the coronary-prone behavior pattern may be related to some of the standard risk factors, but the relationships appear to be too weak to account for much of the elevation of coronary heart disease prevalence.

---

* Some additional supportive evidence is provided by Bengtsson et al.,[8] who attempted to measure the coronary-prone behavior pattern by means of the achievement and aggression scales of the Cesarec-Marke Person Schedule and found aggressiveness to be significantly higher in women with myocardial infarctions than in controls.

**Role and Sex Differences in the
Coronary-Prone Behavior Pattern**

On the average, employed women have been found to display more of the coronary-prone behavior pattern than housewives. Women who had been employed outside the home for over half their adult years had higher scores on the Type A scale used in the Framingham study than housewives.[6] Women currently employed more than 30 hours a week had higher Type A scores on the JAS than women who were not employed full-time.[1] This relationship between current employment and the coronary-prone behavior pattern was observed only for women of higher educational status, a pattern found also in earlier studies of "need for achievement."[11,12] Type A women did not prefer more hours of employment; rather they were more likely to work longer hours than they preferred.[1] This suggests that women who have hard-driving, Type A behavior may be less likely to leave jobs even when they feel overloaded. Also, time pressures and other demands associated with women's employment may increase the coronary-prone behavior pattern.

In the Framingham study, men had higher scores than women.[5] In a sample of employed women and men, the men had significantly higher Type A scores at ages 18 to 25, although sex differences at older ages were not significant when tested within subsamples equated for education and race.[2] Since about half of women in the older age groups are housewives, and since housewives are less Type A than employed women, these data also indicate that women are, on the average, less Type A than men. In two samples of hospitalized patients, significant sex differences were not found, probably because of small sample sizes and selection biases (one sample included only coronary patients) (see Chapter 2). Additional evidence that the coronary-prone behavior pattern is more prevalent among men than among women is provided by psychological studies that show that, on the average, men and boys are more aggressive and competitive than women and girls.[13]

The greater prevalence of the coronary-prone behavior pattern among men than women appears to contribute to the higher rates of coronary heart disease among men.[14] Differences in coronary heart disease rates between employed women and housewives are complex to interpret, since women who become ill tend to leave the labor force, which results in a misleading elevation of disease rates among housewives.[6]

Why is the coronary-prone behavior pattern more common among men than women? Genetic differences appear to make some contribution to sex differences in aggressiveness, but genetic differences have not been shown to play a role in sex differences in other components of the coronary-prone behavior pattern.[13] Twin studies of Type A behavior suggest that genetic factors may make only a small contribution to individual differences in this behavior pattern.[15,16] Cultural factors,[17] including child-rearing practices (see Chapter 16) are related to the development of the coronary-prone behavior pattern in children and young adults. Differences in the socialization of boys and girls probably contribute to sex differences in the coronary-prone behavior pattern. For example, sex differences in competitiveness appear to be fostered by

parents and schools who have typically pushed boys to achieve in the occupational world and girls to seek success in the less competitive family sphere.[14]

It seems likely that Type A behavior is reinforced more in males than in
females, since this hard-driving, aggressive style of behavior appears to contribute to success in traditional male roles, but not in traditional female roles.
For example, adults who are more Type A have repeatedly been found to have
more education, higher status occupations, and more income[1,2,10,18,19] (see
Chapter 2). Limited evidence suggests that this may be due in part to greater
upward socioeconomic mobility of the more Type A individual. Mettlin[18] has
reported a correlation of +0.23 between Type A score and an increase in
income over a 10-year period. Reported correlations between measures of
occupational mobility and Type A have been smaller and not always significant,
probably because of the insensitivity of the measures available (e.g., change in
Hollingshead occupational category over a period of four years)[19] and also
because of cultural differences between white North American men and
Japanese-American men.[20] Intergenerational educational mobility was significantly correlated with Type A interview rating in one sample of women,
although not in another.[1] Also, we have found that students who are more Type
A spend more of their time studying, have higher grade point averages, and win
more academic honors (see Chapter 2). In summary, the coronary-prone behavior pattern is related to educational achievement, high status occupations,
high income, and perhaps also to upward educational and occupational mobility.

In contrast, the coronary-prone behavior pattern does not appear to contribute significantly to success in traditional female roles. Our work shows that
among women in college, those who are more Type A are not significantly
more likely to have a boyfriend or more frequent dates, nor are they more
satisfied with their relationships with men. Among middle-aged women, those
who are more Type A are not more likely to be married, and if married, they have
husbands of equal or lower status than the husbands of less Type A women.[1] In
contrast, middle-aged men who are more Type A are more likely to be married.
If, as these data suggest, the coronary-prone behavior pattern contributes more
to success in traditional male roles than in traditional female roles, it would not
be surprising to find that such behavior is encouraged more in boys than girls.

In conclusion, there appear to be a variety of relationships between the
coronary-prone behavior pattern and social roles. Type A behavior may lead
some women to choose a specific role, such as paid employment, and may lead
to success in certain social roles, for example, as college students. In addition,
rewards or pressures associated with certain social roles may enhance the
coronary-prone behavior pattern. Finally, anticipated social roles may influence socialization practices that may contribute to the development of sex
differences in the coronary-prone behavior pattern.

Proposals for Further Research

The interview and rating of the interview should be better standardized for
women. Further validation is required for use of the JAS for women, particu-

larly for the N form. The proposed multidimensional approach to assessment (see Chapter 8) appears promising and, if found to be useful for men, should also be standardized and validated for women.

The relationship between the coronary-prone behavior pattern and the incidence of coronary heart disease should be assessed for women. This has been begun with incidence data from the Framingham study.[22]

The findings of sex differences in coronary-prone behavior pattern and differences between employed women and housewives require replication. It would also be useful to identify the age span in which sex differences in the coronary-prone behavior pattern emerge, and to study sex differences in aspects of socialization that have been shown to be associated with the coronary-prone behavior pattern (see Chapter 16). For example, do parents or schoolteachers tend to escalate standards of performance more for boys than for girls?

Longitudinal studies of the coronary-prone behavior pattern in women as they enter and leave the labor force, or of men and women as they change jobs, would provide an excellent opportunity to test previously postulated environmental effects on behavior pattern. New studies using better measures of occupational and educational mobility could clarify the extent to which the coronary-prone behavior pattern may be reinforced by greater success in our society.

References

1. Waldron, I.: The coronary-prone behavior pattern, blood pressure, employment, and socioeconomic status in women. *J Psychosom Res* **22**:79–87, 1978.
2. Waldron, I., Zyzanski, S., Shekelle, R.B., Jenkins, C.D., Tannenbaum, S.: The coronary-prone behavior pattern in employed men and women. *J Human Stress* **3**(4):2–18, 1977.
3. Rosenman, R.H., Friedman, M.: Association of specific behavior pattern in women with blood and cardiovascular findings. *Circulation* **24**:1173–1184, 1961.
4. Kenigsberg, D., Zyzanski, S.J., Jenkins, C.D., Wardwell, W.I., Licciardello, A.T.: The coronary-prone behavior pattern in hospitalized patients with and without coronary heart disease. *Psychosom Med* **36**:344–351, 1974.
5. Haynes, S.G., Levine, S., Scotch, N.A., Feinleib, M., Kannel, W.B.: The relationship of psychosocial factors to coronary heart disease in the Framingham Study. I. Methods and Risk Factors. *Am J Epidemiol* **107**:362–383, 1978.
6. Haynes, S.G., Feinleib, M., Levine, S., Scotch, N.A., Kannel, W.B.: The relationship of psychosocial factors to coronary heart disease in the Framingham study II. Prevalence of coronary heart disease. *Am J Epidemiol* **107**:384–402, 1978.
7. Blumenthal, J.A., Kong, Y., Rosenman, R.H., et al.: Type A behavior pattern and angiographically documented coronary disease. Presented at the American Psychosomatic Society meeting, New Orleans, March 1975, and personal communication, 1977.
8. Bengtsson, C., Hallstrom, T., Tibblin, G.: Social factors, stress experience, and personality traits in women with ischaemic heart disease, compared to a population sample of women. *Acta Med Scand* (Suppl) **549**:82–92, 1973.
9. Rosenman, R.H., Brand, R.J., Jenkins, C.D., Friedman, M., Straus, R., Wurm, M.: Coronary heart disease in the Western Collaborative Group Study. *JAMA* **233**:872–877, 1975.
10. Shekelle, R.B., Schoenberger, J.A., Stamler, J.: Correlates of the JAS Type A behavior pattern score. *J Chronic Dis* **29**:381–394, 1976.

11. Baruch, R.: The achievement motive in women: implications for career development. *J Pers Soc Psychol* **5**:260–267, 1967.
12. Kriger, S.F.: *nAch* and perceived parental child-rearing attitudes of career women and home-makers. *J Voc Behav* **2**:419–432, 1972.
13. Maccoby, E.E., Jacklin, C.N.: The Psychology of Sex Differences. Stanford, Ca.: Stanford University Press, 1974.
14. Waldron, I.: Why do women live longer than men? Part I. *J Human Stress* **2**:2–13, 1976.
15. Rahe, R., Rosenman, R.H.: Heritability of Type A behavior. (Abstract) *Psychosom Med* **37**:78–79, 1975.
16. Matthews, K.A., Krantz, D.S.: Resemblances of twins and their parents in Pattern A behavior. *Psychosom Med.* **38**:140–144, 1976.
17. Butensky, A., Faralli, V., Heebner, D., Waldron, I.: Elements of the coronary-prone behavior pattern in children and teenagers. *J Psychosom Res* **20**:439–444, 1976.
18. Mettlin, C.: Occupational careers and the prevention of coronary-prone behavior. *Soc Sci Med* **10**:367–372, 1976.
19. Williams, C.A.: The relationship of occupational change to blood pressure, serum cholesterol, a specific overt behavior pattern, and coronary heart disease. Unpublished Ph.D. thesis, Department of Epidemiology, University of North Carolina at Chapel Hill, North Carolina, 1968.
20. Cohen, J.B.: Sociocultural change and behavior patterns in disease etiology: An epidemiologic study of coronary disease among Japanese-Americans. Unpublished Ph.D. thesis, Department of Epidemiology, University of California at Berkeley, California, 1974.
21. Glass, D.C.: Stress, behavior patterns and coronary disease. *Am Sci* **65**:177–187, 1977.
22. Haynes, S.G.: National Heart, Lung, and Blood Institute, personal communication, 1977.

Chapter 16

Assessment and Developmental Antecedents of the Coronary-Prone Behavior Pattern in Children

Karen A. Matthews

On occasion, I speak to groups of housewives and elementary school teachers about Type A behavior. Afterwards, members of the audience have commented, "Yes, I know the behavior pattern you are describing—I have two Type A sons," or "Last year my classroom contained largely Type B children, but this year, well, I am exhausted." Although these women report easy recognition of Type A children, the assessment techniques of children's Type A behavior are immature. Research on the developmental antecedents of Type A is also in its youth. The goals of the present paper are to thoroughly review the literature relevant to the etiology of Type A, and to suggest directions for future research. We begin with a description and critique of the current methods for assessing Type A, in children, followed by an outline of research on Type A behavior in children. Then, the literature on components of Type A, that is, children's competitive achievement-striving, aggression, and time perception, is reviewed and its implications for the development of Type A are discussed. Finally, directions for future research are suggested.

Measurement of Type A in Children

Several assessment methods for detecting Type A in children are currently being developed. Butensky et al.[1] have adapted a ten-question interview for children from the Rosenman-Friedman adult interview[2] and the Jenkins Activity Survey (JAS).[3] The answer to each interview question is scored largely on the basis of its content, on a scale of zero (extreme Type B response) to one (extreme Type A response), with an intervening half unit rating in most cases. There is one additional rating for interruptions by the respondent on two questions, designed to elicit Type A's characteristic impatience. Possible interview scores range from zero to 11. Reliability and validity data are not published.

An interview has several positive features for the assessment of children's behavior patterns. First, according to Friedman and Rosenman,[4] Type A behavior is displayed by susceptible individuals only in the appropriately challenging environment. The interview provides this environment. For example, the hesitancy of the interviewer at several points can elicit the impatience of Type A children. The challenging of several of the responses by the interviewer can elicit competitiveness. Second, the interview allows probing for potentially relevant information. Third, the interviewer is an observer of the child's Type A behavior in the interview and can check the accuracy of the child's self-perception. Thus, the interview assessment is likely to be more valid than self-reports because the assessments are made on the basis of Type A behavior in the interview in addition to self-reports. However, the Butensky interview does not exploit some of the inherent advantages of the adult interview because it is highly standardized and currently includes only one rating for speech style.

There are several disadvantages of an interview for children. First, young children may not have sufficiently mature speech for reliable interviews.[5] Second, children tend to be shy with adult strangers, particularly in a formal situation such as an interview. For this reason, the interview responses may reflect the child's sociability and lack of fear, as well as Type A behavior. Thus, an interview may not be appropriate for children younger than 9 or 10 years old.

A second assessment method is the Matthews Youth Test for Health, or MYTH.[6] It has undergone several revisions. It contains 17 rating scales of children's competitiveness, achievement-striving, impatience, and anger displayed in the classroom. Two examples are: "When this child has to wait for others, he or she becomes impatient. When this child plays, he or she is competitive." The children's classroom teacher completes the ratings of how characteristic the statement is of the children on a scale of one ("very uncharacteristic") to five ("very characteristic"). Test-retest reliability has been computed for 438 male and female children at grades K, 2, 4, and 6. Each child was rated twice by the same teacher, with ratings 2 to 3 weeks apart. The correlation was .87 between the two scores. Comparable correlations were computed for males and females separately and for each grade level. Currently we are validating the MYTH with laboratory measures of Type A behavior and developing scoring systems for individual Type A characteristics.

A questionnaire like the MYTH has some obvious advantages. It is economical to administer. The scores are not based on children's self-perceptions. Indeed, children have difficulties completing such inventories prior to the age of nine.[7] Teachers should be adequate raters because they have extensive experience with a range of children's personalities. Yet, much is unknown about the MYTH's psychometric qualities, including the interrater reliability of the instrument. Final assessment of its advantages and disadvantages must await further research.

Another method of assessment of Type A in children is a battery of four performance tasks developed by Bortner.[8,9] Each task is related theoretically to an aspect of Type A. For example, impatience is reflected by the relative inability to slow down when requested to write "United States of America" slower than normal writing speed. For a small sample of men, the agreement rate between the interview and the Bortner task assessments was 66% but there was no relationship between the Bortner and the JAS measures.[8] The task battery has been used with male children as young as nine years of age.[10]

The Bortner battery has both strengths and weaknesses as a measure of Type A behavior in children. It places minimal reliance on verbal ability and is relatively unaffected by social desirability response biases. On the other hand, at least one task in the battery is substantially affected by intelligence. The embedded figures test, one of the four tasks, has a substantial correlation with the intelligence tests.[11] Another difficulty is that the reliability of the tasks in the battery is unknown. Finally, the greatest weakness is that the task battery is the most cumbersome, time consuming, and expensive technique of the three discussed.

At this point, it is appropriate to discuss the inherent difficulties in establishing valid measures of children's Type A behavior. With adult tests of Type A, the appropriate validity criterion is clear—myocardial infarction, angina pectoris, or silent MI. If Type A is a predictor of later heart disease onset in a prospective study, then evidence for predictive criterion-related validity is established. A prospective study assumes that Type A behavior is a relatively stable disposition, which it appears to be in adult men.[12] For children's measures, predictive validity is relevant only if children's behavior pattern is stable over a long period of time. If Type A and heart disease are measured concurrently in a retrospective study, then evidence of concurrent criterion-related validity is sought. For children, coronary heart disease is obviously not the appropriate concurrent criterion. Type A adults and heart disease patients exhibit similar physiological characteristics.[13–15] Perhaps these characteristics are an appropriate concurrent-criterion for Type A behavior in children. However, if no association is established, one could argue that pathology only begins after several decades of continual Type A behavior. Thus, criterion-related validity is not an essential psychometric quality for measures of Type A in children. On the other hand, construct and content validities are appropriate for children's measures of Type A. Glass's[13] experimentation on the construct validity of his student version of the JAS is an excellent example of the needed systemic validation research on the children's interview or the MYTH.

In view of the above discussion, my recommendations are to continue to develop both the Butensky interview and the MYTH. The interview appears to be appropriate for children nine years old and older, whereas the MYTH can assess Type A behavior of the younger children. The interview assessment should include some of the advantages of the adult interview previously outlined. This is particularly true since the single speech style rating of the children's interview was one of several individual ratings that differentiated suburban and rural groups in the Butensky study (see p. 8).[1] Reliability, content validity, and construct validity data need to be gathered for the interview and the MYTH. Criterion-related validation is not necessary to establish the adequacy of the measurement.

Childhood Antecedents of Type A Behavior

The following discussion will focus primarily on environmental determinants of Type A behavior in children. Prior to a review of the literature, we should clarify the position of the present paper on two theoretical issues. First, are the antecedents of adult Type A merely Type A behavior in childhood, or are they some other combination of organized behavior, which later in life emerges as Type A? The latter approach is complex and assumes stages of development. The former is simpler and assumes continuity of behavior over time. The approach of the present paper is the former because of the need for parsimony in a new area of research.

The second issue concerns Type A assessment. An individual is classified as a Type A if he has a simple preponderance of Type A characteristics. It is theoretically possible to have one Type A who is competitive and achievement oriented, but patient. On the other hand, it is feasible that another Type A could be aggressive and easily irritated, but not achievement oriented. Until we know the necessary and sufficient combination of characteristics to classify the adult individual into the Type A category, it is appropriate to study the etiology of individual characteristics. Therefore, research on the development of components of Type A as well as research on Type A children are reviewed.

Research on Type A Behavior of Children

Age, social class, and child–parent relationships have been investigated as potential contributors to Type A in children. The relationship of age and Type A is unclear. Bortner and Rosenman[8] found that age and degree of Type A behavior on the Bortner test battery were moderately related in a sample of males 11 to 21 years old. However, there may be a confounding of intelligence with at least one of the tests. Older children could have outperformed younger children and received a higher Type A score due to intelligence alone. Butensky, et al.[1] did not find an association of age and Type A interview behavior in children. They did find that children and teenagers from suburban, middle-class homes were more Type A than age- and sex-matched counterparts from rural, working class homes. The authors argue that the rural students were less Type A because of the limited and well-defined goals characteristic of a working class community in contrast to a suburban community. This interesting notion should be tested in further research.

A frequently studied and obvious factor in personality and social development is the parent–child relationship. Several theorists have suggested that parents might be a model of Type A behavior for their children. Thus, parents and children should be similar on the Type A dimension. The available evidence suggests modest similarity when both the Type A measurement technique is identical for parents and their children and the children are older than 11.[9,16] When the measurement technique is different for parents and their children and the children are younger than 11, there is no relationship between their scores.[10,17] It is unclear whether the above relationships are due to the use of same/different measurement techniques or to the age of the children. A more fruitful approach, however, is to examine similarity on specific Type A components because of the different "types" of Type A individuals.

Child-rearing practices of the parents are likely to play a critical role in the development of Type A. Type A adults and children respond similarly to modest losses of control[10,18,19] (see Chapter 12). Disapproval or loss of approval is conceptually analogous to a loss of control. Perhaps the upbringing of Type A's is distinguished by disapproval or losses of approval. In addition, to produce a child struggling to achieve ever-escalating goals, approval should be contingent on improvement in speed or accuracy of performance. If the above arguments are true, then parental child-rearing practices associated with Type A children should be characterized by frequent use of disapproval and approval contingent upon improving performance relative to the children's previous performance or the standards of others.

There is evidence consistent with the above formulations. Type A college students report that they evaluate their performance relative to others more often than Type B's.[20] In contrast to Type B's, Type A college students report that they feel guilty when they do not meet their parent's approval and that their parents are more strict. However, a small group of hospitalized patients with coronary heart disease did not report greater guilt and parental strictness than a matched control group.[21] Veroff[22] suggests that considerable parental reinforcement for relative performance evaluation can cause the development of social comparison as a general disposition in young children. Finally, Type A and B male children ages 4 to 10 years were observed while working with their mothers on three psychomotor tasks. Mothers of extreme Type A children more frequently disapproved and encouraged them to try harder following a good performance than the mothers of extreme Type B's. In addition, mothers less frequently evaluated Type A children's performance positively than Type B's.[17]

Because a mother's child-rearing practices may be affected by the behavior pattern of her child,[23] it was not possible to conclude that the above child-rearing practices in the Matthews study[17] had caused the children's behavior pattern. It is equally probable that the son's characteristic behavior pattern had elicited this set of child-rearing practices, particularly in light of the suspected genetic contributions to components of Type A behavior.[24,25] Therefore, two studies were undertaken to examine separately the child's impact on the mother and the mother's impact on the child.[6]

In one study, boys worked on a task with a female experimenter (mother substitute), who gave either frequent or infrequent positive evaluations of their task performance and either frequent or no urging to improve their performance following successful performances. An example of urging is "That's fine, but next time try harder.'' The boys were neither extreme A's nor extreme B's on the MYTH. A second experimenter, blind to the children's group assignment, subsequently measured the boys' competitive achievement-striving and impatience on two other tasks. Boys who were frequently given positive task evaluation and were urged to improve their performance were the most competitive subsequently. Impatience was not affected.

The second study examined the effect of the child's behavior pattern on the mother (substitute).[26] Present mother–child interactions are, of course, a culmination of a long history of interactions. To control for unknown history, a female stranger, who was a mother of another same-age boy, observed a child actor behave on one task in ways typical of either Type A or Type B. Then the female stranger actively worked with the actor on two subsequent tasks and the number of positive evaluations and urging of improvement was coded. The women, particularly Type B's, gave Type A children more positive reinforcements and urged them more often to improve their performance relative to Type B children. Taken together, the pair of studies suggests a snowballing effect. Children react to strangers' frequent positive evaluation and urging of improvement by becoming more competitive. Competitive, impatient children elicit, in turn, more positive evaluation and urging improvement of the performance from strangers.

In summary, the research thus far suggests that setting escalating standards and parental disapproval play an important role in the etiology of Type A. However, the role of frequent positive evaluation by strangers with Type A children is unclear because mothers use infrequent positive evaluation with their own Type A sons. Perhaps the combination of frequent extrafamilial approval and intrafamilial contingent approval/disapproval is the specific dynamic behind Type A's chronic struggle. Further research is needed to clarify the appropriate interpretation.

There is substantial work on the development of components of the behavior pattern. Only the highlights of this research are reviewed. The implications of the research for Type A development are stated.

Achievement Motivation

Heckhausen[27] defines achievement motivation as "striving to increase, or keep high as possible, one's own capabilities in all activities in which a standard of excellence is thought to apply . . . " (p. 5). The above definition is remarkably similar to the definition of Type A. A discussion of need achievement gains significance because two studies have reported an association between achievement motivation and heart disease.[28,29] Achievement behavior is a relatively stable characteristic after the age of 6 to 10.[30]

The literature on parental child-rearing practices associated with children who are high on achievement motivation scales converges on several points. First, the parents of high need achievement sons have greater expectations and aspirations for sons' achievement than the parents of low need achievement sons.[31,32] For girls high on need achievement, similar data are not available.

Second, parents serve as a referent for evaluation of their children's successes and failures. Thus, the parents actively reward successful achievements and disapprove of failures.[31,33,34-36] The mother, in particular, frequently makes remarks designed to motivate her child to improve his performance.[31]

Third, the discipline techniques of parents of achievement-oriented children are authoritative, rather than authoritarian or permissive.[37] Authoritative parents exercise firm control, but also recognize their children's needs and share with them the reasons underlying disciplinary decisions. Authoritarian parents are controlling but not accepting of the child, whereas permissive parents show the reverse pattern.

There are different patterns of maternal and parental interactions with high need-achievement children, according to the sex of the children. The fathers of high need-achievement sons tend to be competent, self-reliant men who encourage independent behavior of their sons. "They tend to beckon from ahead, rather than push from behind" (p. 216).[31] On the other hand, the mothers tend to be very competitive, somewhat controlling, and involved with their son's achievement efforts.[31] Girl's achievement-striving is associated with mild rejection by the mother coupled with the father's interest in his daughter's achievement efforts.[38,39] Several theorists have suggested that mild maternal rejection prevents a debilitating dependency of the girls and encourages independent thinking.[38-40] The described pattern of findings cautions us to examine parental inputs to the development of Type A behavior separately for boys and girls.

In summary, the achievement motivation literature implies that parental standards and evaluations of performance and an authoritative discipline style may be associated with the development of Type A behavior in children. The parent–child relationship differs according to the sex of the child.

Aggression

Children learn aggressive behavior by direct teaching of aggression and by observing models behave in an aggressive fashion.[41] Boys are taught to be physically aggressive in prescribed settings—in self-defense or in the defense of a smaller child or sibling. Their aggression is tolerated. Girls, on the other hand, are taught that it is not appropriate to be aggressive and are strongly discouraged when aggressive. Thus, boys, who are aggressive at 6 to 10 years of age are also aggressive adults, whereas aggressive girls at 6 to 10 are not aggressive adults.[30]

Parents serve as a child's first model of aggressive behavior. In fact, aggressive children tend to have parents who give high permission and strong punishment for aggression.[39,42,43] Thus, the parents may model aggression through their punishment techniques. After a child is enrolled in school, however, peers offer the most frequent modeling of aggression.[44] In addition, television programs provide innumerable aggressive models for children; for example, the typical child has observed 15,000 murders by the age of 15.[45]

Obviously, not all aggressive behavior, although learned, is performed. Children's performance of a model's aggression is most likely when the model is rewarded for his aggression, has an affectionate relationship with the child, is the same sex as the child, is perceived as competent, nurturant, and powerful, and, to a lesser degree, models behavior that is sex-appropriate.[42,46-49]

In brief, the aggressive component of Type A is exhibited when attractive models are aggressive; aggression is rewarded by obtaining attention, esteem, or desired resources; and aggression is allowed and returned in kind in the home. Aggression is a relatively stable characteristic in boys, but not in girls.

Time Urgency

Individual differences in children's sense of time urgency have not been investigated. However, Ornstein's[50] theoretical and experimental work on the perception of time duration has implications for the developmental antecedents of time urgency. According to Ornstein, duration lengthens as the size of the storage space for information occurring in a given time interval increases. The size of the storage space, in turn, depends on the amount of information or the number of occurrences in the interval that reach awareness and the way that information is coded and stored. Time duration is perceived to be greater, that is, more time has passed when there is an increase in amount of information coded, an increase in complexity of the material, or a decrease in efficiency of the processor. Interruptions, lack of experience with the material, and failures increase the complexity of the encoded materials.

Type A's chronically overestimate the length of time that is passing.[51] Perhaps Type A's perceive more complex, nonrepetitive events, more interrupted or incompleted tasks, and fewer true successes than do Type B's. A sense of a rapid time passage then might stem from childhood experiences characterized by (1) high frequency and novelty as, for example, occur in cities and high density living areas; (2) projects and activities with neither a clear ending nor a clear standard by which to evaluate competency; and (3) evaluations of failure, i.e., not reaching goals. Research is obviously necessary to explore these possibilities.

Summary of Findings and of Suggested Future Research

There is converging evidence that parental standards of performance, which are ever-escalating, play a role in the etiology of Type A behavior, particularly in the achievement-striving component. High achievement motivation is associated with the following parental behavior: high expectations and aspirations, frequent approval and disapproval, a competitive and involved attitude, and authoritative discipline techniques. The pattern of maternal and paternal interactions with high need-achievement children differ according to the sex of the child. Achievement behavior is a relatively stable disposition for both boys and girls. Children exhibit the aggressive component of Type A when attractive models are aggressive; aggression is rewarded by obtaining attention, esteem, or a desired resource; and aggression is allowed and returned in kind in the home. Aggression is a relatively stable disposition for boys, but not for girls.

Many possible directions for research were mentioned, but I suggest we restrict our initial efforts to the following:

1. Further development of a reliable, valid measurement of Type A behavior in children. The children's interview should exploit the advantages of the adult interview. Further reliability data and content and construct validity data should be gathered for both the interview and MYTH.
2. An investigation of the stability of Type A behavior in children. A beginning step would be a series of two-year longitudinal studies of children at various age levels. If children's Type A assessment was relatively stable, a long-term study might be warranted and early detection of adult coronary-prone behavior might be possible.
3. Studies of parents' modeling specific aspects of coronary-prone behavior, with particular attention to the sex-appropriateness of the behavior.
4. Experiments on time urgency in children. Are the lives of Type A children, specifically those with a sense of time passing rapidly, characterized by many complex and novel experiences, by projects and activities with neither a clear ending nor a clear standard by which to evaluate competency, and by recurring failures?
5. Further studies of school and parental inputs to Type A. The structure of the American classroom and its reward and value systems probably encourage children's Type A behavior. For example, there is evidence that the American classroom promotes social comparison and competition.[52] Perhaps time urgency is encouraged in school by use of timed tasks, discrete periods for classwork, and a value on rapid learning and performance. Observations of parental behavior with Type A male children aged 4 to 10 have been fruitful. Components of Type A, i.e., aggression, achievement behavior, competitiveness, are relatively stable after the ages of 6 to 10 for boys.[30] Evidently, child-rearing practices associated with children younger than this age range play a role in the acquisition of these dispositions. We should observe the child-rearing practices associated with younger children.

The suggested research should lead to an understanding of the etiology of Type A. Thus, we would know the childhood origins of a behavior pattern that affects the health of millions of American adults each year.

References

1. Butensky, A., Faralli, V., Heebner, D., Waldron, I.: Elements of the coronary prone behavior pattern in children and teenagers. *J Psychosom Res* **20**:439–444, 1976.
2. Friedman, M.: Pathogenesis of Coronary Artery Disease. New York: McGraw-Hill, 1969.
3. Jenkins, C.D., Zyzanski, S.J., Rosenman, R.H.: Progress toward validation of a computer-scored test of the Type A coronary-prone behavior pattern. *Psychosom Med* **36**:344–351, 1971.
4. Friedman, M., Rosenman, R.H.: Type A Behavior and Your Heart. New York: Knopf, 1974.

5. Harris, R.: Personal communication, Kansas State University, Manhattan, Kansas, 1977.
6. Matthews, K.A.: Mother-child interactions as a determinant of Type A-Type B behavior. Unpublished doctoral dissertation. Austin: University of Texas, 1976.
7. Barnett, M.: Personal communication, Kansas State University, Manhattan, Kansas, 1977.
8. Bortner, R.W., Rosenman, R.H.: The measurement of pattern A behavior. *J Chronic Dis* **20**:525–533, 1967.
9. Bortner, R.W., Rosenman, R.H., Friedman, M.: Familial similarity in pattern A behavior. *J Chronic Dis* **23**:39–43, 1970.
10. Matthews, K.A., Glass, D.C.: Learned helplessness and Pattern A behavior in children. *In* Behavior Patterns, Stress, and Coronary Disease (Glass, D.C., ed.): Hillsdale, N.J.: Lawrence Erlbaum Associates, 1977.
11. Kagan, J., Kogan, N.: Individual variation in cognitive process. *In* Carmichael's Manual of Child Psychology (Mussen, P.H., ed.). Vol. 1. New York: Wiley, 1970, pp. 1273–1365.
12. Jenkins, C.D.: Psychologic and social precursors of coronary disease. *N Engl J Med* **284**:244–255, 307–317, 1971.
13. Glass, D.C.: Behavior Patterns, Stress, and Coronary Disease. Hillsdale, N.J.: Lawrence Erlbaum Associates, 1977.
14. Rosenman, R.H., Friedman, M.: Neurogenic factors in pathogenesis of coronary heart disease. *Med Clin North Am* **58**:269–279, 1974.
15. Shekelle, R.B., Schoenberger, J.A., Stamler, J.: Correlates of the JAS Type A behavior pattern score. *J Chronic Dis* **29**:381–394, 1976.
16. Matthews, K.A., Krantz, D.S.: Resemblances of twins and their parents in Pattern A behavior. *Psychosom Med* **28**:140–144, 1976.
17. Matthews, K.A., Glass, D.C., Richins, M.: Behavioral interactions of mothers and children with the coronary-prone behavior pattern. *In* Behavior Patterns, Stress, and Coronary Disease (Glass, D.C., ed.). Hillsdale, N.J.: Lawrence Erlbaum Associates, 1977.
18. Krantz, D.S., Glass, D.C., Snyder, M.L.: Helplessness, stress level, and the coronary-prone behavior pattern. *J Exp Soc Psychol* **10**:284–300, 1974.
19. Matthews, K.A.: Children's reactions to loss of control and the Type A coronary-prone behavior pattern. Unpublished study, Kansas State University, Manhattan, Kansas, 1977.
20. Pennebaker, J.: Department of Psychology, University of Virginia, Charlottesville, Va., personal communication, 1975.
21. Dembroski, T.M., McDougall, J.M.: Unpublished data, St. Petersburg, Florida, Eckerd College, 1977.
22. Veroff, J.: Social comparison and the development of achievement motivation. *In* Achievement-Related Motives in Children (Smith, C.P., ed). New York: Russell Sage Foundation, 1969.
23. Bell, R.Q.: A reinterpretation of the direction of effects in studies of socialization. *Psych Rev* **75**:81–95, 1968.
24. Buss, A., Plomin, R.: A Temperament Theory of Personality Development. New York: Wiley, 1975.
25. Rosenman, R.H., Rahe, R.H., Borhani, N.O., Feinleib, M.: Heritability of Personality and Behavior Pattern. Paper presented at the meeting of the American Psychosomatic Society, New Orleans, March 1975.
26. Matthews, K.A.: Caregiver-child interactions and the Type A coronary prone behavior pattern. *Child Dev* **48**:1752–1756, 1977.
27. Heckhausen, H.: The Anatomy of Achievement Motivation. New York: Academic Press, 1967.
28. Appels, A.: Het hartenfarct eeen cultuurziekte. *Tijdscher Suc Geneesk* **50**:446–448, 1972. Cited by Jenkins, C.D.: Recent evidence supporting psychologic and social risk factors for coronary disease. *N Engl J Med* **294**:1033–1038, 1976.
29. Bohani, M., Rime, B.: Approche exploratoire de la personalite pre-coronarienne par analyse standardisee de domes projectives thematiques. *J Psychosom Res* **16**:103–113, 1972. Cited by Jenkins, C.D.: Recent evidence supporting psychologic and social risk factors for coronary disease. *N Engl J Med* **294**:987–994, 1033–1038, 1976.

30. Kagan, J., Moss, H.A.: Birth to Maturity: A Study of Psychological Development. New York: Wiley, 1962.
31. Rosen, B.C., D'Andrade, R.: The psychological origins of achievement motivation. *Sociometry* **22**:185–218, 1959.
32. Winterbottom, M.: The relation of need for achievement to learning experiences in independency and mastery. *In* Motives in Fantasy, Action, and Society (Atkinson, J., ed.). Princeton, N.J.: D. Van Nostrand, 1958.
33. Crandall, V.J., Preston, A., Rabson, A.: Maternal reactions and the development of independence and achievement behavior in young children. *Child Dev* **31**:243–251, 1960.
34. Hermans, H.J.M., Ter Laak, J.J.F., Maes, P.C.J.M.: Achievement motivation and fear of failure in family and school. *Dev Psychol* **6**:520–528, 1972.
35. Radin, R.: Maternal warmth, achievement motivation, and cognitive functioning in lower-class preschool children. *Child Dev* **42**:1560–1565, 1971.
36. Smith, C.P.: The origin and expression of achievement-related motives in children. *In* Achievement-Related Motives in Children (Smith, C.P., ed.). New York: Russell Sage Foundation, 1969).
37. Baumrind, D.: Current patterns of parental authority. *Dev Psychol Monographs* **4**(1, Part 2), 1971.
38. Hoffman, L.: Early childhood experiences and women's achievement motives. *J Soc Iss* **28**:129–155, 1972.
39. Sears, R.R., Maccoby, E.E., Levin, H.: Patterns of Child-rearing. Evanston, Ill.: Row, Peterson, 1957.
40. Bronfenbrenner, U.: Toward a theoretical model for the analysis of parent-child relationships in a social context. *In* Parental Attitudes and Child Behavior (Glidewell, J.C., ed.). Springfield, Ill.: Charles C Thomas, 1961.
41. Cohen, S.: Social and Personality Development in Childhood. New York: Macmillan, 1976.
42. Bandura, A.: Relationship of family patterns to child behavior disorders. Stanford University, Research Grant M-1734; United States Public Health, Progress Report, 1960. Cited by Cohen, S.: Social and Personality Development in Childhood. New York: Macmillan, 1976.
43. Bandura, A., Walters, R.H.: Adolescent Aggression. New York: Ronald, 1959.
44. Cohen, S.: Peers as modeling and normative influences in the development of aggression. *Psychol Rep* **28**:995–998, 1971.
45. Aronson, E.: The Social Animal. San Francisco: W. H. Freeman, 1976.
46. Bandura, A.: Behavior theory and identification learning. *Am J Orthopsychiatry* **33**:591–601, 1963.
47. Bandura, A.: Influence of model's reinforcement contingencies on the acquisition of imitative responses. *J Pers Soc Psychol* **1**:589–595, 1965.
48. Bandura, A., Ross, D., Ross, S.A.: Transmission of aggression through imitation of aggressive models. *J Abnorm Psychol* **63**:575–582, 1961.
49. Bandura, A., Ross, D., Ross, S.A.: Imitation of film-mediated aggressive models. *J Abnorm Psychol* **66**:3–11, 1963.
50. Ornstein, R.: On the Experience of Time. Baltimore: Penguin Books, 1969.
51. Burnam, M.A., Pennebaker, J.W., Glass, D.C.: Time consciousness, achievement striving, and the Type A coronary-prone behavior pattern. *J Abnorm Psychol* **84**:76–79, 1975.
52. Johnson, D.W., Johnson, R.T.: Goal structures and open education. *J Res Dev Educ* **8**:30–46, 1974.

SECTION V

INTERVENTION

Section Summary: Behavioral Intervention

W. Doyle Gentry and Richard M. Suinn

The investigation of behavioral intervention in the Type A coronary-prone behavior pattern is integrally tied to knowledge about methods of assessment, premises about intervening physiological mechanisms, and the development of the Type A pattern. It does not seem necessary, however, to wait until all of the facts are known concerning the development and identification of Type A behavior and the underlying physiological and psychological mechanisms before embarking on investigative studies in this area. Successful intervention in Type A behavior can help clarify the general concept of coronary-prone behavior and further elucidate its relationship to CHD. However, large-scale intervention studies should await refinement of the concept of coronary-prone behavior and studies to validate the most effective intervention strategies.

The few published or unpublished reports on behavioral intervention in coronary-prone behavior underline the need for more research in this area. Recommendations for changes in Type A behavior are presented in Friedman and Rosenman's recent book.[1] They suggest "drills" for altering certain aspects of the Type A behavior pattern, which include: (1) positive reinforcement of non-Type A behavior, for example, scheduling non-business lunch hours, which can be highly reinforcing if taken in settings that offer cues for non-Type A behavior, such as walks in the park and browsing through bookstores; (2) avoidance responding, described as avoiding situations and interactions that elicit feelings of time pressure, hostility, etc. (Examples include not wearing a watch, not making a "things to do today" list, and not scheduling back-to-back activities throughout the work day.); and (3) other self-control techniques.

The use of stress-reduction techniques and other cognitive behavior-modification strategies for coronary-prone individuals has been reported by Suinn,[2] who found that anxiety management training led to a decrease in cholesterol and triglyceride levels, as well as to subjective, anecdotal reports of changes in Type A behavior. More recently, Suinn[3] found that anxiety management training in healthy Type A volunteers led to a desired change in Jenkins Activity Scale (JAS) scores measuring coronary-prone tendencies (hard driving) and in state and trait anxiety indices. Interestingly, the anxiety management training produced a slight rise in cholesterol and triglyceride values, in contrast to the earlier study. Since both studies were based on small samples and yielded similar results on Type A behaviors, the need for more definitive follow-up studies in this area is clearly apparent. Other reports of success in altering Type A behavior using behavioral intervention strategies have been noted by Roskies[4] at the University of Montreal and by Thompson (unpublished report) at Long Island Jewish Hillside Hospital.

Recommendations for Future Research

A variety of intervention studies are possible, ranging from feasibility studies to combined pharmacological-behavioral research. However, it now appears essential to formulate a conceptual model upon which to propose and evaluate proposed intervention studies based on behavioral methods. One possible model follows:

1) Selection of the target(s) for intervention:
   a) It is desirable to identify those target behaviors that appear, by empirical research, to have a significant association with CHD outcome. For example, a high score on the interview measure of "impatience" appears associated with CHD risk.
   b) It is desirable that such target behaviors be defined in terms that experimenters can operationalize; e.g., impatience may be defined variously as:
      (1) inferred when certain behaviors are displayed, e.g., cramming more tasks into less time,
      (2) inferred when certain cognitions are reported, e.g., thinking about the time left to complete a task (instead of working on the task),
      (3) inferred through the reports of emotional or feeling states, e.g., feeling pressured, tense, anxious,
      (4) inferred through evidence from physiological measures, e.g., cardiac reactivity in a delayed response task.
   c) Finally, the intervention method to be studied should directly relate to the particular target behaviors or processes under study:
      (1) if behavior, then behavioral change interventions would be used, such as operant reinforcement methods and/or contingency contracting,
      (2) if cognitions, then cognitive change interventions would be used such as thought-stopping and/or cognitive restructuring,
      (3) if emotions, then emotional change interventions would be used,

such as anxiety management training and/or systematic desensitization,

(4) if physiological, then physiological change interventions would be
used, such as pharmacological methods and/or biofeedback.

2) Identification of ways to diagnose the "causes" of the target behaviors to
select the intervention techniques relevant to the diagnosis:

a) Classify causes as those that *initiate* Type A behavior and those that
maintain such behavior.

(1) Initiators are conditions that prompt the display of Type A behavior when the conditions are present, but reduce the display
when the conditions are removed. For example, in some individuals, the presence of a deadline might precipitate Type A behavior,
which is reduced when the deadline is removed.

(2) Maintainers are those conditions that strengthen the behaviors
such that they become overlearned and appear even when initiators are absent. These may be rewards or other positive consequences, or anxiety-reduction consequences. In effect, maintainers are factors that indicate "what Type A persons may be getting
out of being Type A."

b) If the initiators or the maintainers of Type A behavior can be identified,
then a study may involve those intervention methods best suited to
those "causative" factors, using *impatience* as a problem for intervention:

(1) *Impatience* may be a general objective or goal for intervention.

(2) The target behavior leading to *impatience* may be cramming more
tasks into less time.

(3) the initiator for *impatience* might be time deadlines in the job
setting.

(4) The intervention method might aim at improving work efficiency
to reduce the number of situations in which deadlines occur.

c) Successful intervention in Type A behavior may depend upon the
adequacy of models used to gain an understanding of the "causes" of
such behavior, and the suitability of intervention techniques for dealing
with such causes.

3) Identification of different behavioral intervention methods that

a) have some validity in the literature as applied to other clinical problems, and appear to be relevant for application to Type A target behaviors.
These methods may include:

(1) behavioral change

(2) emotional change

(3) cognitive change

(4) physiological change

(5) situational management (e.g., how to manage time schedules by
better scheduling)

(6) family intervention (e.g., how to involve spouses in encouraging
change in Type A behavior)

    (7)   institutional intervention (e.g., industries organizing programs for employees)

4) Selection of outcome measures may include:
    a)   indicators of coronary-prone behavior, such as JAS scores, structured interview classification, etc.;
    b)   physiological data (e.g., lipid levels, norepinephrine changes, blood pressure, etc.); or
    c)   data considered to vary concomitantly with the above, such as actual changes in reports of *impatience* in the work setting.

Additional outcome measures might focus on endpoints such as productivity. A common assumption presumes changes in the Type A pattern will lead to reductions in productivity. It is conceivable, however, that alteration of potentially damaging aspects of the Type A pattern could be accomplished without causing such a decrease in performance. Extensive efforts should be directed toward clarifying this important issue.

In summary, carefully designed studies are critical to develop, test, and validate intervention strategies to determine whether alteration of the Type A pattern will, in fact, reduce risk for CHD. A tendency might develop in which various intervention techniques are applied prematurely by some who are ill prepared or unskilled in the use of such techniques. The responsibility for development of an adequate knowledge base before inappropriate applications proliferate rests squarely with the biobehavioral and clinical research communities.

References

1. Friedman, M., Rosenman, R.H.: Type A Behavior and Your Heart. New York: Knopf, 1974.
2. Suinn, R.M.: Type A behavior pattern. *In* Behavioral Approaches to Medical Treatment (Williams, R.B., Gentry, W.D., eds.). Cambridge, Ma.: Ballinger, 1977, pp. 55–65.
3. Suinn, R.M., Bloom, L.J.: Anxiety Management Training for Pattern A Behavior. *J Behav Med* 1:25–35, 1978.
4. Roskies, E., Spevack, M., Surkis, A., et al.: Changing the coronary-prone (Type A) behavior pattern in a non-clinical population. *J Behav Med* (in press).

Chapter 17

Behavior Modification of the Coronary-Prone Behavior Pattern

W. Doyle Gentry

While much research has been done to identify the various pathogenic aspects of the coronary-prone behavior pattern, and further, to describe the "risk factor" relationship between this pattern of behavior and coronary heart disease (CHD),[1,2] almost no attention has been given to how this behavior pattern (or any single aspect of it) might be altered so as to reduce the individual's risk for CHD. Two different literature sources[3,4] suggest how *behavior modification* techniques may be helpful in teaching the coronary-prone individual to change certain aspects of his behavior.

Therapeutic Strategies

Positive Reinforcement

Friedman and Rosenman[3] provide numerous examples of how the coronary-prone individual can reengineer his behavior so that new, nonpathogenic behaviors are followed by reinforcing (positive) consequences. For example, a coronary-prone businessman can schedule fewer people to meet and less work to do in a given time period, or shorten the time allotted for various business activities, so that he has frequent "free periods" to devote to reinforcing activities such as daydreaming, reflecting on past pleasant memories, finishing a pet project that has been left undone for some time, and so forth. The coronary-prone individual can also schedule a longer (one hour) period of time with someone who "will enhance either the opportunities or the worthwhileness of your life" as a *reward* immediately following a shorter (30 minutes) session with someone who tends to elicit coronary-prone behavior, i.e., competitive feelings, hostility, impatience. Scheduled nonbusiness lunch hours can also prove highly reinforcing if taken in settings that offer cues for non-coronary-prone behavior, i.e., walks in the park, browsing through book stores and art galleries, which provide cues for relaxation, enjoyment, and unhurried activity.

Avoidance Responding

Friedman and Rosenman[3] indicate how coronary-prone (CP) individuals can reengineer their daily schedule to avoid many interpersonal relationships and situations that elicit pathogenic aspects of the coronary-prone behavior pattern, e.g., feelings of time pressure, hostility, etc. For example, a person cannot wear a watch or have a clock in his office, and thus, he will not be able to constantly refer to an instrument of time, which in CP individuals generates feelings of being in a hurry, of being late, of being overcommitted, and of being overwhelmed. Similarly, a person can instruct his secretary not to interrupt him when he is with another person or engaged in some other activity, and not to schedule people and activities back-to-back, leaving a little time for relaxation in between. The secretary can also engineer incoming telephone calls so that they do not register in his office (awareness). A ringing telephone constitutes another form of interruption and cue to "hurry up" what he is doing. Papers should not be stacked up on the office desk, cueing the CP individual to "hurry up and get it all done." Finally, visible "things to do today" lists should be avoided, as they serve to drive the coronary-prone person to meet deadlines in the same way that a watch does.

Response-Cost Techniques

A clear example of how a response-cost technique can be used to alter certain aspects of coronary-prone behavior is provided by Friedman and Rosenman[3] (p. 264) in their section on "drills" for changing Type A behavior. They advise that:

> Whenever you catch yourself speeding up your car to get through a yellow light at an intersection, penalize yourself immediately by turning to the right at the next corner. Circle the block and approach the same corner and signal light again. After such penalization, you may find yourself racing a yellow light a second, but probably not a third time.

Another example has to do with the anticipatory act of taking one's car keys out long before the car is in sight, i.e., the coronary-prone individual is in a hurry to "get on with" the act of driving before he is anywhere near the car. Here, response-cost would involve putting the keys back into the pocket each and every time they are prematurely pulled out until the person is standing next to the car. For this "drill" to be effective, the coronary-prone person must return the keys to his pocket, even if he is only a few feet from the automobile.

This "drill" will prevent a person from reinforcing himself for anticipating the act of driving and being in a hurry.

Thought-Stopping

Suinn[4] has recommended thought-stopping in his treatment of coronary-prone individuals. He notes that certain negative thoughts compete with a state of relaxation, which is the goal of his stress-management training program, and in fact, these negative thoughts build up physical tension in the coronary-prone individual. Negative thoughts include thoughts about succeeding, worries about having insufficient time, thoughts about being overcommitted, and so forth. Such thoughts, if left unchecked, lead to increased feelings of stress, a sense of "loss of control," and ultimately, to the overt manifestation of the coronary-prone behavior pattern. The coronary-prone person can be taught to say "STOP!," at first out loud, and later on, subvocally, whenever these negative thoughts come to mind. Suinn suggests that if the coronary-prone individual cannot successfully disrupt these cognitions with thought-stopping, he should deliberately engage in such thoughts, but only in specific and time-limited situations, e.g., in a specific room, while sitting in a specific chair, or only at a certain time of day.

Relaxation Procedures

Suinn[4] has demonstrated that *cardiac stress management training* can be effective in reducing coronary-prone behavior and also in altering certain physiological parameters associated with CHD, i.e., cholesterol and triglyceride levels. He describes a variety of direct and indirect approaches to relaxation training that seem to lead to a decrease in coronary-prone behavior. Direct approaches include Jacobsonian muscle relaxation training, biofeedback, transcendental meditation, physical massage, saunas, yoga, and relaxation imagery. Indirect approaches include music, reading, movies and television, recreational sports, and alcohol.

Cognitive Behavior Modification

It is clear that much of the coronary-prone behavior evidenced by individuals at risk for CHD is directly related to thoughts, attitudes, beliefs, and philosophies they have regarding their relationship to the world around them, e.g., "I have to hurry and get everything done or people will think I am not organized," and "If I do not work at least 16 hours a day, 7 days a week, I will not be successful!" A variety of cognitive behavior modification strategies could be employed to deal with these maladaptive cognitions, to disrupt the effect they have on emotional states (tension, drive) and subsequent overt coronary-prone behavior. In addition to the thought-stopping technique already mentioned, other strategies might include rational-emotive therapy, systematic desensitization, covert reinforcement and covert extinction, and stress inoculation training.

Cognitive behavior modification techniques can also be highly effective in treating the hostility component of the coronary-prone behavior pattern outlined by Friedman and Rosenman.[3] Navaco[5] has recently demonstrated the therapeutic effect of self-instruction combined with relaxation training on a group of individuals indentified as having anger control problems. Self-instruction involved the systematic use of self-statements such as "As long as I keep my cool, I am in control of the situation," and "My anger is a signal of what I need to do. Time for problem solving," to cope with imagined anger situations that the person had trouble dealing with in real life. This combination of procedures was instrumental not only in reducing the level of anger characterizing these patients, but also in producing a decrease in both systolic and diastolic blood pressure.

A Word of Caution

If behavior modification techniques are to prove beneficial in changing coronary-prone behavior, several points should be kept in mind from the outset: First, as Friedman and Rosenman[3] clearly point out, it would be foolish to suggest that this reengineering will be an easy process or a painless one. Coronary-prone individuals most often will resist serious attempts to change their fixed patterns of behavior. What they often want is *not to have CHD:* they do not necessarily want to change their behavior. Their philosophy of life (which is in many cases negative) will often interfere with their total commitment to treatment, no matter what the mode of therapy.

Second, as Friedman and Rosenman also point out: "The battle of new habits against old may have to continue indefinitely" (p. 235). Behavior modification must be a gradual and continuing process with these patients. Teaching coronary-prone patients to relax more is but one facet of the coronary-prone problem, and effective treatment here may be short-lived if other aspects of the coronary-prone behavior pattern are also not changed and continually monitored.

In some cases, behavior modification may naively presume that survival and freedom from CHD are more potent reinforcers than the other consequences of coronary-prone behavior, e.g., higher status, more money, etc. This may in fact not be the case and patients may simply fail to comply with behavioral treatment.

Finally, behavior modification techniques used with coronary-prone patients will need to involve principles of self-regulation in which the coronary-prone individual is the change agent. Also, as Suinn notes, the spouse and family should be important agents in modifying various aspects of the coronary-prone pattern.

References

1. Glass, D.C.: Stress, behavior patterns, and coronary disease. *Am Sc* **65**:177–187, 1977.
2. Jenkins, C.D.: Recent evidence supporting psychologic and social risk factors for coronary disease. *N Engl J Med* **294**:987–994, 1033–1038, 1976.
3. Friedman, M., Rosenman, R.H.: Type A Behavior and Your Heart. New York: Knopf, 1974.
4. Suinn, R.M.: Type A behavior pattern. *In* Behavioral Approaches to Medical Treatment (Williams, R.B., Gentry, W.D., eds.). Cambridge, Ma.: Ballinger, 1977, pp. 55–65.
5. Navaco, R.W.: Treatment of chronic anger through cognitive and relaxation controls. *J Consult Clin Psychol* **44**: 681, 1976.

Chapter 18

The Coronary-Prone Behavior Pattern: A Behavioral Approach to Intervention

Richard M. Suinn

The basic objective of intervention is the achievement of change in behaviors (or emotional states) where psychological interventions are involved. This implies that ongoing methods have not effected changes in the patient. For the Type A patient, this appears to be a correct assumption in that many Type A persons seem unable to alter their life-styles, even following a severe heart attack. Although these persons are intellectually aware of the importance of changing their life-style, many report that habits are too strongly ingrained. A behavioral analysis of this problem generally poses two questions: (1) what maintains the behavior in question, and (2) what alternative new behaviors are desirable and how might these be achieved?

Maintenance of Type A Behaviors

It is my belief that two factors contribute to the maintenance of Type A behaviors—reinforcers and stress. There is little doubt that reinforcement plays a major role in preventing behaviors from being extinguished. On a cultural level, our society offers many inducements and social rewards for display of Type A behaviors and values. For example, we pride ourselves on our work ethic, on success and achievement, and on "getting things done." We say the best way to guarantee work accomplishment is to "give it to the busy man." We offer admiration when we speak of a person as having "high drive." We value the worker who never relaxes on the job. We even now have seen a recent set of articles and best-selling writings extolling the virtues of methods to "get more done in the same amount of time." Whereas Eastern cultures accept the development of the whole man—spiritual, philosophical, material—

Western cultures have promoted the values of material success and accomplishments. It has only been in recent years that exercise has become important for the common man, and even then, it is exercise for a goal other than relaxation.

Reinforcers also occur on the more immediate level. The Type A characteristics lead to outcomes that are profitable. Consider the behavioral characteristics: mental and physical alertness, self-imposed deadlines, preference for activity versus relaxation, emphasis on doing, distress at anything that wastes time. Given such characteristics, it would be expected that Type A persons would be more productive and higher performers. Howard, Cunningham, and Rechnitzer examined 12 different Canadian companies and discovered that 61% of the managers could be classified as Type A's.[1] This is not surprising as it probably reflects the climb upward achievable with Type A behaviors. Basically, what I am suggesting is that such behaviors are in fact productive, and that such productivity is both socially and materially (through promotions, salary raises, etc.) rewarding. In fact, the rewards are so powerful and so frequent that the Type A behaviors become overlearned and therefore comprise an extremely strong habit pattern. This pattern then is generalized across other conditions not normally demanding Type A behaviors, such as in recreational activities, during vacations, in non-work-related reading, etc.

A second major factor in maintaining Type A behaviors is stress. Again consider the characteristics of the Type A's: They have been described as suffering from the "hurry-up sickness,"[2] deadlines are *self-imposed*, calendars often show more appointments than can reasonably be handled, and they are impatient at the rate events move. Would they not be expected to experience stress? And this stress is as much prompted by the conditions in which they have put themselves as by their own driven nature. Stress cannot help but be built up and precipitated by a heavy and overloaded calendar. Similarly, stress responses must be triggered in the person who feels the need to continuously drive himself.

An interesting factor is the potential role stress has as a maintainer of Type A behaviors. I am differentiating between stress responses prompted by cue conditions external to the person (e.g., being told that you are running behind on your appointments) versus stresses prompted by internal cue conditions (i.e., need to achieve, drive to perform, etc.). The former may be remedied through control or change of the environmental conditions of work; the latter requires changes in the person, either behaviorally or emotionally. In the former, an additional burst of effort to reduce the tension by getting the job done leads to both external reinforcement (e.g., from one's employer) and reinforcement by anxiety reduction. The latter involves reinforcement mainly through anxiety reduction. The evidence in psychology is that reinforcement can take two forms: a positive tangible reward, or a reduction of a tension/anxiety, drive, or arousal state. Stress reduction is therefore rewarding, and rewards tend to strengthen habits.

It may well be that stress is not only the mechanism maintaining Type A behaviors, but also a mediating mechanism whereby heart disease develops.

Rahe[3,4] discovered that myocardial infarction patients experienced higher life stress events prior to illness than their close friends, and that increases in life stresses appeared associated with sudden or delayed death following myocardial infarction. Other studies have shown an association between increase of stresses and alterations in cholesterol. Clark et al.[5] found increases in cholesterol level among new cadets admitted to the Air Force Academy during the weeks considered to be high in environmental stresses. Following this period, cholesterol levels decreased. This is consistent with previous reports of similar changes among accountants during the periods prior to and immediately following the high stress month of April, the annual income tax deadline.[6]

Alternative Behavioral Change

Understanding the factors that prevent behavioral change, as indicated in the previous section, may be valuable in designing programs for intervention. First, it is unlikely that threats will induce behavioral shifts in many patients, even after a heart attack. The Type A behavior pattern has been so frequently rewarded that it is resistant to change in the same way that threats from pictures of deaths are relatively unsuccessful in changing driving habits of speeders. Next, the reward structure must be reanalyzed. Type A persons believe that Type A behaviors are the *only* way in which they can retain productivity. In this sense their belief is similar to a superstition. Superstitious behaviors are those that have "worked" a few times so well that the person does not experiment with different solutions that may also work as well. Type A persons need to be guided and encouraged to try out different ways of accomplishing so that they recognize that the goal is not work apathy or unproductivity, but productivity at less severe personal cost.

In recognizing the role of stress, we have utilized Stress Management Training[7] as part of the program for retraining Type A persons. In one study, Stress Management Training and covert rehearsal were programmed towards the needs of Type A patients recovering from heart disease.[8] On an initial sample replicated on another sample of patients from the same rehabilitation center, patients reported reductions in stress and changes in some Type A behaviors. Significant reductions in cholesterol and triglycerides were also noted. As a pilot study, this was a promising report.

Recently, Suinn and Bloom[8] studied a sample of healthy persons from the community involving the stress management component only. Subjects included a city manager, a dentist, a mathematician, a head secretary, a life insurance regional manager, and a farmer. Blood pressures were taken before and after, as were measures on Type A traits and anxiety. Lipid analyses were also conducted. Results indicated reductions in Type A characteristics as measured by the Jenkins Scale, as well as reductions in State Anxiety. Some reductions occurred in blood pressure; subjects were not, however, suffering from hypertension. Although reductions were not statistically significant, 86% of the trained subjects showed reductions in systolic blood pressure as compared to 67% of the controls; comparable figures for diastolic blood pressure were 71% and 17%.

Although both studies can only be considered suggestive, they do offer some indication that stress may indeed be playing an important role in the development of Type A behavior. A final intriguing observation was the lack of support for the earlier studies on lipid level data. Increases were noted following training rather than decreases. Many hypotheses are possible, including changes in diet or eating behavior developed after stress reduction; the patient sample was on careful dietary controls, while the healthy sample was not.

Other stress management approaches directed toward blood pressure reduction have been reported. Roskies et al.[10] with one group of subjects used a behavioral approach similar to the stress management training technique previously mentioned. A second group was treated with psychotherapy aimed at facilitating insight into the origins of Type A behaviors. Although no changes on standard anxiety scales were observed, subjects reported reductions in felt time pressure and greater life satisfaction. In addition, significant reductions were observed in serum cholesterol and systolic blood pressure. The behavioral approach appeared to produce somewhat greater improvements than the psychotherapeutic approach. Benson's[11] relaxation response and various relaxation or biofeedback procedures[12-16] have demonstrated efficacy in reducing blood pressure. Again, one must distinguish between the effects of relaxation alone versus the use of relaxation or other methods as stress-coping devices. With respect to Type A persons, it might be hypothesized that they would profit from relaxation training, since they appear to lack the ability to "unwind," as well as from training in stress-coping skills.

Beyond the methods mentioned above, Type A persons might profit through learning alternative behaviors to not only retain productivity but also to prevent externally (environmentally) induced stress responses. Instead of accepting more and more assignments in a busy schedule, an employee might learn to involve the supervisor in setting priorities. Instead of taking all requests as if they were all equally important, a person might set aside those tasks that can and should be done later. Difficult tasks that the person finds aversive could be scheduled to match the most productive times in the individual's day, taking into account that some persons are "morning" persons while others work better in late morning or afternoon.

Potential Directions for Study

The association between Type A behavior and coronary heart disease appears well-documented; what is lacking is better theorizing regarding the mechanisms—the reasons that Type A persons resist change, the types of alternative new behaviors deemed desirable, and thence, the types of interventions possible.[17] Understanding the mechanisms through which Type A behaviors increase the risk of CHD may not turn out to be the most important or even the best means for designing intervention techniques. For example, if the mechanisms are biochemical/hormonal in nature, requiring medication, but the patient cannot tolerate the medication physically, then nonpharmacological methods may be needed.

On the other hand, if indeed the relationship turns out to be stress leading to endocrine changes that in turn affect lipid levels that in turn lead to CHD, then any number of approaches may be taken. Such approaches may include stress prevention or the development of stress-coping skills for those that cannot or will not change their environment. Another approach might be to directly control the endocrine changes through pharmacological means. A final method may be to reduce the lipid levels through other procedures such as diet control.

Remaining with purely psychological premises, a number of topics need to be further researched:

1. To what *degree* do specific stresses or general life stresses contribute to CHD risk? Data should be collected similar to that collected for other risk factors.
2. What useful measures are there for measuring such specific or general stresses?
3. If stress is a factor, what are the psychological and behavioral mechanisms that lead to increased CHD? For example, is it that increased stress leads to excessive eating?
4. How do the Type A behaviors lead to increased risk, again in terms of psychological or behavioral mechanisms? For example, is there an association between deadline setting and high stress responses?
5. Are intervention methods that reduce stress responses sufficient to reduce the risk level? Or must there be both stress reduction and behavioral change?
6. What is the relative effectiveness of differing stress-coping programs, e.g., relaxation only, relaxation through biofeedback, meditation responses, Anxiety Management Training, cognitive behavior modification? (Given the general characteristics of Type A persons, I would anticipate that intervention methods that produce immediate results will be more acceptable to Type A persons than techniques that cover several months.)
7. What is the relative effectiveness of differing behavioral change programs; exactly what new behaviors are needed? Are we aiming to teach Type A persons relaxation skills; or how to achieve better control over their environment and schedules; or how to be more assertive? One may cope with stress responses triggered by time cues by an emotional reconditioning process[18] or by better planning of one's daily schedule to permit time enough for each task. Each approach may contribute something toward reducing risk of CHD.
8. What are the most effective tools for *initiating* behavioral change and for *maintaining* such changes? Behavioral stop-smoking clinics have been successful in initiating but not maintaining change.
9. What measures are available for demonstrating progress in behavioral change? Are such measures associated with indices of CHD risk reduction?
10. Are intervention methods for cardiac patients similarly valid for healthy

Type A persons? Are there substantial differences in mechanism, and hence, intervention outcomes, where the Type A person already suffers from a specific level of CHD? (For example: Are the behavioral methods effective with borderline or mild hypertension also valid with patients whose blood pressure is clinically pathological?)

11. How can we foster generalization of behavioral changes to other environments? (Are self-management approaches of use in helping the patient to be self-reliant and not dependent upon the therapist's continued services?)

References

1. Howard, J., Cunningham, D., Rechnitzer, P.: Health patterns associated with Type A behavior, a managerial population. *J Human Stress* **2**, 24–31, 1976.
2. Friedman, M., Rosenman, R.: Type A Behavior and Your Heart. New York: Knopf, 1974.
3. Theorelle, T., Rahe, R.: Psychosocial factors and myocardial infarction. An inpatient study in Sweden. *J Psychosom Res* **15**:25–31, 1971.
4. Rahe, R., Romo, R.: Recent life changes and the onset of myocardial infarction and coronary death in Helsinki. *In* Life Stress and Illness (Genderson, E., Rahe, R., eds.). Springfield; Ill.: Charles C Thomas, 1974.
5. Clark, D., Arnold, E., Foulds, E., Brown, D., Eastmead, D., Parry, E.: Serum urate and cholesterol levels in Air Force Academy cadets. *Aviat Space Env Med* 1044–1048, 1975.
6. Friedman, M., Rosenman, R., Carroll, V.: Changes in the serum cholesterol and blood-clotting time in men subjected to cyclic variations of occupational stress. *Circulation* **117**:825–861, 1958.
7. Suinn, R.: Anxiety Management Training for general anxiety. *In* The Innovative Psychological Therapies: Critical and Creative Contributions (Suinn, R., Weigel, R., eds.). New York: Harper, 1975.
8. Suinn, R.: The cardiac stress management program for Type A patients. *Cardiac Rehab* **5**:1975.
9. Suinn, R., Bloom, C.: Anxiety management for Type A persons. *J Behav Med* **1**:25–35, 1978.
10. Roskies, E., Spevack, M., Surkis, A, et al.: Changing the coronary-prone (Type A) behavior pattern in a non-clinical population. *J Behav Med* (in press).
11. Benson, H.: The Relaxation Response. New York: Morrow, 1975.
12. Brady, J., Luborsky, L., Kron, R.: Blood pressure reductions in patients with essential hypertension through metronome-conditioned relaxation: a preliminary report. *Beh Ther* **5**:203–209, 1974.
13. Graham, L., Beiman, I., Ciminero, A.: The generality of therapeutic effects of progressive relaxation training for essential hypertension. *J Beh Ther Exp Psych*, (in press).
14. Patel, C.: Twelve-month follow-up of yoga and biofeedback in the management of hypertension. *Lancet* 62–64, 1975.
15. Shoemaker, J., Tasto, D.: The effects of muscle relaxation on blood pressure of essential hypertensives. *Behav Res Ther* **13**:29–43, 1975.
16. Yarian, R.: The efficacy of electromyographic biofeedback training as a method of deep muscle relaxation for college students displaying either coronary or non-coronary-prone behavior patterns. Unpublished Ph.D. dissertation, University of Maryland, 1976.
17. Suinn, R.: Pattern A behaviors and heart disease: Intervention approaches. In Advances in Behavioral Medicine (Ferguson, J., Taylor, B., eds.). N.J.: Spectrum, in press.
18. Suinn, R.: Treatment of phobias. *In* The Group Treatment of Human Problems: A Social Learning Approach (Harris, G., ed.). New York: Grune & Stratton, 1977.

Index